Schoenberg and His School

Da Capo Press Music Reprint Series

GENERAL EDITOR

FREDERICK FREEDMAN

VASSAR COLLEGE

Schoenberg and His School

THE CONTEMPORARY STAGE
OF THE LANGUAGE OF MUSIC

By René Leibowitz

TRANSLATED FROM THE FRENCH BY
DIKA NEWLIN

𝄡 DA CAPO PRESS · NEW YORK · 1970

A Da Capo Press Reprint Edition

This Da Capo Press edition of René Leibowitz's
Schoenberg and His School
is an unabridged republication of
the first edition published in New York in 1949.
It is reprinted by
special arrangement with the Philosophical Library, Inc.

Library of Congress Catalog Card Number 75-115338
SBN 306-71681-X

Published by Da Capo Press
A Division of Plenum Publishing Corporation
227 West 17th Street
New York, N.Y. 10011
All Rights Reserved

Manufactured in the United States of America

SCHOENBERG AND HIS SCHOOL

AUTHOR'S PREFACE TO THE AMERICAN EDITION

It is gratifying to be able to say that many of the hopes I had when I wrote this book have already been fulfilled. Only a few months after the original French version was published I received letters from readers throughout the world, expressing agreement and telling me they had found this work valuable in revealing the real music of our time. This is all I had hoped to achieve.*

Therefore, when I was given the opportunity to present my work to the American public, I immediately undertook to fill certain gaps which—some through involuntary carelessness on my part, some because of existing circumstances—remained in the first edition. I am both pleased and grateful, now, to believe that the United States, which is privileged to claim Arnold Schoenberg as a citizen, will profit from an improved effort to understand and explain the music of this greatest living master of composition.

In translation, the original process of thought inevitably undergoes some transformation. But this transformation can be fruitful, because the fundamental problem is seen in a new light, thus providing an opportunity for one to become more lucid and to measure more precisely one's own limits.

A translation should not only aim to facilitate communication with the world of a different language; it should be in itself another approach to the basic problem—in this case, the international "language" of music. It is my hope that this translation will deepen and widen the comprehension of some of the most beautiful contemporary works of art. And every step taken in this direction

---

* As for those who, full of preconceived ideas and lacking any genuine knowledge of the subject, have always been hostile to these ideas, this work has increased their hostility. This, too, is a good thing.

brings us nearer to the point where these works will find the high position which should be theirs.

Perhaps only a few readers will appreciate fully the difficulties faced by the translator, as well as the courage, generosity and skill which she has spent on a task from which the cause of true music can only benefit. However, what every reader can know is the sincere and friendly gratitude expressed here to Miss Newlin for her work.

RENÉ LEIBOWITZ
Paris

TRANSLATOR'S PREFACE

How often it occurs that, after a period of comparative silence or neglect, a particular subject is suddenly "in the air" everywhere at once! Thus it can happen that a number of works on such a subject will, though conceived quite independently of each other, appear at almost the same time. Surely this is no mere coincidence, but has to do with certain all-pervasive spiritual or philosophical movements which, at a given time, seem to affect all those of a given turn of mind with a certain inevitability.

It was immediately after the publication of my own book on Schoenberg and his predecessors that my attention was called to the present work, then newly issued. I was forcibly struck by its masterly handling of a theme which I had approached in a somewhat different way—Schoenberg as a continuation of the past equated with Schoenberg as a projection into the future. The further development of this idea—the presentation of Berg as the incarnation of the sense of the past, Webern as that of the future—seemed but the logical consummation of the concept of Tradition and Revolt in Schoenberg, which had occupied my mind for some years.

Here, then, was the book which those of us who consider the Schoenberg tradition the most fruitful trend of today had been wanting for years. That so revelatory a work should have appeared in France seemed a matter of profound significance. The great musical tradition of Vienna had been rooted out of its native country. It was—and is—now up to musicians of other lands to carry it on, and, in so doing, to give fresh proof (if such be needed) of its truly universal values. The great international values of music must not, cannot be destroyed by the aberrations of a single country.

Because of all this, it gives me great joy to have the oppor-

tunity of helping to place the work of René Leibowitz before the
English-speaking public. The sincerity, enthusiasm, and devotion,
coupled with the exact and exhaustive knowledge, which he has
brought to his study of Schoenberg, Berg, and Webern cannot fail
to impress the reader already instructed in these matters. May his
labor of love also win new friends and listeners for three of the
greatest composers of our time!

DIKA NEWLIN
Western Maryland College
August, 1947

AUTHOR'S PREFACE

I have learned this book from those of whom it treats.

In writing this sentence, I do not mean merely to pay tribute to the three great musicians with whom I am concerned here, and who have been and still are—in the most profound and genuine meaning of the term—my masters; I should like, above all, to express something still more real and fundamental.

I am not a music critic, any more than I am a historian or an esthetician. I am a musician. Since this is so, most of my life is spent in direct contact with forms of sound, whether I myself make the effort of inventing and coordinating them or whether I find myself in the presence of the musical scores of others. As far back as I can remember, I have been delving into these scores for the instruction which my conscience demands. So I may be excused for seeming to want to reduce music—as far as it concerns me—to its simple didactic functions. To tell the truth, the reading or the hearing of any kind of musical work—and I have read or heard thousands of them—has never been, to me, an excuse for pleasure, distraction, relaxation, or even a manifestation of my curiosity. If certain readings or hearings of music have perforce brought with them pleasure and relaxation—or, for that matter, boredom and irritation—these qualities are *superimposed* on the musical exercises in question, exercises whose origin and real intention are quite different. Every time I hear music, whether in my imagination or through my senses, I begin anew to question all that I know, all that I am. Such questioning automatically enforces the participation of all one's intellectual faculties, which are thus made keener and stronger by each new experience. It is in this gradual progress towards a greater intellectual lucidity that

the *instructive qualities* of music, to which I referred above, are
to be found.

But there is still more to the question. Composing music and
being a composer, making music and being a musician, are not
necessarily synonymous. It is comparatively easy to compose, to
make music. A minimum of gifts and of technical means (which
latter may be acquired comparatively painlessly) is sufficient. To
be a composer or a musician demands more than that. Now, those
who become composers begin (just like those who do *not* become
composers) by *making* music or composing. But at one time or
another there comes to them what some would call a revelation,
and what I like to call a *sudden consciousness* of the true meaning of the language of music. From that day forward, if the
activity of composing or of making music is carried on with the
intention of solving those profound problems which have confronted the consciousness of the individual, that individual has a
chance to become a composer, a true musician.

In the case of the composer, this sudden consciousness comes
at the moment when, in the work of a contemporary musician, he
discovers what seems to him to be the language of his epoch, the
language which he himself wants to speak. Up to that point, he
may have assimilated, in more or less accurate fashion, the language of the past; he may have believed that he has profited
from certain excursions into a style which seems to him to furnish
fresh possibilities. But his real consciousness of *being a composer*
cannot be foursquare and unshakable until some master of our
time brings him the assurance, the irrefutable evidence of the
necessity and the authenticity of his personal language.

That is what happened to me on my first contact with the
music of Schoenberg, Berg, and Webern. I did not immediately
understand the language which their works speak; I must even
add that it took me a long time to become familiar with it, and
I do not know whether even today I have grasped (in a general
way) its wealth of implications. But without having understood
it completely, I understood from the beginning that it was the
only genuine and inevitable expression of the musical art of our
time. Since then, my certainty of this has grown, to the extent

that my activity transformed the first *intuition* into *knowledge* which became ever more lucid and profound. But I owe all this activity, its very meaning and intensity—this activity, thanks to which I have acquired my knowledge—to the example of the three masters whom I have named. It is in this sense that I can say that I learned this work from them—this work which is nothing but the theoretical synthesis of the present extent of my knowledge with regard to the meaning of this musical language, the assimilation of which is the chief goal of my existence.

These remarks will make the reader understand the spirit in which this book is written. It represents, I believe, the first effort to make a profound study of the three composers who dominate our contemporary musical art. That such an attempt should have taken place in France—a land which is not the home of these three composers, a land which, in a certain sense at least, is not my home either, but in the midst of which I have meditated upon the lesson of my masters, a land whose language I use to preserve the results of these meditations—all this seems to me of the highest significance.

In the first place, it pleases me to see here one more proof that France is the very place where the most violent passions may be unleashed and where the maelstrom of intellectual and artistic life becomes so turbulent as to necessitate (before this problem arises anywhere else) a positive and constructive synthesis of the factors which have led to this state of affairs.

For, if it is in France that the music of Arnold Schoenberg and his school has provoked the most exacerbated hostility, it is also in Paris that there is now springing into being, for the first time since the existence of this school, a group of musicians who claim it as their own, but none of whom has been directly influenced by Schoenberg, Webern, or Berg.

This ought not to give the impression that the following pages are conceived in a spirit of propaganda for the school in question. The works of our masters have no need whatsoever for such support. If I wanted to make propaganda for Schoenberg, Berg, and Webern, I would have nothing to say—except that they are among the most powerful, most original, and most virile composers of whom the history of music may boast. But this would not be nearly enough, and that is why I have set myself quite a different task.

Before I define this task, I shall say that in undertaking it I have been aware of the difficulties which it entails. The works of artists such as those whom we discuss are complex individual worlds. When on top of all this we are concerned with contemporary works, it is possible that we do not have sufficient perspective to view them in their total significance. Trying to comprehend the *unique* features of their meaning seems to me, then, an undertaking which is at least risky, if not foredoomed to failure. That is why I have chosen to approach the works of Schoenberg and his school not by considering them as self-contained phenomena, but by placing them in relation to the tradition which has produced them and of which they represent, in my opinion, the most advanced phase at the present time.

Such a method has a chance of being fruitful, and this is why: the fact that the music of the school which interests us is virtually unknown, not only to the general public, but also to the majority of musicians the world over, is explained chiefly by the innumerable difficulties which this music entails. No other music of today demands such arduous and constant effort—whether on the part of the performer, the listener, or the critic—to be understood, appreciated, and penetrated. The essential difficulty appears in that lost feeling which overwhelms most of those coming in contact for the first time with some page of Schoenberg, Berg, or Webern— a feeling caused by forms of sound which seem to have no relation to those with which we are familiar, and which appear to be quite incapable of producing a musical discourse such as we are generally accustomed to hearing. It is evident that such a state of affairs must be attributed primarily to the specific temperaments of our composers. Once again, I have nothing to say about these temperaments, except that in their force and originality they are comparable to those of all the great masters of all time. But it goes without saying that this force and this originality express themselves in a coherent and perfectly articulated musical language. Now, the very term *language* implies a tradition which possesses a *meaning*, and we are permitted to question this meaning. This *traditional meaning* is a matter of *historicity*, a concept which it becomes of prime importance to define.

Here again I can say that I have learned this book from those of whom it treats. In fact, the reader should not imagine that everything which applies particularly to the abovementioned *historicity*, or merely to questions of history, is the result of erudition in the proper sense of the word. I am not at all erudite, and the least musicologist would doubtless feel himself far above me in this respect (I confess that I gladly grant him this feeling of superiority). However, the music of Schoenberg, Berg, and Webern, the problems which it poses, the acquisitions which it displays— all this has opened my eyes to the problems of composition which belong to *all* periods. The extreme novelty of the language spoken by our three composers is a logical consequence of their specific attitudes; but it is also the quality which belongs to every truly creative act. And nevertheless this language obeys general rules which have existed as long as polyphony itself, principles which we may call immutable because they are common to all the great masters, whatever their epoch.

It is in this way that Schoenberg, Berg, and Webern have taught me to consider the past of the art of music: not as a history of classified events, of interest only to the musicologist; not as the "good old days," the "Golden Age" which can never be surpassed, beloved of those whose creative impotence keeps them from looking ahead; not even as the semi-miraculous trysting-place of several masterpieces, likewise miraculous, which delight the hearts of the esthetes; but as the succession of generations of musicians who were men like us, who strove and struggled, who had to take into account the same problems which confront us, and who carried out their resolves with the means at their disposal, that is to say with those furnished by the language of their time—men who sometimes happened to make mistakes, who followed the wrong road for a time, and who then took hold of themselves and found the right answers. When considered from the viewpoint of compositional problems, the history of the musical past becomes fertile, its knowledge indispensable. That is why I have felt it necessary

to discuss extensively, in the first part of this book, the living
chain of polyphonic activity from which is born the long series
of masterpieces that constitutes the tradition of our musical language. But I must also add that most of the notions about the
compositional problems which concern us are subject to so much
confusion and such misuse of terminology, and are so often in-
sufficiently thought out and badly defined, that I have not considered it superfluous to begin, in the following introductory section, by questioning the fundamental evidence as to the very
structure of the apparent art of music.

After all, should not every serious work, especially when it
attempts to synthesize, begin by approaching all the problems
which have arisen up to this point with the most radical skepticism? It is not until we have put all our "knowledge" in quotation
marks that our conscious judgement can attain that unhackneyed
freshness, allied with propulsive force, which will permit us to
present clearly and lucidly the problems which we are about to
attack.

In this sense, I can say that it is the same effort which has
produced the various parts of this work. The *Introduction*, which
contains the initial question as to "the essential factors of Occidental music and the conditions of their comprehension," is followed logically by the first section, *Prolegomena to Contemporary
Music*, which does not constitute a résumé of historical facts, but
a *reactivation* of the meaning of the evolution of polyphony in its
continual synthesis.

The second part, devoted to Arnold Schoenberg, treats of the
"birth and origins of contemporary music." The way in which the
musical past is realized in Schoenberg's consciousness during his
early works, forming a premise of which the acquisitions evidenced
in the later works are but the logical sequence; these new acquisitions themselves, as well as the evolution which they determine—
all this will make us understand how the contemporary art of
music has succeeded in finding a form of expression which grants
it a legitimate and indispensable place in musical tradition.

The two following parts discuss the works of Alban Berg and
Anton Webern. Besides expounding the individual characteristics

of the two musicians in question, these studies should contribute to a better comprehension of the problems discussed earlier. In effect, Berg and Webern were the very first pupils and disciples of Schoenberg. The interest of this fact is not merely anecdotal, for the uniting of these three names gives us the key to many a personal characteristic of each one of them. The friendship and love which characterize their relationship are remarkable; the fidelity to the teachings of the Master, never betrayed by the younger men, is deeply significant.

It does not seem to me an exaggeration to say that, without the addition of the two others, no one personality of this group would have a complete meaning. Such a hypothesis (which, as we shall see, does not belittle any one of the personalities in question) is obviously most applicable to the rôle of the master with regard to the two disciples. Without the teaching and the example of Arnold Schoenberg, the very existence of the art of Berg and Webern would be inconceivable. Appearing as prolongations of the activity of the Master, and forming contrasts among themselves, the activities of the two disciples, while shedding a new light on the problems posed by Schoenberg, acquire their own distinct and clearly individualized directions. In the same way, the powerful and integral personality of Arnold Schoenberg takes on a higher meaning and a more universal significance through the contributions of those whose genius he was able to discover and to guide.

Finally, the last part, stating in a new and precise form certain notions about musical language, and drawing certain conclusions from the activities observed in the preceding sections, attempts to show how this language is constituted in its basic essentials— those which are valid for our time.

*

* *

No doubt I shall be reproached, as I have often been before, for my exclusiveness, my bias, and Heaven knows what else! To limit oneself to the study of the works of the three artists in question is conceivable, since this limitation is imposed by the boundaries of the task which I have undertaken: but to limit genuine contemporary musical activity to the work of these three artists, to annihilate, so to speak, the rôle played by all the rest of the contemporary musical world, may appear inadmissible.

My answer is this: doubtless there are, among the other musicians of our time, a certain number of important personalities. My silence about their work, and the anathema on them, which this silence implies, is doubtless unjust. I cannot help it, for I do not have the time to concern myself with everything. In my opinion the true artist is the one who not only recognizes and becomes completely aware of the deepest problems of his art, but who also proceeds to their solution with the utmost integrity and with uncompromising *moral strength*. I thus can be concerned only with what appears essential to me, with what seems to me the result of such an attitude in such acceptance of artistic *responsibility*. I find the fullest development of this attitude only in our three musicians, whom I consider the only musical geniuses of our time. (I personally do not find it depressing that our century has produced *only* three musical geniuses. There have never been more at one time in any period of musical history.)

The future will show whether I have made a mistake. It is a risk which this book gladly runs, for it, too, is a complete acceptance of responsibility on my part. And in that respect, as well, I have learned it from those of whom it treats.

RENÉ LEIBOWITZ

Paris, May 1946.

Contents

CONTENTS

PART IV

Anton Webern: The Awareness of the Future in Contemporary Music

PART V

The Structure of Contemporary Musical Speech

INTRODUCTION

THE ESSENTIAL FACTORS OF OCCIDENTAL MUSIC AND THE CONDITIONS OF THEIR COMPREHENSION

Contemporary music is not an isolated phenomenon. By this we mean that it cannot be considered as a sort of excrescence without any connection with the musical art which preceded it. On the contrary, the music of today, issuing from a long tradition, crowns ten centuries of Occidental musical activity. Occidental music differs radically from all other known forms of musical expression. Whether we think of ancient music or of music in its exotic forms—Greek, Hindu, Byzantine, Gregorian, African, Chinese, Balinese, Arab or Inca—all these manifestations of the art of sound have one thing in common: they are *monodic*, that is to say they exclude the notion of simultaneity of sound. If sometimes, as in certain forms of Far-Eastern music (Japanese and Balinese, for example), the mixture of timbres caused by percussion instruments on different levels creates, in passing, the simultaneity of different sounds, this simultaneity is sporadic and accidental. In any case, such an occurrence is hardly ever sought *for its own sake* by the musicians, and it never constitutes an element of the musical structure, since it completely escapes the control of those who cause it. The only elements over which such control is exercised are those melodic and rhythmic elements which are necessary and sufficient for the realization of monody.

Basically different in this respect from all other forms of musical expression, the Occidental art of sound has been *polyphonic* for about a thousand years. This polyphony may be considered as the very key to its existence, which means that, at a given moment, Occidental musicians *consciously* introduced a new

xix

A-7 dimension to their art. This new dimension was *harmony,* which, added to the two previous factors, melody and rhythm, created an inseparable whole which, in its entirety, is constantly under the most absolute control to be found in any form of valid musical activity. This *whole* is polyphony, which, in a way, is the *alpha* and *omega* of these ten centuries of the history of music. Of this polyphony certain trends in contemporary music are merely the most advanced development (for the time being). When this is granted, it becomes evident that any serious study of any phase of Occidental music must begin by questioning the very essence of polyphony, as it is understood at the moment when one begins one's task.

*

*   *

Let us begin at the beginning by questioning the very origin of polyphony. It goes without saying that the question, as we put it here, has no historical or philological interest. It is not a matter of investigating the first polyphonists, or of hunting down the earliest extant essays in polyphony. What matters is to find out the *original meaning* with which polyphony must have made its first historic appearance, with which it has developed through the centuries (thanks to a living tradition), with which it still appears to us today, even though we know almost nothing about its first creators. But what we know of the living tradition of polyphony justifies us in questioning its origins, insofar as they were to be the foundations of all its future development.

At first glance, what we know about polyphony is neither more nor less than what we know at first glance about any other science—that is, it is a tradition, and it is the result of activity. Perforce, it bears the meaning of this activity within itself, even if the tradition has become for us (as is often the case) a petrifaction which has lost its true meaning. Given the possibility of examining this tradition, it becomes clear that the mistake of having permitted the feeling for polyphony to become submerged in our subconscious is not irremediable. All lack of consciousness implies the *possibility of consciousness* becoming explicit and evidencing itself irrefutably.

Our examination will begin with one of these evidences: polyphony as it is offered to us by tradition, the polyphony of which we musicians learn the laws and the technique which were taught to those who, in turn, have taught them to us, constitutes a patrimony of spiritual activity which is continually being enriched by new acquisitions. On the other hand, we may consider poly- ⫟ phony not only as a progress from one acquisition to the next, but also as a *continual synthesis,* in the midst of which all the preceding acquisitions continue to exist and form a whole, so that at any given moment the totality of polyphonic acquisitions is only a premise which may be followed by the acquisitions of the next moment in history. It is clear that this perpetual motion, this ceaseless march towards the horizon of the musical *future* belongs to the very essence of polyphony, which is thus connected with an endless chain of generations of musicians—known or unknown —working each for the other.

Like every acquisition of the human spirit, polyphony possesses its historic beginning. Its meaning, then, originates in a first *intentional creative effort,* at first a *project* [1] and then a *realization.* If we remember what was said above, that the evolution of polyphony occurs in the form of living progress, century by century, from one acquisition to the next, it becomes evident that the total meaning of polyphony could hardly exist from the beginning even as a project, far less as a realization. This explains the primitive forms of beginning polyphony, as well as its growing complexity. But this growing complexity implies another problem. Every realization of a project is a piece of evidence in favor of its creator; in that sense the very first polyphonic realization, as primitive as it might be, was such a piece of evidence. This permits us to state that the ulterior complexity which polyphony exhibits during the course of its development was implied in its

[1] This term will be used throughout this book in its strictly Heideggerian sense (Entwurf), i.e.: by existing, the human body *pro-jects* its world, causes the world to *be there:* this *pro-ject* is man's faculty of *being;* by continuously projecting himself in all his actions he becomes aware of his reality and of the reality of his actions which exist as the *present* and determine the *future.*

very origins, since, from its first appearance, polyphony succeeded in presenting problems which would be valid for its future existence.

*

*   *

The last assertions lead us to ask new questions. The project of a work of art and its realization are unfolded purely in the mind of the artist. However, the existence of a work of art is not a psychic personal existence which cannot take place outside the individual consciousness. The life of a musical work, for example, is translated into sound-forms which *exist for everyone,* for every real or potential musician, for every music-lover. In its original meaning, every musical work exists above and beyond time; in principle, it is accessible to all men of all nations and all times. Every new musical form acquires, as soon as it is created, this same *objectivity.*

But it is a sort of *ideal objectivity,* which must not be confused with the objectivity of commonplace objects. The latter—tools, for example—may be copied innumerable times, while the *Ninth Symphony,* and all other music, exists but a single time. No matter how many times a musical work may be performed and no matter how the degree of perfection of the performances may vary, the piece remains *exactly the same* throughout all the performances. Now, it is precisely the act of performance which confers on musical forms a kind of *palpable incarnation,* thanks to which their language becomes accessible to everyone. It is this palpable incarnation which brings about the "localization" and the "temporalization" of something which is, in its essence, neither "local" nor "temporal."

Nevertheless, the function of musical language could not be firmly established [2] were it not for *repeated performances*; for it is only the possibility of repeating a musical performance a large number of times which creates the unanimity of feeling (*Ein-*

[2] We limit ourselves here to a consideration of the *musical language* as something given, but we shall return to it in a more profound sense in the last section of this work.

fühlung) of an entire community with respect to a musical work. In postulating the identity of the work during all its repetitions, we understand easily that, from one person to another, the work finally becomes objectified insofar as it appears from one consciousness to the next in identical form.

The musical performance is a *re-creation* of the work. First created in the spirit of the artist, the musical work is re-created at each new performance and hearing by the performers and the audience. Does this complete the objectivity of the "ideal object" which is the sound-form? Apparently not. This life still lacks *persistence*. In other words, it lacks a durable existence which can outlast the lifetime of the author of a work and his contemporaries.

The primordial function of musical notation is precisely to make possible this *lasting objectification* of ideal forms. Once it has been noted down, the ideal object is given objective existence "in the world" and may be re-created at any moment.

Here we touch on an important aspect of the very essence of polyphony, an aspect which will complete our comprehension of what was said above on this subject.

Occidental music alone [3] has been able to create a genuine musical notation for itself. This notation soon becomes elaborated by the perfection of a special system of signs, completely unrelated to other graphic systems. This is because of the care for exactitude which Occidental musicians devote to the notation of their polyphonic realizations. Indeed, these realizations cannot be perpetuated by oral tradition alone.

But this is not the only reason which necessitated the perfection

---

[3] There were, indeed, several previous attempts: for example, Greek music. The Greeks were doubtless the first to attempt a lasting record of sound-forms; they tried to write them down with the help of the letters of their alphabet. However, their borrowing, for the notation of sound-forms, of a system invented for something else explains the inexactness of the results. Thus it can happen that the same musical text (e.g. the Delphic hymn of Apollo) varies considerably in the different transcriptions of modern musicologists. The effort of the Greeks is understandable, for they introduce into their art a kind of heterophony, considered by some as a precursor of polyphony. On the other hand, the inaccuracy of their system of notation is equally understandable, since their music, being monodic, could if necessary do entirely without this system.

of notation. Let us remember that, in sharp contrast to that cen-
turies-old petrifaction which characterizes most forms of musical
art, the Occidental art of sound is in a perpetual state of *becoming*.
Therefore it must have that lasting objectification, that constant
essential presence, so that, at every moment of its history, the
whole body of polyphony existing up to that time may become
immediately accessible to anyone who, establishing his premises
on this synthesis, uses it to forge ahead on the paths of musical
possibilities.[4]

*

*   *

However, all this entails a serious danger, the effects of which
we feel far too often. Sound-forms, as well as the graphic signs
which express them, are the palpably incarnate forms of ideal
objects, which are, in their essence, impalpable. Nevertheless, the
more familiar hearers and readers are with these incarnations, the
less genuine perception of them will they experience.[5] Their familiarity with the sounds and signs makes them comprehend these
symbols (if I may say so) *passively*. The perception of the content
of the sounds and signs is too often less an active, a living re-creation of the musical work—as it should be—than a merely passive
reproduction of graphic signs (i.e. musical notation), the true
meaning of which has become sedimented. But, every such sedi-
mentation is—to a certain extent—a form of oblivion.

[4] It is interesting to observe that our system of notation has evolved in every
respect according to the needs of polyphony. Still imprecise in its beginnings, the system
was sufficient for the notation of a very simple polyphony. But just as polyphony
became more complex—and so more difficult to write down—notation became ever
more exact and complex. For example, score-form, which did not come into general use
until the sixteenth century, constitutes a great step forward, as well as a definite
acquisition necessitated by the newly won importance of vertical writing. But it is
sufficient to compare the earliest scores with those of a far later date to see the immense
progress that musical notation has made since then. It is this, too, which makes us
comprehend the necessity which Schoenberg feels for the introduction of many innovations in this realm—innovations which we shall consider later.

[5] For proof, we need only look at most performers, who "sight read" and "practise" pieces of music in a quasi-automatic fashion, without being in the slightest aware
of the structure of these pieces. What is true of performers is even more true of most
listeners, who merely *undergo* passively the music that they hear.

This does not prevent the hearer or reader from having the faculty of remembering what has been forgotten, of digging out the neglected experience buried beneath its layers of sediment and reactivating it.

In introducing here the idea of reactivation, we call attention to the principal concern which should guide us in our research. We know how seductive many of the so-called "brilliant" ideas of today—ideas which nearly always operate with ready-made notions—can be, and that is why it has seemed important to us to elaborate this long exordium, in order to introduce into the total question a certain number of precise definitions. We are firmly convinced that every musical work is a definitive phenomenon which exists once and for all, that at each performance it is identically repeated, and that it can indubitably be "reactivated" in the identity of its true meaning.

But then how far can our power of reactivation go? And besides, is it really necessary, in every new musical enterprise, to attempt the reactivation of the entire musical past? Must we pass through all the links of the chain of centuries, back to the original premises, before we can begin our work at the spot assigned to us by history? Such an enterprise, even if it might have been possible during the first centuries of polyphonic activity, would be a Sisyphean labor today!

Never fear: we have seen—and we shall return to this point— that a new phase of musical history is not made up of new acquisitions alone, but is always a living synthesis of everything that preceded it. The links of the lengthy chain are bound together not only by chronology and gradual changes, but also, and above all, by a *meaning* common to all of them, by a *qualitative identity*.

Therefore, it is possible to say that, from the first evidence of the earliest polyphonic experimentation to the most advanced realization of the music of our time, through ten centuries of musical activity, a *logical* chain of evidence connects the genuine origins of polyphony with the manifestations which polyphony has produced.

If we wish to arrive at a real understanding of the problems posed by the most radical and genuine contemporary musical expression as it is incarnated in the works of Arnold Schoenberg and his school, it is less important for us to pass through the different phases of musical history than for us to try to reactivate the *meaning* of that continuity which we have just been emphasizing.

That is the effort to which the first section of this work will be devoted.

PART I

Prolegomena to Contemporary Music

To Simone de Beauvoir and
Jean-Paul Sartre

Our music critics complained about dissonances when the problem of the one-movement symphony confronted them; they complained about dissonances when new possibilities of melodic development manifested themselves. And they also complained about dissonances when there were none to be found. Thus, on the occasion of a concert of my pupils' works, a particularly sharp-eared critic defined a piece for string quartet—the harmony of which, as can be proved, is barely more complex than that of Schubert—as the product of my evil influence.

ARNOLD SCHOENBERG
"On Music Criticism" *Der Merker*, October 25, 1909.

CHAPTER I

Modal Music

1. *Definition of polyphony.*—In current usage only those passages are called polyphonic which exhibit a contrapuntal style. Those which are harmonically conceived are called homophonic.

But, literally and etymologically, the term *polyphony* is applicable to all music which employs simultaneity of sound. It makes little difference whether this simultaneity is obtained by superimposing melodic lines one upon the other (counterpoint) or by connecting chords with one another (harmony); the genuine notion of polyphony is predominant in both systems. Only monody deserves to be called homophonic.

Henceforth, therefore, we shall apply the term *polyphony* to any musical passage which, contrapuntally or harmonically, or combining the two systems, displays the simultaneity of several sounds.

For us, the notion of polyphony includes the unity of the three elements which constitute music: melody, harmony, rhythm. Melody means the horizontal unfoldment of intervals; harmony means the vertical disposition of intervals;[1] rhythm means the articulation of sound-forms in time. So it goes without saying that if we speak of the evolution of polyphony (of its growing complexity, for example) we intend to keep in view all three of these factors. The evolution of these three factors is always parallel, and it

---

[1] The notion of harmony, as we use it here, includes not only what is generally called "harmonic writing," i.e., writing in chords, but also the vertical aspect of contrapuntal writing. This seems fully justified to us, since, no matter what system of writing is used, the vertical structure implies, by its very definition, the idea of harmony. The most genuinely contrapuntal passage is constantly creating—consciously or not—harmonic aggregations, which means that such a contrapuntal passage can be analyzed from one end to the other in terms of vertical aggregations, whether or not these vertical aggregations can be reduced to known chord-types.

is absurd to speak of the progress of one without considering the progress of the two others. A musical composition which is rich rhythmically, but poor melodically, is almost inconceivable, and would in any case betray a weakness on the part of its author. Certainly, a passage may be contrapuntally complex and harmonically simple; one of these elements may, at a given moment, be eclipsed by the other; but then we are dealing with considerations of formal equilibrium, which always demands a certain "relief," a certain apportionment of the constituent elements. However, the hearing of such a passage will, in principle, reveal *its own integral aspect*, and that aspect is its polyphony, which, in its entirety, must belong to a specific stage of polyphonic complexity.

2. *Historic origins of polyphony; first experiments.*—Most musicologists agree in placing the first realizations of polyphony near the end of the ninth century; the first known polyphonic texts date from the tenth century. At one time there prevailed the opinion that the first polyphonic experiments were caused by the necessity of having one of the two parts of an ensemble sung by voices of a different kind. Naturally, female voices sound an octave above male voices. If one wanted to have the same melody sung by both kinds of voices, it was necessary to distribute the parts in different octaves. This way of singing in parallel octaves, for which parallel fifths and fourths were later substituted,[2] may be considered the most primitive expression of polyphony.

However, a new theory tries to seek the origins of polyphony in *heterophony:* a vocal melody is accompanied by an instrument, which plays the same melody with certain variations imposed by the nature of the instrument. Little by little, through the repetition of this process, certain polyphonic figures become established; these are finally used "for their own sake" and constitute the origins of polyphony.[3]

[2] These three intervals, octave, fifth, and fourth, are the principal intervals of the ancient Greek musical system. They determine the limits of the modes and of the tetrachords; they also show the simplest harmonic relationships, already calculated by Pythagoras (1:2, 2:3, 3:4).

[3] We incline definitely to the first hypothesis, for two reasons: 1) the first *organa* (points of departure for the above mentioned polyphonic works) present characteristics

As they are here presented, our two theories describe the first polyphonic experiments as the unfolding of two distinct parts from a single initial sound-form. Whether it is a matter of transposing the same vocal melody an octave, a fifth, or a fourth, or of adding instrumental embroidery to this same vocal melody, the primitive "polyphonic" forms imply at one and the same time the notions of variety and of unity. It seems, therefore, that from the beginning there cannot be any polyphony—that is to say, a certain form of musical variety—without a *unifying principle*.

It will be easy for us to note the constancy with which this function of unity maintains itself, in different forms, through the various phases of polyphony. The first really polyphonic document which we possess is the organum *Rex coeli domine maris* of the *Musica Enchiriadis*, which dates from the end of the ninth century or the beginning of the tenth. Here we see that the strictly parallel motion of the *vox organalis* and the *vox principalis* has been partially abandoned. The *vox principalis*, a Gregorian chant, begins on C, rises to F, goes down to D, and closes on E. The accompanying voice moves in a rhythm which corresponds at every point to that of the principal voice; this constitutes the unifying principle here. On the other hand, if unity is maintained by the rhythm, the harmony can escape the constraint of parallelism from time to time. Thus the *vox organalis* begins in unison with the *vox principalis* (another aspect of the unifying principle); in other words, both voices start on C. This C is maintained in the accompanying voice, while the principal voice rises step-wise to the fourth above, F. Between these two points the harmony has consisted of seconds and thirds. After the fourth is heard, the two voices move in parallel fourths (a vestige of the ancient organum in fourths) and it is only at the end, on the step D-E, that the two voices once more move in unison (a new application of the unifying principle).

Timid though this first essay in the independence of voices

which clearly show that they come from singing in parallel fourths; 2) the idea of polyphony, like every acquisition of the human spirit, is the result of an *intentional* conscious act. It must have been born in one or more musical minds quite outside of any "natural circumstances." But the theory (incompletely presented here) of heterophony as the generator of polyphony seems to us to overemphasize these natural circumstances and to minimize the role of intentional planning.

may be, the treatise *Musica Enchiriadis* is obliged to furnish a relatively complex theoretical justification of it. This justification merits our attention, for it concerns the very structure of the world of sound wherein these first manifestations of polyphony evolve. This world of sound is the world of the *ancient modes,* which we must now examine before we continue our study of the movement of the voices and the resulting harmony.

3. *The structure of the modes and its repercussions on polyphony.* —All music evolves in a sphere of sound made up of a certain number of tones and intervals, which are determined by the musical consciousness. Into such a sphere, into such a world of sound, the musical consciousness always introduces a system charged with organizing this world, with codifying all its tones and intervals according to certain norms.

The world of sound in which the first polyphonic experiments are located is the *diatonic world of seven tones*; the system that organizes it is the *modal system.* Let us recall its essential characteristics: the seven tones (C, D, E, F, G, A, B) may be grouped into seven diatonic modes, if each of these modes is made to begin on a different tone. Thus we obtain, on C, the Ionian mode; on D, the Dorian; on E, the Phrygian; on F, the Lydian; on G, the Mixolydian; on A, the Aeolian; on B, the Hypophrygian.[4] Because of the different placement of the half-steps in each of these modes, every one acquires its own special melodic characteristics. For example, in the mode on C the half-steps occur between the third and fourth degrees (E-F) and between the seventh and first degrees (B-C). In contrast, the half-steps of the Dorian mode occur between the sixth and seventh degrees—and so on through all the modes.

It is evident that these characteristics are, by their very definition, of a melodic nature. Furthermore, we may say that as long as monody reigned supreme the structure of the modes was respected. Indeed, new melodies could be composed, and might even

---

[4] Our classification is not that of Greek music or Gregorian music, but that deduced by later theorists (Glareanus, Fux, etc.) from the common practice of fifteenth and sixteenth century composers.

introduce some new characteristics; but as long as the musical consciousness of the various composers felt at home in that sphere of sound from which they drew their structural elements, all their melodies remained under the sway of the abovementioned modal characteristics. It is striking that the monodic musical consciousness has always felt at home in its particular sphere of sound over a long period of time; the idea of undertaking the slightest modification in its surroundings never occurs to it. This explains the previously-emphasized petrifaction of monodic forms of musical expression over a period of centuries.

But with the advent of polyphony all this will change. The polyphonic consciousness cannot adapt itself over such a long period of time to an immutable world of sound; or, rather, polyphony carries within itself the germ of a necessary evolution. Since there is evolution, the structure of the world of sound itself will be affected. This world, too, will be obliged to evolve. Therefore, it is now possible for us to affirm that any musical system which permits or establishes polyphony bears within itself, even at the hour of its birth, the seeds of its own destruction. This is self-evident, since every system of this kind implies the evolutionary possibilities of polyphony, and it is this evolution, permitted or favored by the system, which finally produces elements that are of such a nature as to break out of the system.

This impossibility of the self-perpetuation of a polyphonic system (at first in a stable form, later in its very essence) is a new, and very important, aspect of the Occidental art of sound.

The primitive organum of the *Musica Enchiriadis*, analyzed above, already reacts in a very specific way upon the laws of the system to which it submits. The essential characteristic of this organum seemed to us to consist of a certain use of the independence of voices which constituted a fundamental principle of all polyphony. Furthermore, we drew attention to the fact that it appeared necessary to the author of the *Musica Enchiriadis* to justify this innovation theoretically. Here are the essential points of this justification.

The motion of the voices in parallel octaves, fifths, or fourths is easily explained by the consonant character of these intervals, the intonation of which is easy because of their simple acoustical relationships. But the parallel evolution of fifths, and especially of fourths, implies the danger of *dissonant* obstacles. The diatonic modes are constituted in such a way that the superposition of fourths produces, within each mode (between B and F), an augmented fourth, or tritone, which is a false interval according to simple systems of measurement. In fact, the acoustical structure of the tritone is complicated, and the interval is difficult to sing simultaneously in two voices. The author of the *Musica Enchiriadis*, who cut his teeth on the system of organum in fourths, is keenly aware of the danger of the tritone. It is in order to avoid it that he does not make his voices parallel everywhere. And, what is more, since he has to compose a counterpoint to a melody which unfolds between C and A, passing through F, the author of the organum in question makes his counterpoint begin at the unison, on C, that is to say *above B,* so that any possibility of the false relation of the tritone F-B may be eliminated from the beginning.

Elsewhere, the author of the *Musica Enchiriadis* undertakes numerous reforms in the world of sound at his disposal, in order to get around the difficulty of the tritone. The fourth F-B is false (it is *augmented*); the same goes for the fifth B-F (it is *diminished*). Why not try to correct them by diminishing the augmented fourth and augmenting the diminished fifth? Thus we obtain F-B flat and B natural-F sharp. These modifications do not lead to final results, for if they eliminate certain obstacles they create others. B flat provokes a false relation with E, F sharp with C.

But, whatever the results, it is clear that profound reforms within the modal system are about to occur. Although the first alterations, which we have just pointed out, are of a benign character and do not imminently threaten the security of the system, that system is nonetheless weakened in its very foundations, so that we may say that with the advent of the first really polyphonic element (the independence of voices) the seed of the destruction of the system was sown.

We have just remarked that the damage to the system was slight. This is largely because the author of the *Musica Enchiria-*

dis (as well as a number of later authors) will do anything to safeguard the special characteristics of each mode. Indeed, these authors evaluate very clearly the different influences which the tritone exerts on the different modes. Thence comes their concern with composing *voces organales* which are clearly differentiated according to the modes for which they are intended. Such differentiation is easy to maintain, since polyphony is still very simple. However, the havoc created by the harmonic notion of the tritone, and the resultant alterations, drive polyphony on to a road which, rising to ever dizzier heights, leads ineluctably out of the system of sound from which polyphony issued.

4. *The progress of the independence of voices and the stages of counterpoint.*—Practised sparingly at first, organum (or, more precisely, the independence of voices which it sometimes exhibits) may be considered the point of departure for the entire evolution of polyphony. Though it is true that even in the most advanced example of the *Musica Enchiriadis* the two voices still display but little independence, because of their largely parallel motion and completely identical rhythm, the tiny deviation of the *vox organalis* from the *vox principalis* is a symptom the importance of which can never be overestimated.

Besides, the independence of voices makes very rapid progress. The lower range soon becomes too limited to satisfy the new demands of the *vox organalis*. The latter then begins to cross the *vox principalis*, and, towards the beginning of the eleventh century, definitely requires greater freedom. Then the given liturgical melody becomes the lower voice, with the contrapuntally invented melody placed above it, where it can evolve more freely.

One innovation follows another. We have seen that in the beginning, when the two voices were parallel, they were distinguished only by their register. Next, each voice has a different melody, with identical rhythm; finally, the rhythm itself varies from one voice to the next. This evolution clearly takes place between 900 and 1200. The parallel motion of organum disappears, and contrary motion, applied as often as possible, is considered essentially polyphonic.

In the twelfth century, new possibilities of polyphonic evolution unfold. Perotin's work has the merit of having notably amplified the musical language of his time. The art of Perotin originates in the acquisitions of his predecessor at the organ of Notre-Dame, Leonin. In Leonin's work, the practise of organum evolves from the type which we have just described, and attains a high level. Starting from this premise, Perotin, far from contenting himself with perfecting the legacy of Leonin, tries to forge ahead on the road of polyphonic possibilities. Up till now, polyphony had been content with two-voiced writing. Perotin was the first musician to use three and even four voices. To the practise of inventing a single counterpoint to the given chant, there is now added that of inventing two or even three such counterpoints simultaneously. But this increase in complexity introduces a new factor with which we must now concern ourselves.

The reader will recall what has been said about the *unifying principle*, to which we have assigned a role of primary importance in all polyphonic construction. We have seen that this principle manifested itself clearly in the organum *Rex coeli*, for it is quite easy for simple polyphony to cling to a *principle*. But how is it possible in a complex work? A glance at one of the four-voiced compositions of Perotin will show us that in a complex work—a work, that is, with a wealth of means at its disposal—the unifying principle is allied with the notion of *economy*. The astonishing *quadruplum* of Perotin, *Vide prophecie*, is exemplary in the economy with which it uses the varied and rich means at its disposal. Over a given chant in the lowest voice, three upper voices expose three counterpoints. In the second and third measures, these counterpoints, reading from top to bottom, form the following pattern: first voice, a short phrase which we shall call c; second voice, a phrase with identical rhythm but different intervals, a; third voice, a transposition of a. Measures 3-4: first voice, repetition of c; second voice, a new phrase, b; third voice, a. Measures 5-6: first voice, a new transposition of a; second voice, a; third voice, b—and so on. Thus we see that Perotin works with a minimum of given material, which nevertheless has a rich appearance because of the four-voiced writing. This sort of work, which is the source of double, triple, and quadruple counterpoint, will have powerful repercussions on the evolution of polyphony.

However, the author of the *quadruplum* which we are analyzing discovers another contrapuntal principle of paramount importance. Thus, in measures 15 and 22, the second and third voices develop by *imitation*, with the third voice imitating the second; but a little further along (measures 47-53) the reverse takes place—the second voice imitates the third, and in addition (measures 53-54) an imitation occurs between the first and second voices.

It is from such principles that the science of counterpoint is developed. About a century after the art of Perotin, that of Guillaume de Machaut represents a new stage of fundamental progress.

Like Perotin (and many other less illustrious composers who link the two masters) Machaut freely uses the principles elaborated by his great forerunner. Imitation has become commonplace in contrapuntal writing, but Machaut augments its possibilities still further. In fact, the only kind of imitation in use up till then was *direct imitation*, in which the voice which is supposed to imitate a melody stated by another voice repeats this statement literally (at most, transposing it). However, in a three-voiced canon, Machaut inaugurates the practice of retrograde imitation, in which one voice takes the statement of the other and unfolds it in the reverse direction, from the last note to the first. Starting from the premise of *imitation*, there is introduced here, in the most logical fashion possible, a new polyphonic acquisition, a perfect means of establishing a true economy in the midst of real musical riches.

Thinking along the same lines, Machaut was to create another important architectonic element, all his own. His Mass is, in fact, the first really long work of which the art of music may boast. In its dimensions this work far surpasses anything that the art of sound had produced up to that time. In order to relate such vast proportions to a unifying principle, Machaut has recourse to the following procedure: the different parts of the mass are bound together by a single *cantus firmus*. This *cantus firmus* consists of a liturgical chant, which Machaut, after the fashion of his predecessors, uses as a basis for his contrapuntal construction. It is, however, interesting to note that this *cantus firmus* undergoes slight rhythmic variations from one movement to the next.

The composition of masses constructed in this manner will become the special feature of the Flemish school which arises about 1430 and which, emigrating to Italy, will reach the heights of *a cappella* vocal style during the second half of the sixteenth century. The primary role of this school is the definitive codification of all contrapuntal procedures. Imitation is still the basic element of this style, but the Flemings and their Italian successors deserve credit for having added other methods of imitation to those with which we are already familiar (direct and retrograde). The most important of these is *inversion*, which reproduces the original intervals in the opposite direction. In addition there are imitations by augmentation or diminution, in which the answer imitates the statement while shortening or lengthening its time-values.

Furthermore, the Flemish school attains such perfection in contrapuntal writing that this style culminates in works for six, eight, ten, and even twelve voices. These works, despite their prodigious complexity, are elaborated on principles of economy. One of the most complex works of this period that I know, the twelve-voiced motet *Laudate Dominum* which closes the *Magnum opus Musicum* of Orlando di Lasso, begins with an exposition of the twelve voices in different kinds of strict imitation.

Thus ends a great era of polyphony, which might be called the *modal and contrapuntal polyphonic era*. After comparatively slow beginnings in the eleventh and twelfth centuries, polyphony, after rising rapidly for three more centuries, succeeds in transforming radically the very structure of the world into which it was born, and is thus forced in addition to transform some of its own essential elements in an equally radical manner.

In the next section we shall study the way in which these transformations are accomplished, and the factors which compel their occurrence.

5. Vertical aspects of counterpoint. Crystallization of harmonic formulae, and their repercussions on the modal system.—From the very beginning, polyphony appears in the form of simultaneous motion of several voices (that is to say in a *contrapuntal* form). However, at the same time it is concerned with the vertical aggregations produced by the meeting of two voices, which result from this simultaneous motion. We have already observed this concern for *harmony* in connection with the tritone, or diminished fifth; other problems of a similar nature were not long in arising.

What is the essence of these problems? It is the fact that every harmonic aggregation appears as a problem to singers, according to whether (empirically speaking) its intonation proves to be easy or difficult. Since medieval music was primarily *vocal*, such problems were found to exert a paramount influence on the development of polyphony. The subdivision of harmonic intervals into two empirical categories corresponds to a subdivision justified by scientific calculation. Thus, the easy intervals correspond to the consonances (unisons, octaves, fifths, and fourths); the difficult intervals correspond to the dissonances (thirds, sixths, seconds, sevenths, and augmented and diminished intervals). This proves that, in its very origins—and by its very definition—polyphony could not obey the laws of melody only, but had also to come to terms with the idea of harmony. Little by little, preoccupation with harmony gained the upper hand over every other consideration in music, and forced the overthrow of the modal system, to which harmonic ideas were not at all adapted (since the system had originally been constructed for an entirely different purpose) and within which they could not unfold with all the freedom— and strictness—to which they aspired.

The division of vertical intervals into consonances and dissonances [5] proves that from the beginning vertical aggregation is a conscious process. But conscious though it may be, the use of these aggregations in the first expressions of polyphony is not governed by precisely formulated laws. There seems to be only one fixed rule—the use of the unison at the beginning and end of a piece, which is justified by the prevalent conception of the unison as the consonant interval *par excellence*. Since it is easily intoned by the

---

[5] This division was also applied to horizontal intervals, in the same way, during the monodic period.

singer, the unison is considered as the ideal *point of departure*, both esthetically and practically speaking. Given this point of departure, *tension* develops. Other intervals, dissonances among them, are heard, and, in order to achieve a successful ending (again, not only because of the esthetic meaning but also because of the practical demands) relaxation takes place once more, in the form of the unison. From the harmonic viewpoint, this final unison is a sort of magnetic point on which two currents are supposed to converge; and this convergence produces the first harmonic *formula*. How is it elaborated?

In order to break the habit of parallel motion, the earliest polyphonists used *oblique motion*, such as we have noted in the organum *Rex coeli* (the *vox organalis* remained stationary while the *vox principalis* moved). Shortly after, another kind of motion, which is the origin of true polyphony, was to be adopted: *contrary motion*, the usage of which is already prescribed by Cotto around 1100: "Ubi in recta modulatione est elevatio, ibi in organica fiat depositio et e converso." (If the principal voice goes up, the organal voice must go down, and vice versa.)

Thus, the piece of music resembles a fan opening and closing: unison—unfoldment (contrary motion)—unison. Accordingly the final unison is frequently approached by contrary motion. But—and this is very important—the last step of the *vox principalis* is *predetermined*. We know that the *vox principalis* is always taken from the liturgical repertory—that is, it is in the Gregorian tradition. It is a fact that the Gregorian repertory is identified with a distinct type of monody which operates with fixed rules. Thus, every Gregorian melody ends on the first note of the mode to which it belongs and this *fundamental* of the mode is most frequently approached through the second note of the mode, which we call the *upper leading-tone*. This state of affairs once given as an almost inviolable rule, the problem of the final harmonic formula is to find a *fixed movement* of the *vox organalis* which may invariably and adequately accompany the cadence in the other voice. Here, too, one element is predetermined—the necessity for the counterpoint to close on the fundamental of the mode. But, this time, the fundamental will be approached by *contrary motion*, through the seventh note of the mode, which we call the *lower leading-tone*. In this way the characteristic motion of a descending second, heard in the given chant, is felicitously varied, in an essentially polyphonic manner, by the counterpoint. This practice, speedily becoming universal, gives rise to the typical harmonic formula of third followed by unison—a dissonance resolving to a consonance. (Later, when the principal voice is relegated to the lower part, the third is replaced by the sixth, the unison by the octave. Thus the essence of the succession dissonance-consonance remains.)

Before tracing the further evolution of such formulae, let us ask the following question: wherein consists the necessity of these formulae? Two factors clarify the answer: 1) the need for singers to operate with familiar and accustomed intervals, in order to be in a position to "render" polyphony with a certain assurance; 2) the need for composers to feel the same familiarity with vertical intervals, in view of the essence of polyphonic evolution. In fact, we know that the polyphonist must have absolute control of all the polyphonic acquisitions of his time, so that these acquisitions can serve as a basis for his future additions. Therefore, it is understandable that each generation of polyphonists should seek to systematize the acquired materials. What more logical way to systematize than to elaborate a certain number of fixed formulae and grant them the status of laws? These laws are capable of formulation and may easily be perpetuated through oral or written instruction.

Evidently, the more complicated and rich polyphony grew, the more necessary it became to enlarge the scope of these fixed harmonic formulae. What are the consequences of this state of mind?

First, the following observation must be made: if singers, as well as composers, are to be given the possibility of a certain familiarity with the vertical aggregations and of a certain self-confidence in handling them, it is necessary that these aggregations be listed in a certain number of easily comprehensive categories. Now, the differences of structure in the various modes *have a tendency to disparity*. The third-unison succession of the final

cadence is not identical in all modes. According to the characteristics of the diatonic world, such a cadence includes a minor third
in the Phrygian, Ionian, and Lydian modes—that is, in all modes
where the lower leading-tone (or, as in the Phrygian mode, the
upper leading-tone) is a half-step from the fundamental. On the
other hand, the third is major in the Dorian, Mixolydian, and
Aeolian modes—that is, in those where the lower leading-tone is
a whole-step from the fundamental. This divergence proves to be
embarrassing. The movement of a half-step between lower leading-
tone and fundamental is judged to be the most satisfactory for
the rising cadence of the counterpoint. It is then decided to reproduce this movement of the counterpoint in the modes where
the leading-tone is a whole-step from the fundamental. In the
Dorian, Mixolydian, and Aeolian modes, then, the leading-tone is
raised in the course of the final cadence. This gives us C sharp
in Dorian, F sharp in Mixolydian, G sharp in Aeolian (since this
G sharp creates the augmented second F-G sharp between the
sixth and seventh degrees, the F is raised to F sharp). The
Phrygian mode alone is protected from such transformation, since
raising its leading-tone produces a false (diminished) third, D
sharp-F, in the final cadence. Because of this difficulty, this
mode is used less and less; when, much later, it was decided to
raise its lower leading-tone, it was also necessary to raise its upper
leading-tone in order to get the right minor third, D sharp-F sharp.
Let us also recall the frequent transformation of B into B flat in
order to avoid the danger of the tritone, particularly evident in
the Dorian and Lydian modes. We find ourselves, then, confronted
with the following result: the various alterations within all the
modes *entirely suppress the individual characteristics of these
modes* and reduce them all to two prototypes:

    1. Modes with a major third: Ionian, Lydian (identical with
Ionian when it uses B flat), and Mixolydian (identical with the
others when it uses F sharp). *Major type.*

    2. Modes with a minor third: Aeolian (ascending: A B C D E
F♯ G♯ A; descending: A G♮ F♮ E D C B A); Dorian (identical
with Aeolian where its ascending form uses B natural and C sharp
and its descending form uses C natural and B flat); and, if neces-

sary, Phrygian with F sharp (identical with the two others when its ascending form uses C sharp and D sharp and its descending form uses D natural and C natural). *Minor type.*

All this leads us to the conclusion that the necessity for polyphony to create fixed harmonic formulae gradually engenders certain factors which ineluctably bring about the dissolution of the modal system.

6. *The generalization of harmonic formulae and its ultimate consequences. Fux's Gradus ad Parnassum. Recapitulation.*—We have not yet envisaged *all* the harmonic aspects of modal polyphony. One of the important problems of this polyphony is the evolution of the notion of *dissonance.* We have seen that in the beginning this notion was applied to all intervals except the octave, fifth, and fourth. However, this theory soon became expanded through the systematic use, in polyphony, of other vertical aggregations. Thus, thirds and sixths are promoted to the rank of *consonances.*[6] The repercussion of this evolution on harmonic formulae is striking. For example, if thirds and sixths are considered as consonances, their function in the final cadence is altered. It is no longer correct to speak of a *relaxation* produced by the succession of dissonance-consonance, since the first member of the succession is itself a consonance. The succession is expanded; it is preceded by a third member, a real dissonance. Thirds and sixths become the resolutions of seconds and sevenths respectively, so that the successions are from now on numbered 2, 3, 1 and 7, 6, 8.

What applies to two-voiced writing applies equally to polyphony in three, four and even more voices. In three voices, the "typical" final aggregation frequently gives rise to the superposi-

[6] It is true that they are called imperfect consonances in relation to octaves, fifths, and fourths, which are perfect consonances. However, this distinction soon proves to be more theoretical than practical, given the circumstance that composers use both types of intervals with equal freedom. All these details are significant, for the same thing occurs constantly in the evolution of polyphony. Certain intervals pass constantly—at least in practise—from the dissonant to the consonant ranks. By this I mean that one of the essential traits of Occidental musicians is to use ever more vertical aggregations until all possible harmonic combinations have been tried. Often "theories" stand in the way, but that does not keep practical music from forging ahead to new harmonic discoveries.

tion of fifth and fourth. It is then numbered 5, 8, and thus unites all the perfect consonances. But, in four voices, it is not uncommon for the third to be added to this structure, and soon such an aggregation is considered as an even more perfect consonance. What is more, all these aggregations are now found not only at the ends of pieces, but also in more general use, so that in the last period of modal music one can analyze an entire piece according to typical successions of vertical aggregations—that is, chord-progressions.

In this connection, it is interesting to devote a few moments to examining Fux's *Gradus ad Parnassum,* published at Vienna in 1725. The very date of publication indicates a certain anachronism; though he was a contemporary of Bach and of a musical speech considerably advanced beyond modal polyphony, Fux (who shows himself, in his music, bolder and more advanced) tries to found his whole system of instruction on the musical principles basic to the art of Palestrina—in other words, sixteenth-century principles. His treatise, though already outstripped by practical music at the moment of its publication, nevertheless succeeds in constituting a complete synthesis of modal contrapuntal style, so that at the present time it furnishes us with the essential elements of that style. Now, the rules pronounced by Fux agree exactly with the results which we have obtained here.

The style expounded by Fux is certainly contrapuntal, since the emphasis is continually being placed on voice-leading. But this counterpoint is only a *project* [7] with Fux; the final result proves to be harmonic. Every vertical aggregation is meticulously controlled, and is automatically reduced to a predetermined type; that is, all chords are classified. [8] Furthermore, we find in most of the chords, as well as in most of the voice-leading, formulae which

---

[7] See footnote 1, Introduction, p. xxi.

[8] It is interesting to note that this state of affairs had already existed nearly a century earlier. Thus, in 1600, the English poet and theorist Thomas Campion published his *Treatise of counterpoint, A new way of making fowre parts in counterpoint by a most familiar and infaillible rule.* This rule is a perfect example of a completely harmonic consciousness still expressing itself in terms of a contrapuntal plan. Here is the rule: given the bass and the position of the four voices in the first chord, one must harmonize this bass note against note (and even with passing tones), without breaking the laws of counterpoint, in such a way as to obtain a "full chord" with every vertical aggregation. The rule is formulated in contrapuntal terms, but the results are entirely harmonic. Here is the first "postulate": "If the bass must rise a second, a third, or a

are completely analogous with those which we are accustomed to hearing in tonal music. One of the most striking examples of this state of affairs is to be found, I think, in the different cadences, of which Fux gives us a theoretical formulation based on his conception of the common practise of Palestrina and his contemporaries. But these cadences, which Fux justifies by voice-leading, are really harmonic formulae. Already in Fux's time, composers used such cadences freely in purely harmonic writing, ignoring voice-leading and explaining the cadences according to the functions of the chord-progressions of which they are made.

We may also add that Fux tries to preserve, in all his examples, the special characteristics of the different modes. However, in a general way (except in the Phrygian mode, the original character of which he safeguards) he practises all the alterations in the modes which we described above. Thus, he admits implicitly only the two principal types, *major* (Ionian, Lydian, Mixolydian) and *minor* (Aeolian and Dorian).

To sum up, then:

1. The counterpoint which constitutes the origin of polyphony never exists in a pure state. It can exist in the pure state only as a project, the realization of which always gives rise to a system which cannot be satisfied with contrapuntal ideas alone.

2. Polyphony, born of counterpoint, tends from the very beginning towards harmony; this is proved by the harmonic formulae which it engenders almost immediately.

3. If the preoccupation with horizontality can continue within the modal system, the vertical aggregations tend to break out of bounds. Harmony, to expand, requires other laws than those of the modal system. Once harmony is employed, consciously or unconsciously, it needs another system to explain its use.

---

fourth, the voice a third or tenth above the bass will pass to the octave, the voice a fifth above will pass to the third, and the voice an octave above will pass to the fifth."

Here is a scheme:

8	3	5
3	5	8

Progressions of the individual voices.
Intervals formed by the different voices with the bass

The following "postulates" apply to a descending bass, etc.

It seems that the theories of Campion are not entirely original or "first-hand." This does not matter, since his sources probably display the same state of mind.

4. Preoccupation with harmony necessitated alterations in the various modes. These alterations accomplish two essential transformations:

a) The *specialization* of the modal system is reduced. Instead of a large number of special modes, two prototypes only remain.

b) The diatonic world of seven tones is considerably enlarged. Instead of seven tones, twelve tones are in current use. This' state of affairs has a profound effect on voice-leading, which often becomes *chromatic* instead of *diatonic*.

5. The transformations which we have just pointed out imply that the last modal music

a) constantly breaks out of the modal system and out of the diatonic world;

b) tends towards another system and another world;

c) is often inexplicable except by means of ideas borrowed from another system;

d) displays a total body of acquisitions which may be considered as a basis for certain new acquisitions, which we shall study in the following chapter.

CHAPTER II

Tonal Music

7. *General characteristics of the new system. Opposition between modality and tonality; transition from one to the other.*

Chromaticism.—All the latest acquisitions of modal polyphony can unfold freely in the *tempered chromatic* world of sound, and can be clearly justified on the basis of the *major-minor tonal system.*

We have seen that the alterations of the modes necessitated the use of five new tones, which were at first hardly understood in the diatonic world. Zarlino (1517–1590) was the first to group the twelve available tones in a coherent way. It is needless to stress the rather complex process which causes this grouping; suffice it to say that the *tempered* chromatic scale irons out the few acoustical inaccuracies which result from the transposition of the intervals to the various chromatic degrees. Indeed, in a twelve-tone system, such as the chromatic scale, it is impossible to reproduce precisely the same intervals on any degree whatsoever. The system of equal temperament strikes the balance among the various inaccuracies and thus succeeds in reestablishing equilibrium for all ears.

This new world of sound is organized according to the major-minor tonal system, the logical outcome of the last modal experiments. Used for the first time in its strict form by Johann Sebastian Bach and formulated for the first time in the theory of Rameau, this system may be, in its essence, reduced to a series of principles some of which are prolongations of the modal system, while others prove to be radical innovations.

The distinction between the two types, major and minor, is preserved. This is the principal survival of *modal specialization.*

However, these two modes are capable of being transposed, twelve times each, to the twelve degrees of the chromatic scale. The result is that the essential character of music composed in the new system is due less to its *modal color* than to its *tonal function*. This is easily understandable, since modal nuances now prove to be extremely limited and obvious, while the possibility of transposing the same key twelve times creates a great number of tonal nuances. The essential characteristic of a tonal work, then, is the key to which it belongs. This means that every such work relates the sound-forms of which it consists to a unifying principle, incarnate in a certain transposition of the major or minor scale, from which the chief structural elements will be derived. Thus we see that instead of *modal specialization* the new system introduces *tonal universality,* since—aside from the difference between major and minor—all keys are created equal, being differentiated merely by *transposition.* The differences, then, are only relative.

All this is but the straightforward and systematic consecration of a state of affairs which, in a less straight-forward and systematic form, had already existed for some time. The first tonal music, before Bach and Rameau, really differs very little from the last modal music. But the new system permits: 1) a more complete and precise "classification" of the latest acquisitions of polyphony; 2) an easier approach to new acquisitions.

Hence we see that continuity—not a violent break—is the principal element in the transition from one musical system to another. This is obvious, since a new system does not issue from pure speculation, but is merely the theoretical consecration of practical usage.

This idea of *continuity* is confirmed by the fact that the universalizing tonal system still admits a certain amount of modal particularity. However, let us say at once that the tonal system soon tends to the realization of its essence, which is precisely its universalism, by showing at first a pronounced preference for major (eliminating minor almost entirely) and, above all, by gradually reducing all its components to the common denominator of chromaticism.

This last point deserves further attention. Chromaticism, little used in the earliest tonal works (which had inherited it from the

last modal works), becomes more and more important
evolves. According to what we have just said (which w
ther proved by the subsequent stages of this evolution)
nothing surprising in this, since, in identifying itself with c
icism, the tonal system is only expressing its own "uni ᵤsal"
essence. Let us remark in passing that chromaticism justifies itself
completely in tonal music, since such music evolves in a sphere of
sound the circumference of which is the chromatic scale. On the
other hand, we must admit that from the beginning chromaticism
is a *destructive* element, a germ which, in its own growth, will kill
the system. Let us not forget that tonal music, if it is to remain
tonal, must submit to the unifying principle of tonality. But
tonality is elaborated on the basis of *a certain transposition* of the
major or minor mode, that is, on the basis of a seven-tone scale.
However, an extremely advanced use of chromaticism obliterates
the contours of such a scale, and assimilates it with every other
transposition, so that not only every modal element, but also every
fixed point of tonality is eliminated. Indeed, it is chromaticism
which confronts us once again with the destruction of a musical
system. The tonal system (just like the modal system at the
beginning of polyphony), because it contains elements capable of
favoring the growth of polyphony, is foredoomed, and will one day
die from those very elements which made it live.

8. *Harmonic structure of the tonal system.*—Modal functions were
essentially melodic. With the progress of polyphony, these functions are obliterated, in order not to interfere with the increasingly
important harmonic possibilities. But the modal system proves
powerless to create harmonic functions, because, not being "made"
for polyphony in the first place, it can hardly dominate all aspects
of polyphony. This is the principal necessity for the advent of the
tonal system,[1] for, in fact, after the work of Bach, this system

[1] One can also say that what is usually called the last modal era (from the end
of the sixteenth century to the beginning of the seventeenth) is really the first, un-
recognized, tonal era. In fact, harmony is most often used then according to its tonal
functions, but these functions are still not explicit. The theoretical formulation of the
tonal system is merely the consecration of a state of affairs which existed before this
formulation.

implies a precise harmonic structure, which imparts a functional value to harmony.

What is this structure? We know that tonality is represented melodically by a *scale,* major or minor. Harmonically, it will be represented by a series of chords built on each degree of such a scale. What sort of chords are these? Their prototypes are incarnate in aggregations known as perfect triads. Such a triad is the result of superimposing, on a fundamental, its fifth and its third—a superposition (since the third is now a consonance) of the most consonant sounds in existence.

In order to justify this new appreciation of a consonant harmonic combination, scientific reasons are invoked; a fundamental tone emits harmonics, and the closest harmonics to the fundamental are precisely the fifth and the third. Thus, the triad is the perfect symbol of the structure of the world of sound, because it reproduces an image of Nature.[2] These justifications are unimportant. It is sufficient to remember 1) that the perfect triad is one of the end-results of polyphony at the beginning of the tonal system, 2) that it was in general and preponderant use throughout the sixteenth and seventeenth centuries, and 3) that it is legitimate for the tonal system to attempt the codification of its use, and to base the principles of the system on the very existence of the perfect triad.

The harmonic expression of tonality is, then, incarnate in a series of chords built on all the degrees of the scale. The principal chord is the tonic triad—the fundamental of the key—inasmuch as it strictly determines the very essence of tonality. In fact, most pieces composed in the tonal system begin and end with the tonic chord, major or minor.

The reproduction of this chord on other degrees gives analogous results on the fourth and fifth degrees (in major, IV and V are major; in minor, they are minor). After I, IV and V take over the most important functions. That is understandable, for these two chords constitute a danger to tonality. Since tonality is essen-

---

[2] It is interesting to note that the same state of mind exists in all arts at this period. The plastic arts of the Renaissance are concerned with exact imitation of Nature. They base this imitation upon many scientific notions—anatomy, perspective, and so on.

tially expressed by I, any other chord constructed like the tonic chord runs the risk of sounding like the tonic of a new key. Hence, a *tension* is set up among the three most powerful functional regions of tonality: tonic region (I), dominant region (V), subdominant region (IV). In every truly tonal composition, this tension must be resolved by the absolute triumph of the tonic.

The chords built on other degrees are imperfect imitations of the structure of the tonic chord. In major, II, III, and VI are minor; VII is diminished. In minor, III, VI, and VII are major; II is diminished. Their functions are less important; for they are automatically out of danger of being confused with the tonic. According to their structure, they are attached to one or another of the three principal regions.

From this division of tonality into three principal regions there result the principal harmonic functions of tonality. It is obvious that this is only possible thanks to the relative universality of the tonal system which allows these different functions to be transposed from one key to the next, since one key is merely the transposition of another key. Thus the unity and identity of these functions are guaranteed for all keys. Let us recall once more that this state of affairs could not exist in a "specializing" system such as the modal system, where the differences between the various modes exclude that concept of *function* which presupposes the notion of *identity*.

A single chord cannot constitute a piece of music. In order that music may exist, there must be movement, there must be displacement in time. Therefore, the tonic chord must be followed by other chords. We have said that chord-progressions provoke tension, which must culminate in the triumph of the tonic. It is on this basis that the architecture of a tonal composition is erected.

9. *The contrapuntal problems of the tonal system.*—We have just seen that a tonal work owes its existence principally to harmonic factors. Must we draw the conclusion that tonal polyphony is entirely dominated by these factors? Is nothing left of the original contrapuntal aspect of polyphony?

At the end of the preceding chapter, we had remarked that the last so-called modal works were no longer contrapuntal except insofar as counterpoint existed as a *project* in the mind of the composer. In effect, the works of a Palestrina, of a Victoria, and especially of certain Venetians and madrigalists, such as Gabrieli, Luca Marenzio, and others, prove to be essentially harmonic, although their project may be explained by voice-leading. From this we may deduce that voice-leading and the chords which result from it are not incompatible. A musician may *think* in independent voices and produce chord-progressions. We shall also see that he can think in terms of harmonic functions and produce independent voices.

Let us examine the first possibility. It is in the work of Bach that all the functions of the tonal system are first realized. Bach, more than any of his predecessors and contemporaries, has a firm grasp on the functions of tonality, and establishes them in a manner which is decisive for the subsequent evolution of tonality.

Now that this has been established, let us see what polyphonic forms Bach uses to permit the significant affirmation of tonal functions. There is no doubt that it is the *fugue* which constitutes the most perfect and original expression of Bach's work. This form is derived from a modal form already used by the Flemings in the fifteenth century. At that time, canonic pieces were called fugues. This indicates the purely contrapuntal plan of such compositions. In the initial pre-Bach tonal period the fugue evolves, undergoing some slight changes, but never modifying its own contrapuntal pattern.

Like his predecessors, Bach composes fugues with a contrapuntal plan. Some of them (I am thinking above all of certain examples in the *Art of Fugue*) display a very advanced contrapuntal style, even more complex than that used by the most accomplished contrapuntists of the past. However, it may be observed that no matter how complex these fugues are contrapuntally they can constantly be reduced to typical tonal chords, to harmonic progressions which are entirely under control and which are carefully realized according to the strictest harmonic functions of tonality. What is more, Bach uses the fugue as the ideal opportunity to establish once and for all the essentially tonal tension between tonic and dominant. In fact, the theme of the fugue is nearly always exposed alternately in these two regions.[3]

All this proves that a contrapuntal plan can exist simultaneously with a harmonic plan; the two ideas are not mutually contradictory.

However, let us not deceive ourselves; in the entire history of music up to the twentieth century, this state of affairs existed only once. The work of Bach, situated at the junction of two roads of music—a work the existence of which seems to have been prepared for by centuries of arduous labor, and in which the fertility of many lands is consummated—realizes the synthesis of two fundamental expressions of polyphony with unparalleled felicity. That is the secret of the impression of absolute perfection which we receive from the music of Bach.

It goes without saying that this felicity, this euphoria, could not last long. After Bach, not only do counterpoint and harmony tend to become separated, but counterpoint itself disappears (except for a few rare instances) from the list of our musical preoccupations. How could it be otherwise? We have seen that the tonal system was created primarily to justify the harmonic nature of music from the sixteenth century onward. Since it was created for harmony, in order to make harmonic writing more explicit and to favor its evolution, the tonal system really does not seem to fit counterpoint. How, indeed, can melodic voices unfold freely if their superposition must at every instant be under the control of *chord-types* and *tonal functions?* We must then aver that counterpoint, already mired in the modal system, becomes almost impossible in the tonal system.

However, the reader will remember what was said above; there can be cases of harmonic ideas which produce an autonomous movement of voices. In fact, this happens rather often. At random, I cite a measure of Schumann (whom one could certainly not call a contrapuntist, and whose work is the product of a time when contrapuntal ideas appear but rarely)—measure 12 of the song Op. 42 no. 4 (part of *Frauenliebe und Leben*), which, although

---

[3] The region of the subdominant also plays a certain role, but its function is not systematically included in music until the rise of the Haydn type of *classical sonata*.

harmonically conceived, is a perfect specimen of contrapuntal
writing. The chord-functions here are of the IV-V-I type; no more
harmonic idea can be imagined, especially as this is a tonal cliché,
a mechanical formula for such a skilled harmonist as Schumann.
But these chords are elaborated by a voice-leading which even
Fux could not have criticized, and which he would have classified
in the category of three-part counterpoint of the second species
(two notes against one) .[4]

Mes. 12

Such examples are abundant in all tonal music. One may then
ask if this is not real counterpoint, or, if it is tonal music sprung
from contrapuntal music, whether it does not sometimes remain
contrapuntal in spite of itself. Neither of these explanations is
valid. Such passages are nothing but survivals of modal formulae.
Even in their origins, these formulae were so harmonic that they
could easily maintain themselves in music which used harmony
in a conscious manner.

Therefore, from whatever angle we approach the problem, it
becomes evident that counterpoint and tonality could not ride
tandem. However, a certain autonomy of the voices is not excluded from the possibilities of harmonic writing. On the contrary,
it is often sought for. On the other hand, after Bach, composers
like Haydn, Mozart, Beethoven, Schubert—and, later, Schumann,
Brahms, Wagner, Franck—will occasionally, especially towards the
end of their careers, feel an urgent need of coming to terms with
counterpoint. This is quite normal. Polyphony was realized, in the
beginning, thanks to counterpoint; counterpoint, therefore, is the
polyphonic element *par excellence*. To exclude this element from
polyphony would be the equivalent of cutting off an arm or a leg.

---

[4] There is even present the license permitted by Fux in this species—that of
progressing in fifths between the *cantus firmus* and the rapidly moving voice, which
proceeds in such a way as to permit that progression.

This explains why, even during moments of contrapuntal "eclipse," counterpoint led a secret life of its own, manifesting itself in those harmonic passages where harmony was realized by a movement of autonomous voices (as in the Schumann example), but sometimes breaking out violently as in some of the late works of Mozart and Beethoven.

Later, we shall see that it is the concern with the realization of a truly contrapuntal style—a concern never absent from the greatest musical minds of the eighteenth and nineteenth centuries —which is one of the chief causes of the abandonment of the tonal system.

10. *The principles of harmonic evolution.*—Harmonically, tonality is expressed by a series of chords built on the different degrees of a certain scale. All these chords are constructed according to a certain "model" which attempts to imitate a "natural image" as closely as possible. We must now discuss this last characteristic. It is nonsense to believe that the idea of the "imitation of nature" according to scientific laws was consciously manifested by the first harmonists. Their use of perfect triads was not dictated by mathematical and physical considerations, but was imposed by *practical laws* of musical composition. How else can we explain the use of minor and diminished chords, which occupy four degrees of the scale (when major chords occupy only three) and which do not constitute an acoustically exact reproduction of the structure of the world of sound? It is a matter of skill, of practical convenience, which ignores scientific considerations and obeys only the laws of composition.

Furthermore, tonal harmony, from its beginnings, is not satisfied with perfect triads alone. Other aggregations were inherited from the modal system by the tonal system. One of them is at least as important as the perfect triad: the seventh chord, whose role is an essential one. It is true that a certain seventh chord—the one which consists of a minor third superimposed on a major triad—is also a perfect imitation of nature, since a certain seventh appears shortly after the third in the overtone series; but, here again, this is only *a single chord* of the scale (V), while harmonic usage reproduces this type on all degrees of the scale. The use of seventh chords is no more dictated by scientific considerations than the use of triads—rather, it is the product of compositional necessity.

Such a necessity was already felt by composers of the sixteenth and seventeenth centuries. It is explained by the principle of *tension and relaxation* which governs all polyphonic composition. We have seen this principle operating in all the earliest polyphonic works, where the tension set up by certain dissonant intervals resolved to the relaxation of the final unison. The same thing happens in the tonal system. The unison is no longer the only possible resolution. The notion of dissonance—we have already indicated this and we shall see it all the time from now on—is no longer absolute, but merely relative. Although the third was at first considered a dissonance, later an imperfect consonance, at the end of the fifteenth century we encounter a state of affairs in which the triad, made up of two superimposed thirds, is presented as the consonance *par excellence*. It is, therefore, the need of setting up tension—dissonance—with respect to the triad, which explains and justifies the frequent use of the seventh chord.[5]

One point should now attract our attention; both the triad and the seventh chord can be reduced to a system of superimposed thirds. If the triad is the result of superimposing two thirds, the seventh chord is the result of superimposing three thirds. It is this system of thirds which will serve as the basis for every consideration of tonal harmony. Let us observe that this also possesses a certain scientific justification. Here is the overtone-series produced by the fundamental C: C–c (octave) –g–c–e–g–b flat–c–d–e–f sharp–g, etc.

We observe that, from the B flat onward, all the new tones of the series are superimposed by thirds on the previous new tones. Thus ninth chords, eleventh chords, etc., are equally justified by the "image of nature." But, again, this holds only for *some of these*

[5] We may also mention another compositional justification; the seventh chord is capable of furnishing a different tone to each voice of a four-part ensemble. Since the vocal quartet was the preferred form of the Flemish polyphonists and their immediate successors, the seventh chord obviously played an important role in their work.

chords, while the structure of other ninth and eleventh chords, which are used just as much, is far removed from that of the overtone series. However, the chords of this kind—which we call "artificial" for lack of a better term—may also be reduced to the system of thirds, and it is for this reason that they may finally be reduced to the tonal system, since they may always be considered in relation to a fundamental degree.

One oversimplified theory, which betrays the fossilization of musical ideas, maintains that the evolution of tonal harmony was determined by the fact that each new generation of composers took a fancy to add a third to the chords used by the preceding generation. In fact, composers cared very little about the system of thirds. Although this system permits the theoretical classification of harmonic acquisitions, the acquisitions themselves were made in a very different way.

The causes of the increasing complexity of tonal harmony must, again, be sought in the evolution of *all* polyphonic problems. We know that modal music was essentially vocal. But already in the fifteenth century instrumental music was beginning to develop. This is understandable, for polyphony had then reached a stage of such complexity that it was difficult for it to submit to vocal demands. Although the hearing ability of singers, and their skill at intonation, had developed considerably since the beginnings of polyphony, it is nonetheless true that certain chords, whatever the polyphonic period, *always* present difficulties of intonation for an *a cappella* vocal ensemble. On the other hand, such difficulties do not exist for instruments. The extraordinary rise of instrumental music from the eighteenth century onward is easily explained by these considerations.

Furthermore, all this implies a sort of reciprocal action. On the one hand, the evolution of polyphony necessitated the abandonment of the vocal ensemble as the chief means of musical expression; on the other hand, the increasingly generalized practise of instrumental music showed musicians new directions for the evolution of polyphony.

What are these new directions? First of all, they are melodic.

The different parts of an instrumental ensemble can move with infinitely more freedom than vocal parts. Style, range, intonation of horizontal intervals—new possibilities everywhere. Let us not forget rhythm, either, with its various factors—speed of performance, complexity of metric values, etc. There, too, the instrumental part enjoys infinitely more freedom. When we add the previously described harmonic possibilities we get a striking picture of the novelty of instrumental polyphony.

Many of these new possibilities are already used in the work of Bach. From then on, each new generation of composers continues to blaze a trail in the same direction. However, I do not believe that all these generations were consciously concerned with specifically *harmonic* evolution. Such a problem was not to be approached in that way until much later, after the work of Debussy —that is, at a moment when polyphony had become completely detached from its contrapuntal origins. But this is not yet the case in the seventeenth and eighteenth centuries or even during most of the nineteenth century, when, as we have observed, voice-leading was still a matter for careful planning in the minds of musicians.

Therefore, we must now state that tonal harmony (the principal element of tonal polyphony) evolves from the impulse of voice-leading, which, when destined for instruments, becomes ever freer and ever richer in melodic, rhythmic, and harmonic possibilities.

Apparently, then, nothing has changed in this respect since the days of the predominance of vocal music, when harmonic aggregations were produced in the same way. However, there is a difference. The new chords which result from instrumental polyphony are quickly captured by the tonal consciousness, which is constantly seeking to reduce them to the principles of its system. This soon permits the creation of the abovementioned "artificial" chords. We have seen that "acoustical genesis" could be artificial; the same now proves to be true of "contrapuntal genesis." In the first case, a "natural image" was imitated on a degree where it could not be reproduced without altering the scale. In the second case, a chord produced by voice-leading, the existence of which is more or less fortuitous and which may, with some exaggeration, be described as the product of chance or of a momentary caprice, may be recreated artificially with no thought of its source.

11. *Stages of harmonic evolution.*—In many ways, the tonal system is a prolongation of the modal system rather than a break with it. If our thesis (that certain essential elements of modes survive in keys) is correct, it is possible to consider the tonal world as a synthesis of the modal world and of a number of more recent acquisitions.

At first, a tonality admits only those chord-types built upon its own degrees; but tonal music has not contented itself with these boundaries for a long time. The zones which rival the tonic— dominant and subdominant—frequently win out in the struggle. Then there is *modulation,* which increases the tension and which gives a higher value to the final triumph of the original tonality. During this first stage of tonal evolution, only very simple modulations were used. For example, one could modulate from a major key to the two abovementioned regions and to the relative minor. But the minor mode is a mere survival of the Aeolian mode; it appears in two forms, the ascending (which raises VI and VII a half step) and the descending (which keeps the natural tones). Thus, the minor tonality automatically allows two different harmonizations: a series of "natural" chords (in A minor, chords with F natural and G natural) and a series of "raised" chords (in A minor, chords with F sharp and G sharp).

However, the major mode is used more frequently than the minor, because it is more fundamentally tonal (a state of affairs which may also be justified scientifically but which is really explained by compositional preferences stemming from the sixteenth century). But composers do not wish to deprive themselves, in major, of the rich variety afforded by minor. The descending minor scale is made up of the notes of its relative major. From this viewpoint, the two keys might be confused. So why not incorporate the *raised* minor chords into the major mode? Here is an even more convincing explanation of this possibility: a major key, when it includes the raised degrees of its relative minor, is merely taking advantage of certain Aeolian characteristics. This process may, then, be extended to all the modes, and thus furnishes a quantity of new chords on all degrees. Dorian and Lydian furnish B flat and C sharp; Phrygian, Mixolydian and Aeolian furnish D sharp, F sharp and G sharp.

The introduction not only of modal chords but also of many other chords becomes more and more frequent when it occurs chromatically. "Natural" or "scientific" considerations are then abandoned because they prove powerless to justify a world of sound where everything has become "artificial." The degrees of tonality, which were, up till now, clearly differentiated by their chord-types (a state of affairs which is not seriously disturbed by the incorporated modal elements), now all become alike, for they can all be harmonized with many different chords. One of these chords met with on every degree is the diminished seventh chord, the first great trouble-maker in tonality. Because of its structure, every diminished seventh chord can belong to every major or minor key. It is the first of those "roving" chords which will destroy the system.

The first phase of chromaticism—the third stage of tonal harmony—begins in the work of Bach. At the same moment, a new element begins to appear, an element the introduction of which will result in a fourth stage. The art of modulating is no longer satisfied with simple modulations. Stronger and stronger tensions are set up by means of excursions into regions ever more distant from the fundamental key. Before this process is carried to extremes, as is the case after Weber and Schubert, the modulation to the *subdominant minor* is freely used by Bach and Mozart. Now the borrowings from the old modes, although they sufficed to exhaust the possibilities of the dominant region, did nothing to tap the resources of the subdominant minor region, the relationships of which with the tonic appear in modulation only. These relationships may quite naturally be incorporated into the major mode. Once this has been carried out, any major key thus con-

stituted may be blended with any other, since they all contain all
the chord-types of every key. This new stage is clearly revealed
in the work of Schumann, and above all in that of Brahms.[6]
Finally, with Wagner, there begins the fifth stage of tonality—
that is, the second great phase of chromaticism. Chromaticism
now conquers all realms. We find it at work everywhere, whether
in voice-leading or in chordal structure. Harmony now becomes
extremely complicated; not, as it is frequently believed, because
more thirds are added (larger aggregations than the ninth chord
are rare in Wagner), but because chromaticism begins to eat away
the very system of thirds. For example, the second degree of C
major, D–F–A–C, can be altered chromatically to D sharp–
F sharp–A flat–C sharp. Of course, this can still be explained
by the system of thirds; but actually there is only one third
(D sharp–F sharp) left in the chord, the other intervals being
a second (F sharp–A flat=G sharp) and a fourth (G sharp=
A flat–C sharp). One can—and, indeed, in Wagner's time one
usually had to—confer a precise tonal function upon this chord,
for example by treating it as a "real" second degree of C. In a
chromatic progression, this can always be arranged. The chord in
question is transformed into the first degree of C if D sharp goes
up to E, if F sharp goes up to G, if A flat goes down to G and
if C sharp (enharmonically interpreted as D flat) goes down to C.
But one also may—and Wagner often does—avoid a precise functional explanation. The issue is then left in doubt. The first chord
goes to another equally vague chord, and so on. A series of such
"roving" chords creates complete tonal chaos. When, in addition,

---

[6] The contemporaries of Brahms were much impressed by this. In one of his
essays, *Einige seltsamen Noten bei Brahms*, Riemann describes these striking phenomena
rather accurately. Pertinently, he reduces them to the *minor-major* system elaborated
by another theorist of that time, Hauptmann, who, starting with observations analogous
to Riemann's, explains all the harmony of his period on the basis of the idea that
tonality as manifested in the works of his contemporaries is merely a synthesis of the
regions of the subdominant minor and the tonic and dominant major. The studies of
Hauptmann and Riemann are extremely interesting, for they give rise to logical, coherent and convincing systems. For example, they are often able to explain certain
tonal functions (that of the Neapolitan sixth, for example) without ever contradicting
the practical use to which composers have put these functions.

the melody—that "endless melody" of Wagner's dream—has no fixed points, the middle voices are mobile and varied, and the rhythm is irregular, we are forced to admit that tonality, even though it still survives in Wagner, must eventually give way under the pressure of such complex polyphony.

12. *Recapitulation of the important aspects of the evolution of polyphony.*—With the work of Wagner we find ourselves at the threshold of contemporary music; for nearly all the composers who have participated in the evolution of polyphony since Wagner were or are our contemporaries, and Wagner's work has posed problems the development and solution of which are the special property of the musicians of our time.

Later, I shall show how numerous composers have undertaken the task of digging deeper into the polyphonic possibilities of Wagner's work; and we shall also see how a more limited number of composers have been able to take the inevitable consequences of this state of affairs.

So that we can subsequently approach these questions, we must now draw a blueprint of the reactivation of the meaning of polyphonic evolution, a subject to which we have given so much time.

In its entirety, the history of polyphony presents the appearance of a living chain of acquisitions. With each new acquisition, a new stage, which synthesizes all preceding stages, is set up; and this synthesis constitutes a necessary premise for future acquisitions. It goes without saying that no such synthesis should pass for a definite and immutable result beyond which one cannot go. On the contrary, not only do all these syntheses imply the possibility of a continuation, but such a possibility belongs to the very essence of polyphony.[7]

Examined more specifically, the evolution of polyphony, from

---

[7] Our insistence on this point may seem boring. It is amply justified by the fact that most musicians and music-lovers, who freely admit polyphonic evolution up to and a little beyond Wagner, categorically refuse to accept more recent developments, which they consider illegitimate.

But, after all, if music has not stopped evolving for over a thousand years, why should it suddenly stop evolving at this point or even start going backwards?

its beginnings to Wagner, appears to be the history of two distinct musical systems, the modal and the tonal. The former, heir of monodic music, breaks up under the pressure of harmony, and is transformed into a *specifically polyphonic* system. Especially at first, the tonal system maintains certain principles of the modal system, but is not long in introducing specifically new elements. All in all, the essence of the tonal system is universal, that of the modal system specific. However, it appears that even the tonal system cannot serve as a permanent basis for the progress of polyphony. At the very beginning, there is unmasked the *subversive element*—chromaticism—to which tonality is forced, by its very essence, to grant ever greater powers.

When we go into even further detail, the history of polyphony appears to us as the history of two styles: the contrapuntal style and the harmonic style. Neither of them can be elaborated in an utterly pure form, since counterpoint has always been governed by harmonic considerations, while, until the time of Wagner, harmony results from the movement of melodic voices. However, let us note that all through their evolution these two styles tend to express their own essences. This is proved by the following facts:

a) Harmony rapidly creates its own formulae. It evolves continually according to a never-changing process which causes the contrapuntal origin of chords to be forgotten as fast as new chords are created. Once the origin of the formula has been forgotten, it is handled in a purely harmonic fashion. The piano, one of the favored instruments of tonal music, furthers this state of affairs.

b) The contrapuntal project is constantly maintained in tonal music. Not only do all composers from Bach to Wagner devote considerable effort to the perfection of their linear style, but tonal music also creates for itself, at a moment towards the end of the eighteenth century when counterpoint seems to have fallen into utter desuetude, an ideal expression of instrumental ensemble polyphony. The string quartet, the ideal chamber-music group, seems designed especially to preserve and to perpetuate the contrapuntal tradition in tonal music. Even in the work of Wagner, who was hardly a chamber-music composer, we find an evident care for counterpoint, in the form of a constant wealth of inventiveness in the extremely supple and mobile inner voices.

Finally, we must still approach the problem of *form*, which becomes of paramount importance with the development of polyphony. We have been able to observe the constant presence of a *unifying principle* to which all musical creation could be related. This principle implies the notions of tension, relaxation, architectonic economy, etc. They have no absolute meaning; their application undergoes a strictly logical evolution. In fact, ever since the symmetry of a little piece like the organum *Rex coeli*, Occidental music has found its realization in ever longer and more complex works. The *sonata*—the typical form of tonal music —is the very incarnation of this state of mind. The architecture of this essentially large form is produced by the complex interplay of several themes, and, furthermore, the form becomes increasingly complex in the course of its evolution. The sonata, still rather symmetrically formulated by Haydn, becomes more and more asymmetrical in the course of its evolution, insofar as it tends to *vary the recapitulation*.

Finally, let us recall the evolution of the concept of dissonance. Let us remember that, in the beginnings of polyphony, this concept included all intervals except the octave, fifth, and fourth. Ever since then the scope of the idea of consonance has constantly broadened. Though it was possible, at the beginning of the tonal system, to justify consonance and dissonance according to pseudo-scientific considerations, such considerations become meaningless in Wagnerian chromaticism. Chromaticism, the importance of which will obviously be maintained after Wagner, introduces an entirely new perspective, by proving that *every chord* is justified by the chromatic scale and that it would be futile to prohibit the use of any harmony.

If we may say that the evolution of polyphony up to Wagner tends to show that the difference between consonance and dissonance is not a difference founded in nature, but only a gradual change, we may also say that Wagner's work attempts to transcend both consonance and dissonance. Certainly, this work did not yet entirely succeed in overcoming the traditional dualism—many further experiments had to be made before musical consciousness could carry out such a reform; but, nevertheless, Wagner had the honor of establishing the conditions of the problem. That is why we may now consider ourselves on the threshold of a new world of sound—the world of contemporary music.

PART II

ARNOLD SCHOENBERG

The Origin and Foundations
of Contemporary Music

The laws of the man of genius are the laws of future
humanity.

SCHOENBERG,
Theory of Harmony

CHAPTER III

Phases of the Schoenbergian Reactivation

of Polyphonic Evolution

13. *The specific problem of contemporary music.*—If, during the first part of this essay, we have come to understand the laws which have governed the evolution of Occidental music from its beginnings, the reader who has followed the direction of this evolution will readily understand that post-Wagnerian polyphony had to enter upon a new phase, which was, in certain respects, radically different from the preceding phases. Let us not deceive ourselves; from the preceding history of polyphony, it is obvious that there is a real *renewal* of musical thought with each new generation of composers, and accordingly a post-Wagnerian renewal is no more significant or essential than any other past or future stage of the evolution of polyphony. However, in the course of this evolution we have encountered a phase which might be called *privileged* because of the importance of its final results— the phase in which the transition from the modal system to the tonal system is completed. Now, from certain observations made during the course of our last chapter, it becomes evident that the tonal system in Wagner gave rise to elements which tend to destroy it. At this moment, therefore, we are again confronted with a *privileged phase* (in the sense in which that term was used above) in which there will occur a transition from the tonal system to a new system. This transition, like the one we studied previously, is brought about by a long and painful process; and it may be said that at the present time we are still in the midst of such a development, which it might seem premature to discuss. However, it is this very development which essentially characterizes

43

the musical epoch in which we live; therefore, in posing the problem of the transition from the tonal system to a new musical system, we pose the specific problem of contemporary music.

In the following section of this work, then, we shall try to show how this problem is consciously and logically attacked for the first time in the work of Arnold Schoenberg.

14. *The awakening of Schoenberg's musical consciousness; its participation in the polyphony of its time.*—Since we have implied that the activity of every real composer is primarily defined by a complete grasp of all the acquisitions of polyphony before his time, which then serve as a basis for future acquisitions, we must try to determine the presence of such an attitude in the earliest works of Schoenberg.

a) *Childhood and first compositions of adolescence.*—Arnold Schoenberg was born in Vienna on September 13, 1874.[1] The death of his father, which took place when the child was eight years old, resulted in an upbringing under straitened circumstances. When he was twelve, he learned the violin, and composed some pieces for two violins which he played with his teacher. A little later he played chamber music with other young music students; for these occasions he wrote trios and quartets. Still later, he taught himself the 'cello and wrote sonatas for this instrument. Egon Wellesz[2] has already pointed out how Schoenberg's youthful preoccupation with chamber music was to exert a preponderant influence on all his future activity. While most of the young people of his generation and background owed their first vivid musical impressions to hearing a Wagner opera or a Bruckner symphony, and were thus led to an "al fresco" method of musical composition which most of them approached without the necessary technique, Schoenberg, little by little and quietly, forged for himself the essential tools of musical composition before he tried his hand at large works. Furthermore, his early acquaintance with chamber music always kept him from making the fatal

---

[1] I owe most of my biographical details to Egon Wellesz' book *Arnold Schoenberg* (E. P. Tal, Leipzig, Vienna and Zurich, 1921.)

[2] *Loc. cit.*

error of using the orchestra in a chaotic, sloppy fashion; therefore, even in his orchestral works, he remained faithful to the spirit of chamber music, imparting a life of its own to each individual strand of the polyphonic web.

Schoenberg, deciding to consecrate his whole life to music, left high school before the completion of his course and composed for several years all by himself, without any outside advice. But one day a friend of his introduced him to Alexander von Zemlinsky,[3] who was amazed by the talent of the young musician and decided to teach him counterpoint. This instruction, which lasted a few months only, represents Schoenberg's only formal study of composition.

From this period (1897) dates the composition of a string quartet in D major, written during the summer at Payerbach, where Schoenberg had gone with Zemlinsky in order to make a piano reduction of the latter's opera *Sarema*. This quartet, unfortunately lost since then, is the only work of Schoenberg's which Zemlinsky looked over and corrected. Schoenberg began once more to work by himself. The quartet was played in public the following year, and was even rather successful, for it still operated with a tonal vocabulary familiar to audiences of that day.[4]

b) *The first songs.*—A first attempt at a symphonic poem, immediately after the composition of the quartet, was abortive. On the other hand, at this time there appeared a large number of songs, many of which are unpublished while others go to make up the collections of Op. 1, 2, and 3. Some of them were performed in 1898 in a recital given by the singing-teacher Gaertner, with Zemlinsky at the piano. At the end of this performance there was a slight disturbance, "and ever since then," Schoenberg said smilingly one day, "the riots have never ceased!"

Most of these songs already exhibit perfect mastery of technical means and complete assimilation of the chief acquisitions of post-Wagnerian polyphony. Two examples may elucidate this. The

[3] Alexander von Zemlinsky (1872–1942), an extremely gifted composer and conductor (at the Vienna Opera in 1908), was then rated high by all the *avant-garde* young people. Schoenberg married his sister Mathilde in 1901.

[4] Everyone who knows this quartet has told me that it already contained that intense melodic warmth so characteristic of Schoenberg's later works.

first displays, over an E flat pedal-point, the chromatic transformation of the tonic chord into another chord which really cannot be analyzed according to the system of thirds. However, since
it is produced by a simple chromatic displacement of its compo-
nent parts, it still has a precise tonal function although it is not
one of the chord-types of the tonal system. Each of its tones is a
lower or upper leading-tone to a note of the tonic chord.[5]

Ex. 1

We see, then, that such an example displays Schoenberg's
clear conception of the problems created by chromaticism. In this
sense we may say that his work is imbued with the latest acquisitions of polyphony.

The same song emphasizes certain other fundamental musical
principles. One of them, which will eventually become the key-
stone of the Schoenbergian edifice, is what we have called the
unifying principle, which is the basis for every genuine musical
composition. Now, at the moment when tonality as a unifying
principle is being steadily undermined, Schoenberg makes up for
this disorganization with his intense feeling for *compositional
unity* and *architectonic economy.* Thus, the entire song in question is dominated by the chord-progression which we have just
been examining. This chord-progression also furnishes the sub-
stance of the vocal part, which, at the end of the song, unfolds
an expressive melody derived from the flutelike arabesque of the
first measure. We shall see later the tremendous consequences of
this compositional attitude on the part of Schoenberg.

[5] In this sense, such a chord, although in a way it is a new phenomenon, is not yet
a *pure harmonic invention.* We shall later see the significance of this.

A glance at Example 2 will confirm all of the preceding statements.

Ex. 2

zwei blut ro _ te nel _ ken schick, ich dir   mein Blut ___ du,

The role played here by chromaticism in the extremely independent motion of the inner voices (one of the fundamental acquisitions of Wagner) need scarcely be emphasized. However, I should like to draw attention to the fact that these three measures are elaborated from the variation of an initial motive which is exposed by the voice in the first measure (with its upbeat). The last note of this motive may be considered as the upbeat of the following measure, where the first motive undergoes an enlargement of its second interval as well as a melodic elimination (suppression of the second strong beat) which transforms the iambic meter into dactylic meter. Finally the third measure, preceded by a chromatic elaboration of the upbeat in the piano (which thus introduces the anapestic meter), varies the initial motive, retracing its intervals in reverse order and returning to iambic meter (on the second strong beat). The imitation of the vocal part by the inner voice in the third measure, as well as the change of register in the right hand of the piano in the second measure, are but fresh proofs of the most stringent economy of means applied to the most extravagant wealth of invention. These are, indeed, the principal characteristics of all the great masters of music; and Schoenberg's youthful works display them to a surprising degree.

c) *The Sextet, Op. 4.*—During the summer of 1899, Schoenberg is again at Payerbach with Zemlinsky. In three weeks there, he composes his first important work, the string sextet *Verklärte*

Nacht (*Transfigured Night*), Op. 4, which is the only example of a symphonic poem in chamber music. For the listener of today, it is obvious that this work is written in the Wagnerian language, for it consistently uses all the different idioms of that language which we have already pointed out. This is quite evident, and only goes to show what a firm grasp Schoenberg had on the musical language of his time. However, at the time it was written this work shocked most listeners, who, far from hearing its relationship with Wagner, were disturbed by its daring harmonies, by the excessive complexity of its polyphonic web (which seems quite transparent to us today), and by its completely unfamiliar sonorities. Even then, Schoenberg could not content himself with submitting passively to the influence of Wagner, but actively recreated the heritage of his illustrious predecessor, unfolding its possibilities of evolution to their furthest length. The following example clearly proves this. The ninth chord is an important acquisition of romantic harmony, but, in fact, Schoenberg's predecessors used it very sparingly, and generally in root position. It is in root position that it makes its first appearance in music; this form is produced by a suspension or an anticipation in the voice which carries the ninth. However, Schoenberg seizes upon this acquisition, the ninth chord, and *consciously* decides to draw all possible consequences from it. In other words, this chord will appear, in his music, not only in root position but also in *all* possible inversions. *Verklärte Nacht* introduces one of these inversions of the ninth chord, that in which the ninth is used in the bass (see Ex. 3., N.B.). But this is the very inversion which was strictly forbidden by the theorists of that day! [6]

Ex. 3   N.B.

[6] Schoenberg tells how this chord caused a concert society to refuse to perform the piece. "It is self-evident; there is no such thing as the inversion of a ninth chord; therefore, there is no such thing as a performance of it; for one really cannot perform something that does not exist. So I had to wait several years."

All this proves how deeply Schoenberg's musical consciousness is already imbued with the true meaning of the evolution of polyphony.

d) *Gurre-Lieder.*—In March, 1900, Schoenberg undertook the composition of the *Gurre-Lieder,* the largest work that he had written up till that time. He composed the first and second parts, as well as the beginning of the third, during the spring, but financial need obliged him to interrupt his work for a year to orchestrate nearly six thousand pages of operettas, some of which bear names famous in their day. The composition of the *Gurre-Lieder* could not be completed until March, 1901. The score of this work demands more performers than anything of the sort written before or since. In addition to five solo voices, three four-part male choruses, and an eight-part mixed chorus, it calls for an orchestral apparatus of four piccolos, four flutes, three oboes, two English horns, three A and B flat clarinets, two E flat clarinets, two bass clarinets, three bassoons and two contra-bassoons, ten horns, six trumpets, one bass trumpet, one alto trombone, four tenor trombones, one bass trombone, one contrabass trombone, one tuba, six tympani, bass drum, cymbals, triangle, glockenspiel, side-drum, tambour, xylophone, tam-tam, four harps, celesta, and a proportionate number of strings in the usual quintet.

In order to construct such a score, Schoenberg had to order, from Breitkopf and Härtel, special music paper with forty-eight staves, twice the size of the usual format. As soon as the paper arrived (August, 1901) he began the orchestration, which he had to interrupt several times—first in December, when, immediately after his marriage, he left with his wife for Berlin, where he hoped to make a better living. There he became conductor at the *Buntes Theater* of the famous Wolzogen, where he was supposed to accompany songs.[7] Although, in spite of his job, he resumed work on the *Gurre-Lieder,* he had to stop again in 1902 in order to orchestrate more operettas. It was not until much later (1910), after having shown the first two parts of the work to Richard Strauss (who procured for him not only the Liszt Prize but also

---

[7] He himself wrote one (with trumpet obbligato) which was considered too difficult and received but a single performance.

a professorship at the Stern Conservatory in Berlin), that he could definitely resume the orchestration and complete it (1911).

It would be quite impossible, within the framework of the present study, to give even an approximate idea of this grandiose work.[8] Let us try briefly to locate it in the musical tradition to which it belongs. Generally speaking, we may say that the *Gurre-Lieder* represent a prolongation of the melodic, harmonic, rhythmic and compositional tendencies which we have observed in the preceding works.

In this sense, the examination of Berg's analytical pamphlet cannot be too highly recommended; for its detailed analyses reveal many procedures which, in their subsequent development, become extremely important constituents of Schoenberg's musical activity. It is remarkable, for example, to see how the first part, though composed in the form of a series of independent vocal pieces, attains extraordinary unity by means of all kinds of subtle thematic relationships. Furthermore, it is important to observe the persistence of certain harmonic forms (the chord of the beginning and also what Berg calls the "small seventh chord") which are not only a basic element of the structural unity of the whole, but which also frequently tend to unfold in melodic forms, thus adumbrating an essential characteristic of Schoenberg's future polyphony. No less significant in this respect are the contrapuntal superpositions of various themes of the work. These superpositions reveal a principle which we shall have many further occasions to discuss. In any case, let us note that all the features listed here furnish proof of Schoenberg's extraordinary compositional lucidity, as well as of his conscious will to base the act of composition upon a profound reactivation of the most fundamental principles of musical architecture. In addition, there is the desire to use up all the conceivable sonorities of the Wagnerian orchestra. From this point of view, we may say that, because of the gigantic proportions of its instrumental forces, this work exhausts all such possibilities; but we must also add that it discovers some new ones. I am thinking not only of the extraordinary *col legno* and *sul*

[8] Alban Berg has devoted an analytical booklet to this task. (Universal-Edition, Vienna.)

ponticello effects in the strings, used for the first time here, but also of the typically Schoenbergian treatment of the monster orchestra, which depends for much of its effect on the juxtaposition of various solo instruments. Example 4 shows such a state of affairs; here we discover, in addition to a concern for counter-

Ex. 4

Tove: *Nun sag' ich dir zum ersten Mal* (*Gurre-Lieder*, Part 1)

point, a type of melodic and harmonic progression which is extremely characteristic of Schoenberg. The harmony, indeed, already adumbrates that of the second theme of the *Kammersymphonie*, Op. 9; the wide skips in the melody prove to be characteristic of much later works.

The reader is advised to study this example very carefully; for, in addition to the abovementioned qualities, which are Schoen-

berg's personal acquisitions, there is to be seen an extremely firm
and self-contained melodic structure, which points the way towards new discoveries. While most melodies of this period, even
those written by Schoenberg's greatest contemporaries (Strauss,
and even Debussy), have little meaning by themselves and acquire real significance only with their harmonic accompaniment,
this melody is a perfect *thing in itself*. The comparison of this
melody with most of the melodies of Strauss's songs, for example,
proves highly significant. One cannot help being shocked by the
melodic poverty of Strauss's vocal lines—even in such a famous
song as the "ravishing" *Morgen*!

14. *The first Schoenbergian innovations.*—Up until this time, the
activity of Schoenberg, in spite of a few bold strokes, has largely
been confined to the "ultra-consequent" realization of the principal
acquisitions of Wagnerian polyphony. We have seen that he sometimes surpassed these acquisitions in his search for new horizons,
but we have not yet observed any truly radical discoveries. In
Pelleas und Melisande, Op. 5, such discoveries are manifest.

Schoenberg composed this work (his only symphonic poem)
at Berlin in 1902; the instrumentation (for a very large orchestra) [10] was completed at the beginning of 1903. The larger architecture (which uses the cyclic principle, and blends the various
movements of the symphony into a single one) displays a profound
concern with counterpoint, which hereafter will never disappear
from Schoenberg's work. We shall have many occasions to return
to this subject; for the moment, let us consider it from the viewpoint of its meaning in the evolution of polyphony.

At the end of the first section of this work, we emphasized that
counterpoint, although it could not be realized in its pure form
within the tonal system, maintained itself, in spite of everything,
as a mode of thought common to most composers. But, although
we have also noted that Wagner's work displays a concern for
counterpoint in its mobile inner voices, such a concept of counterpoint has but little to do with the essence of genuine counter-

---

[10] Fourfold woodwinds (five clarinets), eight horns, four trumpets, five drums,
tuba, four tympani, other percussion instruments, glockenspiel, two harps, and strings.

Ex. 5

point. The successors of Wagner moved even farther away from this essence, which they forgot so completely that counterpoint almost entirely disappeared from most of their works. It is not the least merit of Arnold Schoenberg that he was aware of the urgent necessity of restoring rank and dignity to one of the paramount systems of polyphony, and that he reactivated the laws of polyphony in their inner meaning. *Pelleas und Melisande* is a striking example of this; doubtless there are not many scores as contrapuntal as this one. Every motive is surrounded by numerous countersubjects; in the elaboration sections, vast melodic "ensembles" are combined one with another; at one moment there is even a superposition of five different motives—each of which is then imitated separately.[11] Our Example 5 is a characteristic illustration of this state of affairs.

In addition to all this, it goes without saying that *Pelleas und Melisande* offers us novel instrumental effects—for example, the trombone *glissandi*, which are used here for the first time. However, aside from the recrudescence of counterpoint, its most radical innovation is a harmonic detail which at first sight seems insignificant. What we find here is the first conscious example of chords created by the superposition of fourths, in the following form:

Now, these chords present a problem of the first importance.[12] In the second chapter, I emphasized the fact that all the chords of the tonal system, up to and including the work of Wagner, owed their origin to the superposition of individual voice-leadings.

[11] For the analysis of this work, see the pamphlet of Alban Berg (Universal-Edition). No wonder that such a complex work was not understood in its day! Apparently even Mahler, when he followed the performance with the score, had some difficulty in understanding all the interweavings of the melodic lines.

[12] I have explained my views on this problem in a recent article consecrated to Stravinsky. (*Les Temps Modernes*, No. 7.) The present passage repeats several points of this explanation.

I stated also that, in most instances, the "contrapuntal" origin of the vertical aggregations was speedily forgotten, and that these aggregations were later handled with no thought of their origin, but with consideration for their tonal functions. But the consciousness of harmony "for harmony's sake" was still not strong enough for composers to discover new chords in a specifically harmonic way. Such a plan could only burgeon in a post-Wagnerian mind; and that is exactly what happens in the mind of Schoenberg. The fourth-chords to which we allude *are created out of whole cloth*; they result from *pure harmonic speculation*. (Schoenberg himself tells us in his *Theory of Harmony* how he hesitated to write them down.) They are not justified by any voice-leading or even by any *a priori* tonal function.[13] And yet, this is the logical and consequent end-result to which polyphony had to come sooner or later. In this sense, we may say that Schoenberg has now started in a direction which, though it implies the reactivation of all the polyphonic acquisitions of the past, clearly points the way towards future discoveries. Later, we shall see how such harmonic projects smash the last vestiges of the tonal edifice; however, we must now mention another important harmonic innovation displayed by *Pelleas und Melisande,* an innovation which is produced by the genuine tradition of polyphony and which also tends to destroy tonality.

For the first time in his work (and at about the same time as Debussy), Schoenberg introduces the whole-tone scale. Harmonically, it is realized as follows:

We see that the scale in question is realized here by the superposition of two *different* augmented fifth chords. This is remark-

---

[13] Although it is true that, in this particular example, the chords assume relatively precise tonal functions, this takes place only *a posteriori*.

able, and proves once more that Schoenberg's musical consciousness participates with the greatest lucidity in the movement of
the history of polyphony. The augmented fifth chords, used for
the first time in a conscious and consequent way by Wagner, were
bound to be superimposed in this way sooner or later, and thus
to engender the *whole-tone scale*. Such superpositions can eventually give rise to the idea of a *purely harmonic project*. However,
I do not believe that this is really what happens, for 1) the invention of these superpositions may, strictly speaking, be reduced
to the pattern of "contrapuntal" inventions, since they are made
up of two augmented fifth chords, which have a "contrapuntal"
origin; 2) we clearly see, in the above examples, that these movements are created by chromatic displacement, and by the contrary motion of two analogous augmented fifth chords.

Be that as it may, the two chord-types which we have just
examined introduce—in a more radical way than ever before—
types of aggregations which have nothing more in common with
the prototypes of the tonal system. In this sense, such chords
constitute a *roving* element in any given tonality; if necessary,
they can still assume the functions of such a tonality (inasmuch
as they are comparatively rare for the moment), but infallibly
and ineluctably they lead away from the tonal system in its present form.

15. *The consolidation of the first Schoenbergian innovations.*—
However, Schoenberg was not up to that point yet. Before he
succeeded in surpassing the tonal system, his wonderful compositional consciousness had to indulge in many more experiments.
In the meantime, while he strives to draw the utmost consequences
from every new acquisition, he constantly succeeds in consolidating all his acquisitions in a masterly fashion.

Let us try to understand all this through an examination of
the eight works which followed Op. 5. In order of composition,
they are the *Six Orchestral Songs*, Op. 8 (1904), the First Quartet,
in D minor, Op. 7 (1904–1905), the *Eight Songs*, Op. 6 (1905),
the *Two Ballads* for voice and piano, Op. 12 (1906–1907), the
Kammersymphonie, Op. 9 (1906), the *a cappella* chorus *Friede*

auf Erden, Op. 13 (1907), the *Two Songs*, Op. 14 (1907), and the Second Quartet, in F sharp minor, Op. 10 (1907–1908).

These years (1904–1908) also bring the unfoldment of Schoenberg's career as teacher. In fact, pupils flock to him; the principal members of the group are Alban Berg and Anton Webern.[14] From another viewpoint, this period marks the beginning of the growing fame of the name of Schoenberg—but also the beginning of the constant opposition provoked, then as now, by that name at its every appearance. Schoenberg's material situation remains difficult. It is significant to note that the first of the *Two Ballads* (Op. 12) and Op. 13 were written for contests. The prizes offered, though not large, would have materially alleviated his situation. Needless to say, he did not receive any of them! But, on the other hand, he wins devoted friends in all quarters. Some of his songs begin to figure in the standard repertory of a small group of singers, and the famous Rosé Quartet devotes (in 1906) more than forty rehearsals to Op. 7, which it will perform as often as possible.[15]

At this time Schoenberg's activity displays extreme concentration. All the acquisitions of the preceding works are not only consolidated but also carried further. Above all, Schoenberg becomes completely conscious of a fundamental compositional principle which, *implicit* in all the previous evolution of polyphony, becomes *explicit* in his work for the first time. This is the principle of *perpetual development*. It may, in fact, be said that polyphony, since its very beginnings, has tended to formulate a compositional method which, beginning with an initial motivic cell (or basic musical idea), succeeds in constructing a work of rich and abundant musical invention from nothing but the *varied developments* of this initial cell. That is why the art of music has always called upon new unifying principles such as tonality, thematic unity, and

[14] Some others are Karl Horwitz, Heinrich Jalowetz, Karl Linke, Josef Polnauer, and Erwin Polnauer. Some of them later became top-ranking conductors, while others devoted themselves to theory.

[15] This score, which may seem comparatively simple today, is nonetheless so rich in polyphony that the impressive number of rehearsals does not seem excessive. Mahler said one day to Schoenberg, "I am accustomed to reading scores on thirty staves, but the four staves of your Op. 7 have given me infinitely more trouble."

others. In creating the tone-row technique, Schoenberg will succeed in embodying a unifying principle which contains all the realms of polyphony (the world of sound in which it evolves and its various constituent elements, melody, harmony, and counterpoint, as well as the general articulation of its speech and the structure which it erects). But for the moment Schoenberg contents himself with trying to master all the compositional means which he has inherited from tradition. In this sense, his Op. 7, 9, 13 and 14 are more radical than anything else tried up till that time. There is not a single note or figuration which does not result from the development and variation of the basic motive. The classic distinction between principal voices and accompaniments, which made the latter somewhat arbitrary, is entirely abolished here. Everything in a piece of music is essential; every part, even though it be of subordinate importance, must be conceived as intensely and elaborated as conscientiously as though it were the principal element. After all, is there any such thing as principal and secondary elements? In fact, *every note that one writes* must be essential—otherwise why write it? Although it may be necessary, in a given polyphonic structure, to bring one part into relief at the expense of another, and although the architecture of the piece may sometimes necessitate a firmly established theme (which may appear primary) and sometimes a more loosely constructed transition (which may appear secondary), all these distinctions are caused by the necessity for clarity, relief, variety, and so on. But, just as in a well-constructed building the least brick and the least beam must have a profound organic reason for their presence, even so the least note in a piece of music must be so necessary that it could not be removed without destroying the whole structure.

Another aspect of this compositional attitude appears in the extreme care which Schoenberg devotes to the *variation of the recapitulation*. At the end of the first part of this book, we explained that it was this idea which determined the evolution of form throughout the different phases of the evolution of polyphony. Derived from the principle of *perpetual development*, the idea of the varied recapitulation, although quite evident in the great masters of the past, appears in their works only implicitly or partially (particularly in Wagner, who explicitly applies the idea of perpetual development to the melody alone). On the other hand, in Schoenberg's work the varied recapitulation becomes explicit for the first time in its total meaning, and so we see once more how powerful is his spirit of reactivation. In fact, one of Schoenberg's greatest merits is that he has a clear conception of *all* the problems which arise in the activity of a composer. "Never do what a copyist can do instead," he says to his pupils when he finds an unvaried re-exposition in their works. From the simplest harmony exercise to the most complex work in large form, Schoenberg demands of his pupils that same constant effort to endow each tone with the maximum of intensity and expressive power which is found in his works. "You are a composer, and that means that your work must force you to bring all your faculties into play at every moment." In this sense Schoenberg is not a run-of-the-mill "professor," but it is because he "professes" his faith in the *dignity* of the composer as he admires this quality in the masters who have served as his models, that his activity becomes, in turn, the model for others.

It goes without saying that, in the recapitulation, such a mind cannot be satisfied with work which a copyist could do. The "recapitulations" (one cannot help putting this term in quotation marks in any discussion of Schoenberg), even in those works which we are now about to study, are variations—often quite elaborate— of the expositions. When, for example, a thematic form is literally repeated, it is harmonized differently or it appears as a counterpoint to other themes—and so it goes throughout. It is this fanciful asymmetry which makes Schoenberg's early works difficult of approach even today.

It is by necessities of this order that all of Schoenberg's work is governed, and the works which concern us at present represent Schoenberg's first complete comprehension of these necessities. I cannot possibly give a profound analysis of these works here; [16]

[16] For such an analysis, see the abovementioned pamphlets of Berg (in addition to his essay on Schoenberg's Op. 7, which is to be found in *Alban Berg* by Willi Reich), the analyses of Webern in the collection of essays dedicated to Schoenberg (Munich, 1912), and those of Wellesz, *loc. cit.*

I shall merely give a superficial indication of some of their characteristics, before I approach the conclusions which must be drawn from them.

The *Six Orchestral Songs,* Op. 8, exhibit an amazing simplification of the orchestral style in comparison with the preceding works.[17] The chamber-orchestra style is elaborated. We also find the bold voice-leading already observed in the *Gurre-Lieder.* This is illustrated by our examples 6a, b, and c; the last of these exhibits ever richer harmonies, elaborated by extremely mobile instrumental parts which display the most sensitive nuances of orchestral color.

Ex. 6

a) lasst die - - - sem Eu - re Gna - - - - de wi - der - fah - ren.

b) und mit Ent - zük - ken ist ganz in ihr des Gei - stes Blick be - fan - gen,

c) Nie ward ich, Her - - - rin,

müd', um Euch zu min - - - nen,

---

[17] The orchestra, reduced in size, uses threefold winds, four horns, three trumpets, three trombones, three tympani, a few other percussion instruments, and the normal complement of strings.

The Quartet in D minor, Op. 7, consolidates cyclic form by amalgamating all the architectonic divisions. The following scheme is used:

I

1. A. Principal theme-group. B. Transition. C. Secondary theme-group.
2. First development section.

II

1. Scherzo. 2. Development. 3. Recapitulation of the principal theme-group.

III

1. Adagio. 2. Recapitulation of the secondary theme-group. 3. Transition.

IV

1. Rondo-Finale. 2. Development of previous motives. 3. Coda. The whole is played without interruption.

There is no doubt that this is Schoenberg's richest work to date. In order to give an idea of it, I cannot do better than cite some of the observations made by Alban Berg in his essay *Why Is Schoenberg's Music So Hard to Understand?* [18]

The first thematic group, Example 7a, displays extraordinary wealth of invention in the asymmetrical structure of the melodic voices (NB 1), in the subtle variation of the motives (NB 2 and NB 3), in the incredible density of the polyphonic texture, and, finally, in the rich variety of the harmony, which uses a great many different degrees.

In order to illustrate this characteristic of the harmony, Berg uses the striking "chorale" Example 7b, which is not the chordal foundation of a vast Adagio—as one might easily be led to imagine —but is merely the harmonic skeleton of the beginning of the quartet.

[18] *Arnold Schönberg zum fünfzigsten Geburtstage: 13 September 1924.*

Ex. 7a

From the contrapuntal viewpoint, Berg observes that the combination of the three elements (1, 2, 3) which constitute the first measures of the quartet—wherein they appear disposed according to the scheme $\frac{1}{2}$—undergoes many variants in the course of the work. On page 5 it appears as $\frac{3}{2}$ (in octaves); on page 8, "the secondary voices, although they keep the same melodic tones, are radically varied." The arrangement becomes

Ex. 7a (cont'd)

2 (varied in sixteenth-notes)

1 (in octaves)

3 (circumscribed with eighth-note triplets)

"Finally, in the course of the last recapitulation of the principal thematic group, the principal and secondary voices appear—aside from their innumerable combinations with other themes of the work—in the following arrangement:

3 (varied in eighth-note triplets, but in a different way from the preceding variant in this rhythm)

1 (in octaves)

2 (inversion and diminution) ."

It is hardly necessary to state all the implications of this analysis; in any case, we shall have frequent occasion to return to the problems which it raises. Even in a résumé such as we have had to confine ourselves to here, Berg's analysis ought to give us an understanding of the remarkable intensity of Schoenberg's musical thinking, and of the serious effort to reactivate the basic

Ex. 7b

principles of polyphony which is exerted in such a composition as this.

This kind of work is carried even farther in the *Kammersymphonie*, Op. 9, where each element is reduced to its very essentials, and where the thematic structure itself attains unparalleled concision. This symphony, which also amalgamates the four traditional movements into one, presents the following scheme:

I. Exposition
II. Scherzo
III. Development (which also includes elements of the Scherzo)
IV. Adagio
V. Recapitulation (themes of I in a different order, contrapuntally varied, with incorporation of the themes of the Adagio).

In addition, the work displays a new purely harmonic invention, the six-tone chord made up of successive fourths, which gives rise to an analogous melodic figure. Both these elements play a considerable part in the structure of the symphony.[19]

Ex. 8

With the *Kammersymphonie*, Schoenberg enters upon a new phase of polyphonic evolution. In order to understand the importance of this innovation, we must remember the orchestral hypertrophy in which post-Wagnerian style had culminated. The instrumental apparatus of symphonic music and chamber music alike had become stereotyped; for every work, composers turned to instrumental combinations which were given in advance. Schoenberg's Op. 9 changes all this; in it, the *free choice of instruments,*

[19] Cf. Chapter I of my *Introduction to Twelve-Tone Music.*

which had not existed in this form since Mozart, is revived.[20] Later, we shall see the radical outcome of this reactivation in Schoenberg's work; however, we must immediately state that this new concept of instrumental *selectivity* is, in its turn, a fundamental constituent of that compositional economy which we have already tried to describe in other respects. For, in fact, if every thematic or harmonic element is to be reduced to its essentials, the same should be true of the instrumental style. Therefore, although Schoenberg still had recourse to the monster orchestra in *Pelleas und Melisande,* the concision and precision of his subsequent musical ideas obliged him to create this extraordinary combination of *fifteen solo instruments,* which embodies that synthesis of two genres already symbolized by the name *Kammersymphonie.*

Here, too, the analysis of this work by Berg cannot be too highly recommended to the reader. In studying it, he will become convinced of the subtlety, logic, and infinite variety of Schoenberg's compositional procedures. The way in which each musical figure is derived from the preceding one, the breath-taking finesse of the transitions, the extraordinary contrapuntal workmanship— all this, and more, proves to us that in 1906, at the age of thirty-two, Arnold Schoenberg had attained a mastery which already ranked him among the greatest composers of all time. I cannot resist quoting a passage from the development section, in which this mastery is applied to the contrapuntal elaboration of three different thematic ideas. This elaboration calls to our attention how far Schoenberg's musical consciousness had progressed in a few years. When we compare it to the extravagant exuberance of Op. 5, as exhibited in our Example 5a, Example 9 immediately makes us aware of that concision and economy which we have just been stressing.

Having thus sufficiently characterized the essential preoccupations of Schoenberg's musical thinking during the period which concerns us, let us briefly mention the other works composed at about the same time.

---

[20] For the preceding see also my lecture *What Is Twelve-Tone Music?* (Edition Dynamo, Liège), where these problems are more thoroughly discussed.

Ex. 9

The chorus Op. 13 is a model of architecture elaborated from an unusually strong contrapuntal conception.

The songs Op. 6 introduce ever freer tonal relationships, and frequently display a daring treatment of the voice. An example from the first song demonstrates this:

Ex. 10

Es ruht _____ auf mei_nem Mun . de ein Frül .

These statements hold true for the *Two Ballads*, Op. 12, and even more so for the *Two Songs*, Op. 14. In this latter work, we may even say that tonality is completely suspended; harmony for its own sake is given free rein, while the economy of the structure is astonishing. Thanks to the sovereign mastery of contrapuntal technique attained by the genius of Schoenberg, the relationships between voice and piano are extremely close-knit.

Finally, the Quartet, Op. 10, embodies all the acquisitions of the previous works. Its last movement is the first example of consciously suspended tonality.[21]

16. *Results of the consolidation of Schoenberg's first acquisitions.* —The successive stages of Schoenberg's reactivation of the evolution of polyphony have given rise to the following acquisitions:

1. Comprehension of the great compositional laws which affect the general structure.
2. Progressive broadening of tonal relationships.
3. Invention of harmony for its own sake.
4. Restoration to counterpoint of the importance which it had ceased to possess in the nineteenth century.

Taken all together, these acquisitions led Schoenberg to the complete suspension of the tonal system.

Let us examine this situation a little more closely.

The first of these acquisitions was discussed explicitly enough in the preceding section. Let us add only that such an attitude, the ideal incarnation of the dignity of composition, could find its complete expression only in the tone-row system, which, in its turn, implies the suspension of tonality. Thus we see that, although he could not yet foresee the ultimate results of his activity,

[21] See the analysis of Webern (*loc. cit.*), and Chapter I of my *Introduction to Twelve-Tone Music*.

Schoenberg was already directing this activity, teleologically, into a phase beyond that of his immediate evolution.

The second acquisition, the broadening of tonal relationships, is an ineluctable consequence of Schoenberg's energetic reactivation of the evolution of polyphony.[22] Indeed, such a process is characteristic of the various stages through which the tonal system has passed since its origins. Elsewhere we have seen the essential role played by chromaticism in these stages of the tonal system, and we may now say that, up until this point, Schoenberg's activity has devoted itself entirely to drawing the utmost consequences from all the possibilities furnished by the chromatic scale. In this sense, Schoenberg begins his activity at the point where his illustrious predecessors stopped. This way of using the chromatic possibilities produces melodic and harmonic forms which show an increasing tendency to break out of the harmonic system.

The third acquisition, invention of harmony for its own sake, produces the same result.[23] Let us look at any chord elaborated in this way—for example, the basic chord of the *Kammersymphonie* in Example 8. What strikes us first is its quality of "dissonance" as compared to the aggregations with which polyphony up to Wagner has familiarized us. We have already emphasized this aspect of the evolution of polyphony, according to which the dualism consonance-dissonance would one day cease to exist; we have already observed that Wagner did not succeed in "surpassing" this dualism. This is because Wagner lacked the conception of harmony for its own sake, the only conception capable of resolv-

[22] This question is the object of a remarkable study by Schoenberg himself in his latest book, *Structural Functions of the Harmony*. In this work, Schoenberg introduces the concept of *monotonality*, that is, the idea that the broadening of tonal relationships leads to the inclusion of all keys within a single tonality. The idea of the keys to which a piece may *modulate* is replaced by the idea of *regions*, near or remote as the case may be, which, encompassing all possible keys that surround a given tonal center, are grouped about this center and entirely submit to its domination. This process furnishes a completely convincing explanation of the way in which the tonal system, through a development of its utmost possibilities by means of the unmitigated juxtaposition of the most distant tonal regions, is at length surpassed, and is finally metamorphosed into that "pantonality" which is the twelve-tone technique. Schoenberg's book is the most valuable document for the study of this problem, which has largely been misunderstood in contemporary criticism.

[23] The following passage constitutes a development of the discussion of this problem which I approached in the previously cited article on Stravinsky.

ing the ancient conflict which, during the course of its evolution from the origins of polyphony (an evolution which would eventually bring about its complete disappearance), never ceased to oppose "consonant relaxation" to "dissonant tension." But, after 1904 or thereabouts, Schoenberg has no more qualms about using any vertical aggregation whatsoever. This is what he calls the emancipation of dissonance, which was bound to contribute to the suspension of the tonal system.

Before we verify this, let us ask the following question: is the invention of harmony for its own sake sufficient in itself to justify the emancipation of dissonance? Yes and no. It permits the invention of chords which have nothing more in common with those presented by the beginnings of the tonal system, but of itself it seems incapable of conferring precise functions upon the new chords or of setting up rules for their use. Indeed, the chords which concern us have been made possible not only by the concept of harmony for its own sake, but also by the increasing consciousness (which we have already emphasized) of *all* the possibilities of the chromatic scale. In fact, it is the chromatic scale alone which can furnish a coherent explanation of all these chords. Hence we are led to the assertion that this scale, as we have already seen, tends to transcend the tonal system; this is verified by the appearance of the chords in question, which bear but little resemblance (and sometimes, as in fourth-chords, no resemblance at all) to the chord-types of any tonality. When we consider the fourth-chords and other chord-types which Schoenberg uses freely after 1904, we find ourselves confronted by a paradox; these chords tend to break out of the tonal system, yet the composer forces them to obey tonal laws. But this situation did not last long, since, after 1908, Schoenberg realized that the tonal system had to be suspended because of the forces liberated by his consequent treatment of the chromatic scale.

Before discussing counterpoint, the fourth acquisition of Schoenberg, we must step aside for a moment to assert that Schoenberg's clear conception of the harmonic problems posed by the evolution of polyphony is unique. Other composers (Debussy, Ravel, Stravinsky, Bartok, Falla, and even Puccini) did not hesitate, following Schoenberg, to use many new chords; but they never used them so freely or so radically. Elsewhere [24] I have shown how equivocal was Stravinsky's use of chords of this sort. The *Petrouchka* chord is a superposition of two triads; the *Sacre* chord may be traced to the combination of an E major (F flat major) triad and a dominant seventh chord on E flat. This shows that Stravinsky's concept of harmony, despite all its seeming boldness, operates with obsolete ideas; or, rather, Stravinsky's concept has never been strong enough to *create an entirely new chord* without consideration for the *so-called immutable essence* of every harmonic structure. This essence is the system of thirds, which supposedly explains the entire apparatus of tonal harmony, and to which Stravinsky's two chords may be reduced.

It must be noted in passing that Schoenberg, for all his radical ideas, nearly made the same mistake. When he saw that the system of thirds was inadequate to explain the "new" chords, he thought for a while that their essence might be discovered in a system of fourths, which would be capable of engendering a chord containing all the notes of the chromatic scale. But, when he made that statement, Schoenberg discovered the real world in which these tones *exist*, and soon perceived that only the chromatic scale can assume the responsibility for all possible chords and thus surpasses the idea of the essence of harmony. Thus it becomes clear that there cannot exist—at least in our time—a harmonic essence which *precedes* the existence of chords, but that this essence resides only *in* their existence.

All this gives us a partial realization of why Schoenberg's efforts did not run into that *impasse* which was to be reached by most of the others who started out on the same road. All the others cling to the classic tonal functions, although they manhandle them violently. Their chords are robots without a life of their own—a life which they might have lived if they had been invented and handled according to the functions of the chromatic scale. Again, only the chromatic scale can justify these chords, when "tonal explanations" remain illogical. For example, it is all very well for the *Petrouchka* chord to superimpose the triads of

[24] *Loc. cit.*

C major and F sharp major, but it still does not belong to either of these keys; the same goes for the *Sacre* chord and all the "polytonal" aggregations of Bartók, Milhaud, etc. There is a compromise, a lack of real choice, which sometimes drives these composers to total chaos. In fact, these lifeless automata of chords proved incapable of *living* by creating new functions; their *mechanical* use finally exhausted even the composers, and that is why many of them came to a dead end in their work.

On the contrary, Schoenberg's awareness of the functional role assumed by the chromatic scale was to bring about quite different results, the first condition of which is that suspension of the tonal system which occurs in his work after 1908.

A few more remarks will clarify the role played by counterpoint in this process.[25] This fourth Schoenbergian acquisition is principally due to the reactivation of polyphonic evolution. In this sense, Schoenberg took note of the fact that the lack of counterpoint in the works of some of his predecessors represented a real impoverishment of polyphony. His genius now sought to remedy this state of affairs. On the other hand, a contrapuntal impulse came to him from what we have called the first of his acquisitions. The structural economy and the extraordinary feeling for development and variation which dominate his work from *Pelleas und Melisande* to the Second Quartet could not be completely realized without the aid of the virtues of counterpoint. If we carefully examine certain pages of the development of the *Kammersymphonie*, where several superimposed themes are continually developed at the same time, we understand the absolute necessity of the contrapuntal style. In the same way—as Alban Berg demonstrated so clearly in his analysis of the beginning of the Quartet in D minor—it is thanks to the contrapuntal concept, used for the first time in many generations by Schoenberg, that the compositional attitude which seeks to animate every part of the tonal structure with its own individual life *can* be completely realized.

But it is easy to understand that this concern for counterpoint can hardly remain forever content with the harmonic functions demanded by the tonal system. In the first part of this book, we

[25] Cf. Chapter II, *Introduction to Twelve-Tone Music.*

have seen that, because of the necessary equilibrium between voice-leading and the vertical aggregations which result from it, counterpoint has *never* had a chance to be realized in its pure form. Arnold Schoenberg decided to obtain entirely different results. He wants counterpoint to *be* counterpoint, he wants to enable this counterpoint to make strict use of all the thematic superpositions required for the architecture of a piece of music, and he wants this counterpoint to express itself—just like melody and harmony —with all the musical means afforded by the chromatic scale. It is from this new facet of his compositional attitude—the last acquisition of Schoenbergian polyphony—that there radiate the death-rays which will finally pierce the inner shell of the tonal system.

CHAPTER IV

The Suspension of the Tonal System

17. *General aspects of the new world of sound.—*
A. *Analogies with the older world of sound.*—We now find ourselves facing a historic moment comparable to the transition from
modal music to tonal music; a great many of the statements which
we made about tonal music are also applicable to that phase of
polyphonic evolution which we are about to study.[1]

To begin with, let us state that all the latest acquisitions of
tonal polyphony can be used freely as soon as Schoenberg consciously suspends the classic functions of tonality. Indeed, the free
disposition of all the materials offered by the chromatic scale
permits the invention *for its own sake* of every imaginable melodic
or harmonic form, as well as the unfolding of a purely contrapuntal style. In the same way, the typically Schoenbergian compositional technique of *perpetual variation* can now be realized
in a more consequent way, since musical structure will no longer
be fettered by the requirements of symmetrical reprises and specific tonal regions, and may, in extreme cases (as in certain works
of Schoenberg and especially of Webern),[2] entirely do away with
the idea of recapitulation.

All this, in fine, is nothing but the straightforward and systematic realization of a state of affairs which—less straightforward
and less systematic—already existed in the last tonal works of
Schoenberg and even, up to a point, in certain works of Wagner.
In this sense it is possible to say that, just as the first tonal music

---

[1] I cannot call this phase anything but *the suspension of the tonal system*, since
the term *atonality* is quite incorrect. Schoenberg himself never accepted it, and, in any
case, we shall see that the state of affairs which we are about to examine could not
possibly be defined by a single word.

[2] Cf. Part IV of this book.

is very similar to the last modal music, even so the first works in which Schoenberg abandons tonality are hardly different from those in which he still maintained it.

Let us prove this with several examples.

First, let us take the last movement of the Second Quartet, in which, for the first time, Schoenberg almost entirely does away with the classic tonal functions.[3] Is the following voice-leading radically different from that quoted in Example 10?

Ex. 11

On the contrary, it seems to me that they are clearly related. Likewise, the following example displays a similar relationship, and even recalls in certain respects the previously quoted melody from the *Gurre-Lieder* (example 4).

Ex. 12

As for the harmonic aspect,[4] it goes without saying that certain chords used frequently in the last tonal works—fourth-chords, for example, and many others—figure just as often in the works which now concern us. But even aside from that, we find definite relationships among harmonic *progressions* in works of different stages of development.

---

[3] In fact, only the last measures of this movement constitute a cadence which brings back the tonality of the entire work, F sharp minor.

[4] It would be easy to cite innumerable such melodic and harmonic examples in further proof of the statement that there is no fundamental difference between the last tonal works of Schoenberg and the first works in which he suspends the tonal system.

In the first of these examples (still tonal) we find a sort of sequence made of chords completely analogous to those used in the two following examples. (Ex. 13b is also a sequence.)

Ex. 13

a)

b)

c)

In a general way, the hearing of a song such as that from which the first example is taken produces an impression analogous to that of most of the songs of Op. 15 (1908), or even of the first two piano pieces of Op. 11 (1909). The only difference is that in Op. 14 Schoenberg still feels obliged to end in a particular key—a constraint which is abandoned in Op. 11 and 15. But already the way in which the final cadence of Op. 14 No. 1 is treated,

Ex. 14

and the scarcity of triads in this piece (there are, in thirty measures, eleven of them, five of which are "passing" and have the value of an eighth-note only, while, of the rest which are openly used, only one, the last, is in root position) makes it possible to speak of tonal suspension even in a piece like this, where tonality still seems to be preserved. Therefore, it is not surprising that the following compositions, where tonal suspension becomes a deliberate and effective process, completely resemble the earlier ones. There are the same melodic and harmonic idioms, the same scarcity of triads—all of which proves once more that continuity, not cleavage, marks the transition from one system of music to another. This is obvious, since a new system is never the result of speculation pure and simple, but is merely the deliberate and systematic embodiment of a common practise which up till then was partially unconscious and less systematic.

18. *General aspects of the new world of sound.—*
B. *Differences from the old world of sound.*—However, if it is possible for us to consider this entire group of works as belonging to a single phase of *dissolution* of tonal functions, nonetheless there are some differences between those works which still preserve tonality and those in which it is suspended. Before examining

these differences, we must state that, just as the modal system finally proved incapable of grouping certain polyphonic acquisitions coherently, even so the tonal system is finally insufficient for the understanding of certain polyphonic phenomena which we have already observed in the last works of Schoenberg. But the modal system, once overthrown, was not followed immediately by the definitive constitution of the tonal system (which does not take place until the work of Bach). There, too, one may speak of a *suspension* of the modal system, and it is in this sense that we must interpret the idea of suspension in those works of Schoenberg that belong to the period with which we are now concerned. These works are no longer tonal—and yet they are, to the extent that they continue to safeguard certain principles of the last tonal music (melodic idioms, harmonic progressions); and their nature is not yet such that there may be deduced from them a completely organized new system, even though, from time to time, they exhibit certain characteristics of such a system (which will be discovered very soon in any case).

The tonal system proves powerless to hold all the elements created by an increasingly bold treatment of the materials of the chromatic scale; therefore, the more pronounced this treatment becomes, the greater will be the differences in question.[5]

Now that we have pointed out certain analogies with the tonal world exhibited by Schoenberg's Op. 10 (last movement), 11, and 15, let us indicate certain completely disparate elements.

Here is the beginning of the fourth movement of Op. 10.

Ex. 16

[5] For a further study of this process of the increasingly elaborated and conseqent treatment of the materials of the chromatic scale, see Chap. I, *Introduction to Twelve-Tone Music.*

Such an unfoldment, within so short a space, of *all the tones* of the chromatic scale here appears for the first time in Schoenberg's work. Furthermore, we find here for the first time a passage which is truly *inconceivable* from the point of view of tonality. Obviously, numerous similar passages may be found in Op. 11 and Op. 15. The following example seems to me particularly significant in this respect:

Ex. 16

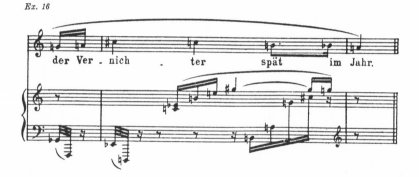

Again, such passages will become more and more frequent in the following works, while reminiscences of tonality—even in its most advanced form—will become more and more infrequent. Thus, little by little, there will unfold works which are really different from the last tonal works.

19. *Special aspects of the new world of sound.—*
C. *The new instrumental style.*—But these differences no longer consist only of the increasingly bold use of chromatic possibilities and the consequent invention of melodic and harmonic forms *for their own sake*—a kind of invention which becomes increasingly free. At least as important is the handling of the technique of variation proper to Schoenberg, a technique which now assumes

vast proportions. In fact, it upsets the whole style; and the transformations—eventually radical—in the instrumental style are
among the most important acquisitions of Schoenbergian polyphony. In the last movement of Op. 10, we may already observe in
certain places a complete change in the method of writing for
string quartet. Unheard-of sonorities are here heard for the first
time. In the same way, the piano style of Op. 11 introduces several
previously neglected possibilities of the piano. In Op. 15, not only
do the piano style and, on occasion, the vocal style present a
novel and original appearance, but the very concept of the song
with piano accompaniment is altered. In fact, the "symphonic
bond" between the human voice and the instrumental accompaniment had always been constructed by means of the simultaneous
development, in both parts, of the same thematic material (or of
interrelated motives), or, even more frequently, by the constant
and consequent development of two entirely different motives in
the two parts. Thus, from Mozart to Mahler, via Beethoven,
Schubert, Schumann, and Brahms, there grew up a tradition rich
in masterpieces, which Schoenberg inherited and to which he contributed actively, from his earliest songs up to Op. 14. But with the
fifteen *George-Lieder*, Op. 15, Schoenberg enriched this tradition
with a new acquisition. In a concert given (1909) by the *Verein
für Kunst und Kultur*, in which were heard the first part of the
Gurre-Lieder (with piano), the *Three Piano Pieces*, Op. 11, and
the *George-Lieder*, Op. 15, Schoenberg, presenting the program,
made the following confession with respect to these songs:

With the *George-Lieder*, I have succeeded for the first time in
approaching an expressive and formal idea which has haunted me for
years. Up until now, I lacked the strength and the self-assurance to
realize it. But now that I have started definitely upon this road, I am
aware that I have burst the bonds of bygone aesthetics; and, although
I am marching towards a goal which seems certain to me, I foresee
the opposition which I shall have to overcome; I feel the heat of the
animosity which even the least temperaments will generate, and I
fear that some who have believed in me up till now will not admit
the necessity of this evolution.

Again, the essential acquisition of these songs seems to me to be their overthrow of the traditional conception of the *genre*. Without falling into simple recitative, as is the case with numerous composers who have tried to "reform" the song with piano accompaniment in our time, Schoenberg succeeds in safeguarding the very essence of the *genre*, the unity of the two parts, by separating these parts completely and not basing either of them on integrated thematic material. Everything which takes place in either of these parts is based on a constant and perpetually varied elaboration of the various characteristic motives of each piece. The amazing independence of voice and piano (of which Example 16 may give some slight idea), and the overwhelming richness and variety of this song-cycle make it not only one of Schoenberg's finest works but also one of the masterworks of that tradition to which we alluded previously. It is scarcely an exaggeration to say that Schoenberg's Op. 15 represents the culmination of that system, for the efforts which it displays and the innovations which it introduces *had to be undertaken sooner or later,* given the previous history of the form. But, in bringing this form to such a culmination, Schoenberg seems to have exhausted the possibilities of a musical *genre,* at least provisionally; and doubtless this is why his heretofore fruitful activity in the field of the song with piano accompaniment now ceases entirely.[6]

The following work, the *Five Orchestral Pieces,* Op. 16 (written in the first half of 1909), displays tremendous innovations in orchestral style. The tendency to a soloistic style is here, for the first time, completely realized. Two examples will clarify this. The first, Example 17a, is the beginning of the second piece, and it is easy to see how distinctly each part of the ensemble is individualized by its specific instrumental color. Most of the time, the superposition of these different timbres excludes even the juxtaposition of two instruments of the same family. Here is still another aspect of the spirit of *variation* peculiar to Schoenberg.

---

[6] In fact, no song of this type has been published by Schoenberg since then; we shall see later that Berg and Webern, each in his own way, merely confirm the attitude of their master in this regard.

Ex. 17

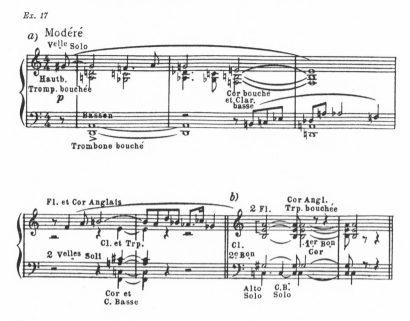

The second example, Ex. 17b, reproduces the beginning of the third piece. Here we are confronted with a single chord which constantly recurs, each time in a different instrumentation. Since each new group of instruments enters (almost imperceptibly) before the preceding group has ceased to sound the chord, there results a continual change of color, remarkable equally for its bewildering variety and for its continuity.

The most advanced piece, in this sense, seems to me to be the fifth. Schoenberg calls it the *Obbligato Recitative*. A principal melody, perpetually new, which never repeats a previously heard figuration, runs throughout the piece. Its instrumentation, too, is constantly changing, whether it passes from one instrument to another or whether, when an important segment is entrusted to a single instrument (or instrumental group), the unisonous doubling of this segment by alternating instrumental groups changes its color. Ex. 18, which reproduces the beginning of the melody, may give some idea of this.

In addition, this melody [7] is constantly accompanied by parts of great expressive force and utter independence, which are orchestrated with equal variety. The astonishing counterpoint which results from this, combined with the instrumental variety which we have emphasized, makes this piece one of the richest examples of polyphony in all music.

20. *Special aspects of the new world of sound.—*
D. *The culmination of the spirit of variation and the idea of chamber music.*—The tendencies found in Op. 16, No. 5, are elaborated, developed, and forced to their utmost consequences in the following works. Thus, the monodrama *Erwartung,* Op. 17, an opera with a single character, maintains the principles of orchestration found in Op. 16, and, in 'addition, tends to complete athematism, in the sense that there is never any kind of recapitulation. This work, which lasts a half hour and was written in about a fortnight (August 27–September 12, 1909) is an extraordinary *tour de force.* A sort of musical inventiveness *unprecedented in the history of music,* an inventiveness the wealth and intensity of which are staggering, makes every measure of this score a perpetual renewal. The soprano voice is heard throughout the work, and, like the principal melody of Op. 16, No. 5, is elaborated

---

[7] In order to clarify the evolution of this melody through the complex appearance of the score, Schoenberg uses here for the first time a special sign, designed to show the reader of the score, the conductor, and the performers in which part the principal voice is to be found. The sign ⌈ indicates the passage of the melody from one instrument to another. Later, Schoenberg introduces the signs H— (*Hauptstimme*) and N— (*Nebenstimme*), which end with ⌉; everything not so marked is to be considered accompaniment. In Schoenberg's American scores, these signs are translated as P ⌉ (principal voice) and S ⌉ (secondary voice).

by means of perpetual variation of the melodic lines. The orchestra, also extremely varied, underlines the voice with remarkable subtlety and plasticity.

Ex. 19

A second dramatic work, *Die Glückliche Hand,* Op. 18 (begun immediately after Op. 17, but not finished till November 18, 1913), takes the form of a musical play with the following characters: a man (baritone), a woman and a "gentleman" (whose parts are enacted in pantomime), and six men and six women (who form the chorus). It may be said that this work represents an effort similar to that of Op. 17; but here there is a greater concern for counterpoint, which is particularly obvious in the writing for chorus. Furthermore, this work displays a desire for extreme concision, which frequently motivates abrupt changes in structure and instrumental style. This is shown in the first entrance of the baritone (Example 20).

The preceding scene, which was dominated by the chorus, has barely finished in a flurry of *tremolos* when the expressive motive of the 'cello is heard. The end of this motive is accented by a heavy chord of four bassoons, which introduces the baritone; he is accompanied in his turn by a widely-spread chord of two clarinets and tuba. Then the orchestration changes completely, and from here on an entirely different musical atmosphere (which, of course, varies constantly) pervades the second scene.

It is also in this work that Schoenberg makes his first consequential use of that *Sprechgesang* which will later be employed systematically in *Pierrot Lunaire*. This new way of treating the voice permits the elaboration of melodramatic scenes according to purely musical principles, which is not the case in classic recitatives. Here, too, Schoenberg reveals himself as one of the most

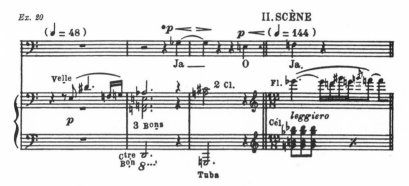

genuine and clear-headed musicians of all time. Although before him all composers, even the greatest, had contented themselves with the recitative every time that dramatic necessity demanded it—a procedure which often obliged them to sacrifice a strong musical structure to dramatic exigencies—Schoenberg does not hesitate to introduce a radical innovation, and creates out of whole cloth a new style of singing, which has the virtue of making possible the amalgamation of the spoken word with a melodic structure as firm as that of any *arioso*.[8]

Our Example 21, taken from the first scene of the drama, exhibits the application of this principle to the choral style, which, combined with the orchestra, produces an unbelievably dense polyphonic texture.[9]

[8] For more details on the *Sprechgesang*, see the preface of *Pierrot Lunaire*. Here are its principal features: the rhythm should be observed as in ordinary singing; while a sung melody maintains its pitches, the spoken melody merely indicates the pitches and then moves up or down from them.

[9] For more details on Schoenberg's Op. 17 and 18, see my study "The Dramatic Works of Arnold Schoenberg," in *Polyphonie*, No. 1, Brussels 1947.

The year 1911 sees the composition of the *Six Little Piano Pieces,* Op. 19, and the song *Herzgewächse* for soprano, celesta, harmonium, and harp, Op. 20.

Here we are confronted with a new phase of Schoenberg's evolution. The spirit of variation, so that it may appear in its purest form, now calls for works of reduced dimensions.[10] This is the only way in which the repetition of the slightest melodic motives can be avoided. In this respect, Op. 19 represents a completely new departure. Each piece of this set lasts but a few moments. However, its sound-forms, pared to the bone, create a firm and clearly articulated structure. Thus, this work, as well as *Herzgewächse,* which again manifests Schoenberg's extraordinary instrumental imagination, prepares the most important composition of this period: *Pierrot Lunaire,* Op. 21.

In the fall of 1911 Schoenberg gave a series of ten lectures on aesthetics and the teaching of musical composition at the Stern Conservatory in Berlin, where he made the acquaintance of the actress Albertine Zehme. It was she who gave him the idea of setting (in the form of melodramas) the cycle of three-times-seven poems of Albert Giraud, *Pierrot Lunaire,* in the German translation (infinitely superior to the original) of Otto Erich Hartleben. The work was written during the spring and summer of 1912; the first piece was composed on March 30, the fourteenth (last to be completed) on September 9.

The work appears, then, in the form of twenty-one melodramas for female voice (*Sprechgesang*). The instrumental accompaniment includes a flute (alternating with piccolo), a clarinet (alternating with bass clarinet), a violin (alternating with viola), a 'cello, and a piano. Except for Op. 20,[11] then, it is Schoenberg's first return to real chamber music since Op. 10. The cycle is divided into three parts, each of which comprises seven poems. Each poem has a different instrumentation, and, even when all

---

[10] This problem is developed in Part IV, in connection with similar works of Webern.

[11] Which, as mentioned before, may be considered as a preliminary study for *Pierrot Lunaire.*

the instruments are used during the course of a poem, the successive entrances have their own special characteristics.[12]

[12] For example, in the first part, the first piece uses the flute, the violin, and the piano, later joined by the 'cello; the second piece begins with the violin and the piano, with the flute and the clarinet entering later; the third is set for piccolo, clarinet and piano; the fourth, for flute, clarinet, and piano; the fifth, for flute, clarinet (later bass clarinet), and piano; the sixth, for flute, bass clarinet, and 'cello, later joined by the piano; the seventh, for flute alone.

All this constitutes a new aspect of that spirit of variation which now becomes intensely active in the instrumental realm. The radical innovation is that variety is obtained with a minimum of material; this is a transplantation to the instrumental field of Schoenberg's chief preoccupation—the creation of rich and abundant musical material with the greatest possible economy of means.[13] With *Pierrot Lunaire,* we view the culmination of that tendency which from *Verklärte Nacht* through the two string quartets, the *Kammersymphonie* and Op. 20, tried to restore chamber music to the niche from which the post-Wagnerian orchestra had ousted it. Later we shall see, examining the works in question from a different viewpoint, what were the other motives and the other results of this restoration.

Before closing this section, we must speak of the last work of this period, which exhibits a veritable paroxysm of instrumental variation.

The *Four Orchestral Songs,* Op. 22, were composed as follows: the first, October 6, 1913; the fourth, August 28, 1914; the third, December 3, 1914; and the second, December 30, 1914–January 1, 1915.

---

[13] It is needless to add that Schoenberg discovers previously unsuspected instrumental possibilities. The renewal of instrumental style, approached in Op. 11 and 15, now takes place at a fantastic rate. Schoenberg's compositional necessities make demands on previously unused instrumental resources. In this sense, it may be said that the instruments are forced to play parts which would previously have been considered beyond them. But the fact that these parts are not only *playable* but are even, after a certain necessary lapse of time, considered by performers to be *eminently adapted* to their instruments, proves the extraordinary mastery achieved by Schoenberg, and also confronts us anew with one of the major laws of the evolution of polyphony—a law which Schoenberg obeys with all his being. This law is to be found in that progressive expansion of instrumental possibilities and resources which has been taking place ever since the seventeenth century. When we recall the progress thus achieved in all fields of instrumental style—piano, strings, or woodwinds—we must immediately understand that instrumental style could not remain at the point which it had reached by the turn of the century. In this sense, Schoenberg's activity in this field is not only legitimate but also replete with historic meaning, since the spirit of reform which characterizes it belongs to the very essence of musical history; it is, indeed, a condition *sine qua non* of that history. The opposition which Schoenberg has often encountered in this realm (and also in that of vocal music) is hardly surprising, for "it was ever thus." The *Sonata Pathétique* of Beethoven was dubbed "unplayable" by Weber (who, after all, was not Tom, Dick, or Harry); the operas of Mozart were considered "unsingable" by certain singers—who, it is true, retreated before certain difficulties, and thought that Mozart did not make their parts beautiful enough.

Here is their orchestral apparatus, which, for the reader who has followed our reasoning, requires no comments.

The first song calls for twenty-four violins (usually *divisi a 6*), twelve 'celli (usually *divisi a 3*), nine double-basses, six clarinets (usually playing in unison, but sometimes fanning out into four-, five-, or six-tone chords), one trumpet, three trombones, one tuba, tympani, cymbals, xylophone, and tam-tam. The second is written for four flutes, one English horn, one piccolo-clarinet, two clarinets, two bass clarinets, one double-bassoon, one harp, three solo 'celli and one double-bass solo; the third, for two piccolos, three flutes, three oboes, two English horns, three bass clarinets, one double-bass clarinet, four solo violins, five solo 'celli and one solo double-bass. It is only the fourth song which uses a more nearly normal orchestration: one piccolo, three flutes, three oboes, one English horn, three clarinets, one bass clarinet, three bassoons, one double-bassoon, four horns, one trumpet, one tuba, and the string quintet.

What leaps to the eye in this astonishing score is a fantasy, an imagination and an inventiveness with respect to sonority which demand our admiration. But this is not pure hedonism on Schoenberg's part; his principal concern, in such esoteric instrumental combinations, is for clarity and economy of means. In order to be completely realized, the clarity of such complex polyphony as this demands the juxtaposition of strongly individualized timbres. Furthermore, the perpetual variation of all the musical forms— motives, themes, chords and the like—demands this enormous variety of timbres in order that the articulation of the musical speech may emerge clearly. On the other hand, Schoenberg's keen awareness of the problems of chamber music prevents him from being satisfied with the ready-made orchestral mold; his feeling for musical economy demands the "reinvention" of the orchestra in every piece, "for the good of the cause." No matter how many instruments are used, they will be used *only if they prove indispensable*.

21. *The search for a means of organizing the chromatic materials and the growth of new laws.*—In my *Introduction to Twelve-Tone*

Music, I have tried to describe as precisely as possible certain structural characteristics of melody and harmony in the works which exhibit the suspension of the tonal system. I have also attempted to show how these different phenomena, which occur more and more often during the course of polyphonic evolution, finally forced the discovery of a technique—the *tone-row technique* —capable of organizing the various acquisitions of "post-tonal" polyphony, and also capable of organizing a system within which these acquisitions might develop freely and lead to further acquisitions. I cannot repeat all this here and therefore take the liberty of referring the reader to my other work. However, I am obliged to recall several of my remarks on this subject, and to explain a number of points which I have not yet had occasion to emphasize.

Let us recall that the works discussed in this chapter were all composed (except Op. 22) between 1908 and 1912. This extremely short period [14] also included various other activities. On the one hand, there is Schoenberg's teaching activity, which takes a great deal of his time (including that devoted to writing his *Theory of Harmony*),[15] and, on the other hand, the more and more frequent invitations to conduct his works both in Germany and in other countries [16] which his growing reputation brings him.

[14] Four years for nine works, at least three of which (the two dramatic works, Op. 17 and 18 and *Pierrot Lunaire*) are built on a grand scale.

[15] Written between 1909 and 1911, this important work, which constitutes a synthesis of the principles of tonal harmony up to Schoenberg's last tonal works, and which goes so far as to prophesy—with surprising accuracy—the eventual evolution of harmony, has the additional merit of basing its instruction on infinitely sounder principles of musical technique than had ever been used before. In more recent theoretical works, *Models for Beginners in Composition* (New York, 1943) and *Structural Functions of the Harmony* (unpublished), Schoenberg makes some important additions to the principles expounded in his first book.

[16] Among the principal trips abroad were those to Amsterdam and St. Petersburg (1912) where Schoenberg was invited to conduct his *Pelleas und Melisande*, Op. 5. Later (1914) the Queen's Hall Promenade Concerts invited him to conduct his *Five Orchestral Pieces*, Op. 16. It must also be mentioned that Schoenberg conducted other works than his own. One of the most memorable occasions of his doing so before 1914 was a concert which took place on March 31, 1913, under the sponsorship of the *Akademischer Verband für Litteratur und Musik*. This concert was organized by Schoenberg in order to give his pupils Berg and Webern a chance to have their works performed. The program included Webern's orchestral pieces, Op. 6, Schoenberg's *Kammersymphonie*, Op. 9, some orchestral songs of Zemlinsky, and Berg's songs, Op. 4; it was to close with the *Kindertotenlieder* of Mahler. There was already rioting during the first two works—a fight between the enthusiastic young people and the older lis-

All this may give us some idea of Schoenberg's feverish activity, of the turbulence of his inspiration and his ideas. In fact, if we look back on all the works from the songs, Op. 15, up to (but not including) *Pierrot Lunaire,* what strikes us with particular force is—in addition to the constant awareness of those problems which we have already discussed—a well-nigh delirious enthusiasm in the midst of the wealth of chromatic material released by the suspension of the tonal system. The only precise statement which one can make about these works is that, in their handling of the musical material at their disposal, they go further and further in the direction that is to mark Schoenberg's later treatment of these matters. Little by little, in this way, all the elements which recall the old order of tonality are eliminated. This state of affairs is not caused by any preconceived esthetic speculations; it is essentially due to purely compositional laws and necessities. Thus, this consequent treatment of all the possibilities of the chromatic scale almost automatically excludes any obvious tonal reminiscences, since, in this way, no tone or chord can acquire a special functional meaning. And if, from a certain moment onwards, this practise becomes conscious and voluntary, it is on account of a genuine compositional attitude. Obviously, if a tone or chord were allowed, at a given moment, to outweigh other tones or chords, this overweight would give that tone or chord a functional value which would (given the use of all chromatic possibilities) be belied by the context. Thus there would be an unevenness in the composition, which would be all the more serious because of its unintentional character. It was legitimate, therefore, for Schoenberg and his principal disciples to attempt the elimination of such solecisms from our musical speech. Likewise, the progressive abandonment of all melodic or harmonic idioms reminiscent of tonal music (triads, for example) may be explained by similar considerations. These idioms, so familiar to the ears of musicians, have become, for these ears, parts of certain almost stereotyped formulae. This means that such idioms automatically imply certain others which usually precede and follow

---

teners who tried to break up the performance by hooting and whistling. Finally the songs of Berg completely upset the applecart—the concert had to be stopped; the rioters marched right to the police-station, and later to court.

them, so that if they are isolated from their context they sound like clichés automatically stamped on a background which does not belong to them. Thus, this gradual abandonment of the most characteristic tonal reminiscences is forced by compositional logic, and, in the long run, by genuine artistic *honesty*.

But the gradual multiplication of such experiments, even their organization into more or less explicit laws, is still the *negative* side of the question. The *positive* side does not appear until Schoenberg becomes keenly aware of the necessity for an "ultra-consequent" treatment of the chromatic materials, which demands the systematic avoidance of the repetition of any tone before the other eleven tones of the chromatic scale have been heard. In fact, the works after Op. 17 conform roughly to these conditions.[17] The positive side appears also in certain increasingly frequent phenomena the later awareness of which was to prove the key to the tone-row technique. These phenomena are produced by the *unity of melody and harmony*. We have seen an early application of this idea in the *Kammersymphonie,* Op. 9, where a "row" of successive fourths produced both harmonic and melodic figures (Ex. 8, a and b). Such instances become more and more frequent in the works which concern us, although they come about almost unconsciously and quite unsystematically.

Finally,[18] we must note the great economy of means practised in melodic construction. This economy can furnish a structural law capable of replacing those means of articulation provided by the tonal system. An example (Example 22), from the beginning of Op. 22 No. 1, is an excellent illustration of this theory.

Here we have a perfectly constructed melodic line, elaborated, with ideal economy, by the variation of a very few motives. The entire first part up to measure 5—the *antecedent*—is built on the

---

[17] I say roughly, for it would be exaggerating to speak of consistent systematization in these works. It is true that they contain numerous long passages which can be almost entirely divided into a series of sections using the twelve tones of the chromatic scale. We also find series of nine, ten, or eleven notes; what matters is the tendency towards the unfoldment of a large number of tones, which is extremely characteristic of Schoenberg's activity at this time.

[18] For all the preceding discussion, the reader will find numerous examples in Chap. I of *Introduction to Twelve-Tone Music.* The following example is new.

single motivic cell of group 1 (minor second and minor third).
Groups 2, 3, 4, 5, 6, and 7 use these intervals only. The second part,
up to measure 8—the *consequent*—is introduced by a contrasting
interval, the tritone (group 8) which will play an important part.
Group 9 takes up the original intervals. Group 10a introduces a new
combination, but is elaborated from the tritone C–G flat, which is
equivalent to group 8. The chromatic transformation of B flat to B
natural builds, with the abovementioned tritone, group 10b, C–G

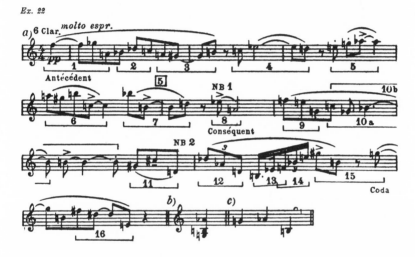

Ex. 22

flat–B natural, which finds its equivalents in groups 11 and 12.
Group 13 is the equivalent of 10a; group 14 is an inversion of 10b
(which equals 11 and 12). The last two notes of the *consequent*
and the first note of the *codetta* build group 15, which is only a
variant of the groups of the beginning, and which reproduces exactly the first chord of the piece (which harmonized group 1) —
unity of melody and harmony! (Cf. Ex. 22, b and c.) In the same
way, group 16 is a variant of the beginning groups (minor third
and minor second). Finally, let us observe that at one point
(NB1–NB2) this melody unfolds a pure twelve-tone row.

It is needless to add that such examples abound all through the
works in question.

Finally, we must speak of the dazzling flights of counterpoint
in this music. Now we know that the awareness of the necessity for

counterpoint has always been one of the basic elements of Schoenberg's "reactivation." This necessity brought the recrudescence of
chamber music, since groups like the string quartet or small ensembles of soloists furnish the most efficient means of performing counterpoint. This counterpoint now proves increasingly necessary to
"post-tonal" music; in the first place, it is only now that counterpoint can unfold freely, and, in the second place, counterpoint can
furnish powerful means of articulation to replace the "articulating"
functions of tonal harmony.

It is *Pierrot Lunaire* which doubtless exhibits Schoenberg's most
advanced contrapuntal style up to that point; numerous passages
are realized in the forms of strictest counterpoint. I shall cite the
most characteristic of these.

The eighth piece is a strict *passacaglia.*

The coda of the thirteenth piece takes up the flute melody of
the seventh piece and keeps it in the flute, while the melody
"sung" by the reciter in the seventh piece is now given to the bass
clarinet, and later to the 'cello with an imitation in the viola.

The seventeenth piece displays an imitation of the *Sprechgesang* by the viola, while the clarinet imitates in contrary motion.
Then there appears a double canon between the reciter and the
piccolo on the one hand and (in contrary motion) the viola and
clarinet on the other hand.

The eighteenth piece is the most remarkable in this respect.
Here we have a double retrograde canon between piccolo and
clarinet on the one hand, violin and 'cello on the other hand.
From the middle of the piece onwards, all the parts are played
backwards (from the last note to the first). To this is added a
"free" melody for the reciter, as well as a three-voice *fugato* in the
piano. These elements do not participate in the retrograde motion.

But it must be emphasized that the strictness and the complexity of such a piece result in a marvelous clarity of sound. For
one to whom this music has become familiar, the musical speech is
extraordinary in its wealth of meaning. In any case, we are here
confronted with the kind of musical realization and inventiveness
which had not been seen in polyphony since Bach.

By reactivating the deeper meanings of counterpoint and by

treating this science with its appropriate dignity, Schoenberg has brought elements of great nobility and power to contemporary music.

These are the elements which were to guide him towards the discovery of the laws of organization of the new world of music— laws which not only present the synthesis of ten centuries of polyphonic activity, but also afford glimpses of entirely new perspectives in musical composition.

It is to the examination of these questions that we must now address ourselves.

CHAPTER V

The Definite Organization of the New World of Sound

22. War years; Schoenberg's resumption of teaching.—The war of 1914 put a sudden stop to Schoenberg's beginning "international" activity. But, in addition to the songs of Op. 22, he was now planning an important choral work, an oratorio. This work, first conceived in 1910, was originally intended to be in three parts, but finally shrank to a single part, *Die Jakobsleiter*. He began writing the text [1] in January, 1915, but, because of being drafted for the first time, could not finish it until July, 1917. As soon as the text was completed, he started to compose the music, but a second mobilization soon put a stop to this effort.[2] After his second demobilization (October, 1917) Schoenberg devoted himself principally to teaching for several years. His pupils steadily increased in number. The "seminar for composition" was founded, and functioned from 1917 to 1920. Besides the usual subjects—harmony, counterpoint, composition, and orchestration—there were evenings of discussion, during which Schoenberg would answer questions, analyze compositions, and so on. Soon, in the course of these evenings, there arose the desire to make music, to play contemporary works unheard in ordinary concerts, and to familiarize the public with new music. For this, two conditions were necessary: 1) perfectly prepared performances of all works and 2) repetitions of these performances (a complicated work could be repeated three or four times). It is in this spirit that the *Verein für musikalische*

---

[1] Schoenberg had already written his own text for *Die Glückliche Hand*. Later, he wrote most of the texts for the choruses, Op. 27, as well as those of Op. 28 and 35.

[2] However, he has resumed it recently.

Privataufführungen was founded. Here were heard, for the first time in Vienna, numerous works of contemporary chamber music: *L'Ile joyeuse, En blanc et noir,* and the violin and 'cello sonatas of Debussy; the string quartet, *Gaspard de la Nuit,* and the *Trois poèmes de Mallarmé* of Ravel; pieces of Satie; piano pieces and the clarinet trio of Reger; the *Bagatelles* of Bartók; the Sonata for 'cello solo of Kodály. Even orchestral works (Schoenberg, Webern, and Mahler) were played, and numerous transcriptions of orchestral works for two pianos (Mahler, Reger, Strauss, Debussy, and Ravel) were made. Each program was introduced by a different pupil,[3] whose duty was to point out, clearly and simply, the essential characteristics of the works to be heard. This "master of ceremonies" also had to direct the first rehearsals for his concert; Schoenberg himself conducted the final ones (there were always ten to twenty for each concert) and the performance itself.

All this activity continued till the fall of 1920, when Schoenberg was invited to Amsterdam to conduct his own works with the *Concertgebouw* orchestra and to give some courses in theory. During all these years, until 1923, no new work was to come from his pen.

23. *The silence of Schoenberg; its cause and effect.*—Today, it seems obvious that this long silence was not due only to the war and its consequences; the activities which were carried on during the period of silence leave no doubt of this. The new world of sound entered in the last movement of the Second Quartet had to be organized, and the implicit laws which governed composition after the suspension of the tonal system had to be codified.

Schoenberg's chief goal was to construct, with the total resources of chromaticism, a new tonal system, obtained by means of a new method of realizing functional unity. The plan was ambitious; before it could be carried out, a new technique, already partially in evidence in some of the works of the preceding ten years, had to be invented. This new technique, quite aside from any question of

---

[3] Among them were the composer Hanns Eisler, the pianists Steuermann and Serkin, the violinist Rudolf Kolisch (founder of the Kolisch Quartet), the composer and conductor Max Deutsch, and the conductor Rankl.

tonality or the absence thereof, is nothing but a *tool* for composition. In considering the twelve-tone technique—for that is what now concerns us—merely as a tool, I am far from minimizing its worth; I simply mean that this technique, which, as we shall see, permits the coherent development of a musical thought, does not of itself guarantee the presence of a particular tonal or post-tonal structure. The erection of such a structure is a more specialized process.

It is in the *Five Piano Pieces*, Op. 23, that the tone-row technique is first used consciously. This is how it works: a series of notes produces a series of intervals, and this latter series is employed functionally throughout an entire composition—that is, it gives rise to all the melodic and harmonic forms of a work conceived in this way. The cause and purpose of such a compositional method are as follows: in the absence of a unifying principle for the total resources of chromaticism, the tone-row may constitute just such a principle. In the first place, it is a principle of economy, because it bears the sole responsibility for everything that happens in the music, and thus engenders *unity*. In the second place, the tone-row permits, and even requires, the invention of numerous forms which are, in the long run, merely *variations* of the initial idea (the tone-row). Thus is engendered *perpetual variation*, an incalculable enrichment of the language of music. In the third place, the tone-row, responsible for the melodic unity of the piece, becomes responsible also for the coherence and the logic of the harmony, which is merely the vertical aspect of the tone-row. And, finally, the tone-row embodies that unity (already adumbrated in the works discussed in the preceding chapter) of melody and harmony, two different aspects of the same musical reality.

24. *Schoenberg's first tone-rows; his first twelve-tone works.*—The *Five Piano Pieces*, Op. 23, use tone-rows. The last piece of the set is built on a series of twelve tones; this means that Schoenberg is extending the principles of the tone-row technique to the total resources of chromaticism, which, as always, serve as the foundation of his work. This piece, then, is the first twelve-tone composi-

tion. Since the *twelve-tone technique* is still used here in a rather rudimentary way, we shall rather explain it in connection with a work wherein it has evolved to a higher level. However, let us take a little time to examine the other characteristics of Op. 23. Quite aside from their firm structure—obviously the consequence of the tone-row technique—these five pieces represent the culmination of that piano style developed in Op. 11, Op. 19, the songs of Op. 15, and *Pierrot Lunaire.* All these works attempted to increase the resources of the piano as much as possible. Especially in *Pierrot Lunaire* do we find a piano style which is highly varied (one may say that each number in which the piano appears brings into play its own special pianistic resources), extremely difficult, and yet perfectly adapted to the pianist's hands. We find all these characteristics even more highly developed in the present work. Its very appearance is radically different from that of the "pre-Schoenberg" piano style. However, there is nothing arbitrary about it; [4] on the contrary, Schoenberg writes in a manner much more appropriate to the piano than that of certain post-romantic composers who, influenced by Liszt, wrote all their piano music in the style of piano reductions. There is nothing of this sort in Schoenberg's Op. 23. Everything that belongs to the pianistic tradition—ornaments, chords, melodies accompanied by solid or broken

Ex. 23

[4] Indeed, the difference between the piano style of these pieces and that of, say, Chopin is certainly no greater than the difference between the piano style of Chopin and that of Mozart.

chords, virtuoso passages, contrapuntal passages—recurs here in its most authentic and traditional form. But, of course, since these devices are all applied to the total resources of chromaticism, the resulting forms can hardly resemble those produced with more limited resources. A few examples will show this. In the first, Example 23, a melodic line which moves from a low register to a high register of the piano (using all possible resources!) is accompanied by a constantly changing rhythmic and harmonic formula (perpetual variation!).

This passage presents no complex problem—only the combinations of intervals, unknown before Schoenberg, may at first appear surprising.

Example 24 is a virtuoso passage. Formerly, such a passage would have been written in octaves, sixths, or thirds. But, in the first place, Schoenberg's feeling for variation does not allow him to limit himself to a mechanical unfoldment of fixed interval-patterns, and, in the second place, the total resources of chromaticism permit him to augment the possibilities of the piano by writing such passages in sevenths (and also, then and later, in seconds and fifths). Many other examples of the fundamental traditionalism of all the devices of Schoenberg's piano style might easily be cited.

The next work, the *Serenade*, Op. 24 (1923) for clarinet, bass clarinet, mandolin, guitar, viola, 'cello, and bass voice (in the fourth movement only), also uses the tone-row technique, and includes passages where the twelve-tone technique is employed, though still in a very rudimentary way. This work belongs to the tradition of chamber music abandoned by Schoenberg about ten years earlier, after *Pierrot Lunaire*. In addition, we see here a return to classical forms, which dominate the following work of Schoenberg. The first movement is a march, the second a minuet, the third a predominantly contrapuntal theme with variations, the fourth a sonnet of Petrarch (No. 217) in which extremely free instrumental counterpoint is embroidered around the voice, the fifth a dance-scene (a sort of waltz, with extraordinary instrumental verve), and the sixth an extremely simple and beautiful *Song Without Words*. The Finale is a variation of the opening march, and contains, just before the end, a slow passage in which the principal elements of the sixth movement are combined contrapuntally with elements of the fifth movement and of the march. All these figures appear, of course, in a form extremely different from that of their first statement.

The instrumental and contrapuntal style need not be further discussed, since, from this point of view, the *Serenade* is clearly in the line of descent of the previous works. As to the much-discussed problem of the classical forms, I shall say here only that, at the moment when Schoenberg introduced into music his most radical innovation, the tone-row technique, his genius at first felt the need of experimenting with this technique within the framework of certain established forms. However, it must also be said that he does not use these forms as ready-made molds; on the other hand, every classical form that he uses is re-created, amplified, and developed until it bears but slight resemblance to the familiar original.

In the next two works, the Suite for piano, Op. 25, and the Wind Quintet, Op. 26 (both 1924), we find the same tendencies manifested. The forms (even more drastically remodelled) are classical, and the contrapuntal and instrumental style is based on principles which we have already discovered.

Op. 25 consists of six movements: Prelude, Gavotte, Musette, Intermezzo, Minuet, and Gigue. The piano style, though always extremely rich and varied, tends to be simpler than that of Op. 23. Contrapuntal passages are frequent; for example, the Trio of the Minuet proves to be a strict two-voice canon in contrary motion.

Op. 26 is in four movements: an Allegro in sonata form, a very elaborate Scherzo, an Adagio in ternary form (A B A) with a highly developed coda, and, for Finale, a Rondo with marvelously varied reprises; the last movement, in particular, makes great use of the principles of strict counterpoint. This work represents the first attempt since the suspension of the tonal system to recapture the large musical forms. At first, the loss of the traditional means of articulation made the composition of large works impossible. It is only the application of the *twelve-tone* technique, which is full-grown in the two abovementioned works, that makes the use of large forms possible again.[5] Further proof that there is *no* problem of the evolution of polyphony to which Schoenberg has not been able to find the answer!

25. The twelve-tone technique.—Schoenberg's Op. 25 and 26 are the first works to be based exclusively on the new technique, the general principles of which are definitely established here. Let us recall its essential characteristics.[6]

A series of twelve tones forms the basis of the composition. All the sound-forms of this composition must, then, consist of successive or simultaneous presentations of the complete row, a fragment of it, or several forms of it. The different forms of the row are as follows:

I. Its original form (O).

II. Its retrograde form (R), produced by reading the original form backwards, from the last note to the first.

III. Its inverted form (I), produced by reversing the direction of the intervals of the original row, so that the ascending intervals become descending and vice versa.

IV. Its retrograde inversion (RI).

---

[5] Cf. *Introduction to Twelve-Tone Music.*

[6] The reader should consult my other work for a more thorough study of the question.

All these forms may be transposed to each of the twelve tones of the chromatic scale, thus making a total of forty-eight possible forms.

It is important to note in this connection that Schoenberg, in creating such a technique, synthesizes not only all of his own fundamental acquisitions but also those of the entire evolution of polyphony. Thus he invents a tool for composition which builds the most "economical" of all possible principles of unification; for all the musical happenings in a given piece are inevitably traced back to one fundamental idea. At the same time, this unifying principle gives a functional meaning to every vertical or horizontal musical structure, for it encompasses them all. Furthermore, it both permits and justifies the invention of *any* melodic-harmonic aggregation and the elaboration of counterpoint *for its own sake*. Because the tone-row includes all twelve tones of the chromatic scale and may be transposed to every degree of that scale, the total resources of chromaticism are finally related to a single norm. Finally, such a unifying principle makes *perpetual variation* the *conditio sine qua non* of its existence, since it may be said that every twelve-tone piece is nothing but a series of variations on the original row. The technique of perpetual variation thus includes all those procedures which permit the alteration of a series of intervals without the destruction of its functions. These procedures are the four types of variation of the tone-row: Original, Retrograde, Inversion, and Retrograde Inversion, which have been used (not always consciously) ever since the beginnings of polyphony, and which, therefore, had to be incorporated into the twelve-tone system.[7]

Finally, generally speaking, it may be stated that the twelve-tone technique constitutes a synthesis of all preceding techniques, since these techniques developed in the world of chromaticism

[7] The most frequent variation before Schoenberg is Inversion. Retrograde has also been used quite often. But Retrograde Inversion, though it may be discovered rather often in a good many compositions, seems not to have forced itself on the attention of "pre-Schoenbergian" composers, and to have been used unconsciously. Just one more example of the tremendous force with which Schoenberg reactivates the whole meaning of polyphonic evolution, thanks to which his work stands as a masterly and living synthesis of all the acquisitions of this evolution.

which they could organize only *in part*, while the new technique organizes it *completely*. Furthermore, the world of sound organized in this way includes the characteristics of the two previous musical systems. The twelve-tone technique preserves, and even accentuates, the *specialization* of the modal system, since it emphasizes the *special arrangement* of intervals, i.e., the particular structure of each tone-row, which even *varies from one work to the next*. On the other hand, the new technique preserves and accentuates the *universalism* of the tonal system, since it encompasses the total resources of chromaticism with the structure of the tone-row, as well as with its transpositions, the differences in which are much slighter than the differences in the scales of the tonal system.[8]

With the creation of the twelve-tone technique, the art of music enters a new phase—not (as one might suppose) because the works composed in the new system are radically different from the works which led to the discovery of this system,[9] but because this discovery itself marks the precise moment when (as with Bach and Rameau in the tonal system) the intuitive acquisitions of a particular polyphonic period are organized, by a consciousness which comprehends them clearly, into a complete synthesis of the premises which made them possible, and become the basis for future acquisitions.

26. *The unfoldment of Schoenberg's twelve-tone activity.—* A.—*The choruses Op. 27 and 28.*—The next two works of Schoenberg, *Four Pieces for Mixed Chorus*, Op. 27, and *Three Satires for Mixed Chorus*, Op. 28 (both 1925), again solve, even more cleverly, the problem of strict counterpoint. Now, thanks to the new technique, this counterpoint can give rise to laws as precise as those which governed earlier forms of counterpoint. In this sense, it must be said that an imitation could rarely be strict in

---

[8] In this sense, it is important not to confuse tonal modulation with the use of a transposed form of the tone-row. Although the two processes sometimes produce analogous results, this does not occur automatically.

[9] Once more there is not a *break*, but *continuity*, between the two systems. Furthermore, as always in such cases, numerous elements of the earlier phase continue to survive in the later phase. We shall return to this.

the modal or tonal systems, while such strictness is obligatory here.[10]

The first three pieces of Op. 27 are to be sung *a cappella*; the last, a kind of little cantata, is accompanied by a mandolin, a clarinet, a viola, and a 'cello. The first piece is a four-voice canon in contrary motion; only the ending is free. The second makes considerable use of canonic principles, but is generally less strict. The third, extremely strict, somewhat resembles a chorale in four verses (the last of which would be a coda). A *cantus firmus* is stated by the tenor in the first verse, accompanied by clearly differentiated counterpoints in the three other voices. In the second verse, the *cantus firmus*, inverted, is in the viola; the other voices unfold the previously heard counterpoints, also inverted (besides, the counterpoint originally in the soprano is now heard in the bass, and vice versa, etc.). Thus, we have before us an example of quadruple counterpoint (the first example of this kind since the finale of Mozart's *Jupiter* symphony). The third verse has the *cantus firmus* (retrograde form) in the soprano; the counterpoints also appear in their retrograde form. Finally, the coda presents a variant of the *cantus firmus*, produced by the retrograde inversion, in the bass. Thus, this piece exhibits a strict contrapuntal form, produced by tradition and by the structure of the new technique.

The last piece of the set is, in spite of great independence of the voices, written in harmonic style. It constitutes the first precise formulation of the rules of twelve-tone harmony,[11] and owes its

[10] In fact, strict modal or tonal imitation depended on the two hexachords, CDEFGA and GABCDE, only in those cases where these hexachords corresponded to the tonic and dominant regions respectively. To produce strict imitations in contrary motion, the following scheme had to be used:

CDEFGABCDE
EDCBAGFEDC

Without the use of these schemes, strict imitation could only be achieved by means of chromatic alterations, unthinkable in modal music, and dangerous to tonality in the tonal system. It is only the twelve-tone system which can create the possibility and the necessity of strict imitation. This is one more demonstration of the purity of twelve-tone counterpoint, which thus becomes the ineluctable consequence of the evolution of polyphony, which *had* to come to such a conclusion.

[11] Rules which result from the fragmentation of the tone-row. Cf. *Introduction to Twelve-Tone Music.*

articulation to the architectonic functions of the variants of the tone-row.

Op. 28 shows even more preoccupation with counterpoint. The first piece, *a cappella*, is an endless canon in four voices. The second, also *a cappella*, is a retrograde canon, one of the most difficult canonic forms.[12] The third is a little cantata accompanied by viola, 'cello, and piano, which ends with a very complex fugue. The collection ends with an appendix. "Since the preceding choruses are strict twelve-tone compositions, and many people believe that it is much easier to accomplish certain contrapuntal tasks when dissonances are placed on the same footing as consonances, the following works show that one who wrote the preceding compositions does not need any such special privileges, and can, with seven tones only, succeed in a task which, to tell the truth, is not very highly prized, but is nevertheless considered difficult." [13] There follow several complex canons realized with the means of tonality.

In a general way, Schoenberg's ideas and compositional attitudes at this time are expressed with such polemic force in the preface to this work that it is sufficient for us to reproduce it here in its entirety.

As for me, this is the danger that I would fear most: some souls who were intended to be the targets of these satires [14] may still wonder whether I was aiming at them.

For more than one who has reason to fear the light may think that he can hide behind the seeming obscurity of words and music; therefore, let us dissipate their fog with a few unveiled words.

1. I was aiming at all those who seek their personal safety in the "middle way." For that is the only road which does not lead to Rome. The ones who set out on it are greedy; they grab at dissonances, hoping thus to pass for "modernists," but they do not have the courage

---

[12] This particular example may be read 1) from back to front, in which case it is a retrograde version of the original (this retrograde version, if it is written after the original and then read upside down. is the same as the original); 2) upside down and back to front, which is the same as right side up.

[13] Schoenberg, Appendix to *Three Satires*, Op. 28.

[14] Let us not forget that the texts of these satires are by Schoenberg himself. Cf. footnote 1, Chapter V.

to take the consequences—the consequences not only of the dissonances but also (even more so!) of the preceding consonances. The same goes for those who pick and choose among dissonances without being able to give any reasons why their own cacophony should be permitted and somebody else's forbidden, and for those who do not "go too far" but cannot explain why they go *so* far, and finally for the pseudo-tonalists, who think that they can do everything to smash tonality just as long as they profess their faith in it by sticking in a triad from time to time, whether it fits or not. What musical ear can endure it? Furthermore, anyone who possesses knowledge and awareness of forms cannot fail to see that such a procedure can hardly satisfy the longing of these people for "form" and "architecture" unless they satisfy it in some other masterly fashion (which is of course quite possible).

2. I am aiming at those who work for a "return to . . ." Let none of them try to convince us that he is capable of deciding how many years behind the times he will soon be, or that he can ally himself with some great master of the past (whose every effort was in the direction of the future). The name of the master is always in his mouth, but in reality he is only treading on the master's toes. When he sees through himself, this champion of the "return to . . ." finds that he lacks training; now he has to go back to experiments with the tonic and dominant. It would be a pleasure to buy him a round-trip ticket through all the styles. But it would be useless to inform him of what mediocre minds call, a little teasingly, the "rules of the game." He knows how to cheat, and we may be sure that he will have recourse to his usual expedient of peeking at the hand of his involuntary partner. And since many a noisily applauded "Renaissance" has speedily turned out to be only a pitiful miscarriage, it may be said that such a musician deliberately forces on his music that poverty to which a poor Conservatory professor is reduced in spite of himself.

3. I also enjoy taking a shot at the folklorists who try to treat the basically primitive ideas of popular music with a technique which is appropriate only to more highly evolved forms of musical thought, whether they are obliged to do so because they have no themes of their own or whether they are not (after all, living musical tradition and culture can easily furnish enough support even for them!).

4. And finally, I refer to all the "—ists," in whom I can see only "mannerists" whose music satisfies principally those to whose minds

it constantly suggests a "label" that conveniently obviates the necessity for further thought.

I cannot judge whether or not it is really nice of me (probably it is no better than anything else I do) to make fun of efforts which are usually sincere, frequently talented, and sometimes estimable. I know how easy it is to mock at everything—even much more serious things—in even more light-hearted fashion. But at least I can make the excuse that, as always, I have expressed myself as well as I can. May others have more fun out of it than I, who am also capable of taking these matters seriously.

And perhaps, after all, that is what I also meant.

27. *The unfoldment of Schoenberg's twelve-tone activity.—*
B. *The expansion of the new technique.*—In my *Introduction to Twelve-Tone Music,* I tried to show how the twelve-tone technique culminates in Schoenberg's *Variations for Orchestra,* Op. 31.[15] By this I mean that the principal devices of this technique, after having been gradually and partially developed in the works preceding Op. 31, are for the first time completely used in this work, so that all twelve-tone works (of Schoenberg and also of his pupils) after the *Variations for Orchestra* merely apply or develop these devices according to the same principles. Since we shall not make such a detailed analysis of the problem in the present study, we may say that the group of works which we shall now examine presents, generally speaking, the culmination of the twelve-tone technique and the solution of its principal problems.

These works are the Suite, Op. 29, for piano, piccolo clarinet, clarinet, bass clarinet, violin, viola, and 'cello (1926), the Third String Quartet, Op. 30 (1926), and the *Variations for Orchestra,* Op. 31 (1927–28). The first two works show that Schoenberg continues to attach great importance to the role of chamber music. In the third, he solves the problem of writing for large orchestra (which he had not done since Op. 22) in the new technique. Furthermore, we may affirm that all the acquisitions of the previous works persist in these works, which are also enriched with new acquisitions. Indeed, whether in counterpoint, in instrumental

[15] The ninth work in which Schoenberg uses the twelve-tone technique, counting the fifth piece of Op. 23 and certain passages of Op. 24.

style, in the technique of variation, in the construction of the
larger forms, or even in the new laws of harmony, they display
new developments.

First, let us glance at the Suite, Op. 29. Schoenberg's fantasy
and instrumental style appear in a new light because of the novel
instrumental ensemble used here. The piano part deserves special
attention, for, although it is in a richly elaborated *concertante*
style, it never sounds like a brilliant solo, and blends admirably
with the ensemble. The proportions of this work are very ample,
which indicates that the large form has won its right to exist in
contemporary music.[16] Certainly, these dimensions are partly due
to the use of classical forms, but let us not deceive ourselves on
this score. If we think about the evolution of these forms since
their creation—an evolution always impelled by the idea of increasingly varied recapitulation—we realize that the new technique, far more advanced in the works which concern us, imparts
to their "classical forms" an aspect far different from that
proper to such forms even in the preceding generation of musicians.[17]

The first movement of Op. 29, *Overture*, is a sonata form,
extremely subtle and strict in construction. The structure of the
first theme, made up of short motives imitated in contrary motion, is already quite remarkable. The second theme, contrasting
in its strongly *cantabile* character, is built on broad lines. The
development (elaboration) introduces a new element, which reappears in the coda. The recapitulation of the beginning occurs
in a very refined manner; striking is the way in which the introduction is amalgamated with the first theme.

The second movement, *Tanzschritte* (*Dance Steps*) is a sort
of Scherzo, bewilderingly rich in rhythmic variation.

The third movement, an Adagio, is a theme with variations, a

[16] It may be said that it never lost its right to exist in much of contemporary
music. But it must also not be forgotten that it was never subjected to such searching
re-examination and was never (to use a philosophical expression) the object of so much
skepticism as in the work of Schoenberg. Cf. our conclusions in the study of Webern
(Part IV of this book).

[17] Indeed, it may be said that Schoenberg's "sonata form" is as different from
that of Mahler or Brahms as theirs was from that of Schubert or Schumann.

form which Schoenberg uses in his next two works as well, and which seems eminently suited to the new system.

The fourth movement is a Gigue, the form of which is again derived from "sonata form" and which displays obvious care for counterpoint. I quote the beginning of the piece in order to show how the twelve-tone technique is capable of embodying such a compositional plan.

Ex. 25

First, the clarinet exposes the principal figure of the theme, which unfolds the original form of the twelve-tone row on which the work is based (Ex. 25b).

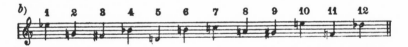

This figure is repeated in contrary motion (an inverted form of the series) by the bass clarinet in the second measure.

Meanwhile, the piano and the clarinet play contrapuntal motives derived from the original tone-row. First the piano plays tones 1–3, the clarinet tone 4, piano 5, clarinet 6 and 7 simultaneously with 8

in the piano which goes on to 9, clarinet 10, piano 11, and clarinet
12. In the third measure the original tone-row comes back in the
piccolo clarinet, while the clarinet and the bass clarinet play the
inversions of the preceding contrapuntal motives, which are derived from the inverted form of the row.

All this fine polyphonic workmanship clearly comes from the
technique of double counterpoint; thus we see how the twelve-
tone technique, through certain elements of its structure, makes
such a compositional attitude possible. The new technique, created
largely to satisfy certain contrapuntal needs, opens new realms to
counterpoint.

The next work, the Quartet, Op. 30, displays similar characteristics. Just like the Suite,[18] it uses the four movements of traditional symphonic form—here, a *Moderato alla breve* (d=100)
in sonata form, an Adagio in the form of variations, an Intermezzo
in the form of a Scherzo, and a Rondo.

Example 26 reproduces a fragment of the second theme as it is
announced by the first violin in the exposition (Ex. 26a) and by
the 'cello in the recapitulation (Ex. 26b). The original form
of the row is that of Ex. 26c, but the first exposition of this particular form begins with an unfoldment of an inverted form (I)
(Ex. 26d).

Ex. 26

<hr>

[18] And also like the earlier Wind Quintet, Op. 26.

c) Original   *d)* Renversement

After this comes the unfoldment of R. On the other hand, the recapitulation of the theme begins with O and continues with RI. Thus we find ourselves confronted with the following "double variation": 1) the recapitulation is the inversion of the exposition, since its two sections are produced by the inversion of the corresponding sections of the exposition; 2) the recapitulation is the exact retrograde of the exposition. Since the rhythm and general tone are the same in both presentations, the recapitulation is really felt as such despite its great divergence from the exposition.

Such an example is well calculated to clarify the meaning of these problems and their solutions, as they have concerned us in these pages.

I shall not stress the *Variations for Orchestra,* Op. 31, since the greater part of my other book is devoted to a detailed analysis of this work. I shall merely reiterate that in this work the principal procedures of twelve-tone technique are, as it were, crystallized. Here too we note the awareness of certain harmonic laws implied by the organization of the new world of sound. Among other passages, the harmonization of the theme of these variations seems to me highly significant in this respect.

28. *The consolidation of twelve-tone technique in Schoenberg's last "European" works.*—I shall not lay much stress on the last works written by Schoenberg before his departure for America, since I devoted many pages of my other book to them. But I should like to recall some of their characteristics.

The first twelve-tone orchestral piece is followed by the first twelve-tone opera, the one-act *opera buffa Von Heute auf Morgen* (*From Today till Tomorrow*), Op. 32, written in three weeks (1929) for the Frankfurt am Main opera house. The opera has five characters: a lady (soprano), her girl-friend (soprano), her husband (baritone), a singer, the girl-friend's boy-friend (tenor), and a child which says only a few words (not sung) at the end of the play. The orchestra, comparatively reduced, consists of twofold wood-winds (but with four clarinets, including piccolo and bass clarinets, and two saxophones), two horns, two trumpets, three trombones and tuba, a good many percussion instruments (used very discreetly), a harp, a piano alternating with celesta, a mandolin, a guitar, and a rather small string group.

This score is remarkable in all the respects which concern us. Its culmination is surely the wonderful final quartet, composed in a close-knit contrapuntal style of marvelously balanced sonority. The orchestra, which supports the vocal quartet, adds two more independent voices to it, so that we really hear a musical structure made up of six voices, each more expressive than the next.

The next opus consists of the two piano pieces 33a and b (composed in 1932). These pieces, very characteristic from the viewpoint of formal evolution,[19] appear as a synthesis of the previous piano works. Paradoxical though this may seem at first, it may be said that they partake both of the complexity of Op. 23 and of the simplification of Op. 25. In fact, this is no paradox, since, though the first twelve-tone experiments automatically entailed a certain simplification of the musical speech, Schoenberg's greater familiarity with and mastery of the means of twelve-tone technique now permit him to return to a style at once freer and more complex. But also, while the complexity of Op. 23 was the result of a certain chaos (relatively speaking, of course) of the new world of sound, the present rigorous and conscious organization makes possible a style of remarkable clarity—a style which may therefore, in a certain sense, be considered *simpler* than that of Op. 23.

Before Op. 32, Schoenberg composed (1930) two other works, the *Accompaniment to a Film-Scene*, Op. 34 (a kind of little symphony for small orchestra) and *Six Pieces for Male Chorus*, Op. 35. They do not tell us anything especially new (which does

---

[19] Cf. my analysis of the first of these pieces in Chapter IX, *Introduction to Twelve-Tone Music*.

not mean that they are insignificant!) [20] and, like the two preceding works, participate in the consolidation of those features of twelve-tone technique which, after Op. 31, belong, so to speak, to the public domain. By this I mean that the principal characteristics of Op. 31 now become the regular constituent elements of the twelve-tone music written by *all* composers of this school, and produce a remarkable solidity of structure in their works. In this sense, Schoenberg's Op. 34 and 35 appear to me highly significant. The ease with which these works were apparently conceived, the clarity of their style, the obvious facility with which the most important problems are stated and resolved—all this adumbrates a classical period of perfect serenity (if I may so term it) in the work of Schoenberg.

After his stay in Holland (1920–21) Schoenberg returned to Berlin. In 1925 he was appointed professor at the Academy of Arts in Berlin (thus succeeding Busoni). In May, 1933, he resigned—which he would have had to do sooner or later, given his Jewish ancestry and his musical tendencies; he left for Paris, and then for America. Perhaps no public or private organization in Europe desired the services of an artist whose importance is unknown to or denied by most; but perhaps, too, Schoenberg foresaw the catastrophes awaiting this continent where he had lived sixty years and where he had fulfilled one of the greatest musical evolutions of all history.

[20] I am thinking especially of the next-to-last piece of Op. 35, written in *eight real voices,* a task which presents staggering difficulties in the twelve-tone technique and within the narrow range of the male chorus. This is one of those astonishing *tours de force* to which Schoenberg's genius has accustomed us, and which, coming from him, no longer surprise us.

CHAPTER VI

Schoenberg's "American" Works

29. *The dialectics of the "American" works.*—Schoenberg arrived in America in October, 1933, and accepted a professorship at the Malkin Conservatory in Boston. In 1935, he went to California for his health, and was appointed professor of composition at the University of Southern California. Finally, in 1936, he accepted a similar position at the University of California at Los Angeles (in which city he still lives). In 1940, he became an American citizen. During his sojourn in America, Schoenberg has devoted himself to compositions of many different kinds. Before we name them and traverse their pages, let us define some of their general characteristics.

At the end of the preceding chapter we alluded to a certain *serenity* of the works which were under our scrutiny. This serenity becomes even more noticeable in the following works. But Schoenberg's constantly alert mind cannot remain satisfied with this state of affairs; or, rather, with the development of his mastery of the technique which he created, a mastery which nearly reaches the point where there are no more problems, Schoenberg finds himself obliged, by a spirit inherent in all his activity, to jeopardize the very foundations of this mastery. Later, we shall see how much courage and honesty this implies.

The re-examination of the compositional means responsible for this serenity is caused by a special intuition. As previously stated, during his long silence between 1915 and 1923 Schoenberg planned to construct, with the total resources of chromaticism, a new tonal system, obtained by a new method of realizing functional unity. What remains of this plan in the works discussed in the previous chapter? Practically nothing. I showed in my other book that these works, despite certain vestiges of tonality, tend, in their entirety, rather to surpass the tonal order than to consolidate it. In other words, the tone-row technique in general and the twelve-tone technique in particular, far from having restored the functions of tonality to the total resources of chromaticism, have transcended and suspended these functions.

Schoenberg, the eternal seeker, cannot accept the certainty of this without submitting it to the most exacting and skeptical scrutiny. In the first place, every point of rest is an object of suspicion to this mind, which always demands the maximum of tension from itself and others; in this sense, his fabulous mastery and ease become disquieting factors. In the second place, the problem of new tonal functions has remained in the balance; it has been avoided but not resolved. This, too, cannot satisfy Schoenberg, because the very difficulty of this problem makes its solution urgent and important.

Here, in my opinion, is the essential characteristic of Schoenberg's activity in America. First of all, we find, running parallel to the increasingly perfected twelve-tone compositions—the Violin Concerto, Op. 36, and the Fourth Quartet, Op. 37—a series of tonal works, including the Suite for Strings (no opus number), the *Kol Nidre* for solo voice, chorus, and orchestra, Op. 39, and the *Variations on a Recitative for Organ*, Op. 40, which tend to incorporate certain twelve-tone elements. Then there is a work, the *Ode to Napoleon* for reciter, string quartet, and piano, Op. 41, which uses both techniques at the same time. Finally, there is the Piano Concerto, Op. 42, which is in strict twelve-tone style but obviously maintains certain principles of tonality.

I said before that this activity was marked by great honesty and courage. From a purely intellectual and personal viewpoint, this is quite obvious from our preceding remarks. But these qualities manifest themselves in still another realm, for it is evident that, to many mediocre minds, some of the last works of Schoenberg seem to be a "retreat" or even a "capitulation." The very people who used to scold him for being too aggressive now scold him for being too mild; those who hated him an an "anarchist" now hate him as a "reactionary." All this wrong-headed stupidity is caused by a preconceived theoretical idea of "tonality" in the minds of many people who *have not heard* the works in question. I doubt very much that listening to one of these works—the *Ode to Napoleon,* for example—would "soothe" them as much as they would like to make us believe.

It does not matter; none of this can touch Schoenberg, who has "been through it all before," and who has always gone his own infallible way in spite of the bitterest and most violent opposition, never losing for an instant his keen awareness of the problems posed by polyphony at every moment of its evolution.

What will be the results of his present activity, what will be the synthesis of its ruling dialectics? We can hardly foresee it, and in any case it is not our duty to voice such conjectures. Let us stick to our task, which is the most precise possible analysis of the essence of the works which concern us; and let us continue to have confidence in a musician whose every action has already demonstrated his genius.

30. *Schoenberg's return to tonal activity.*—Already, one of the choruses of Op. 35 represented an isolated attempt to return to the expression of a precise tonality with the means of the twelve-tone technique.[1] The years 1932 and 1933 also produce two extremely curious and significant works, the 'Cello Concerto (after a cembalo concerto by Georg Matthias Monn),[2] and the Concerto for String Quartet and Orchestra, after Handel's *Concerto Grosso,* Op. 6 No. 7. These two concerti (perhaps preparatory studies for Op. 36 and 42) mark, then, the return of Schoenberg's "tonal consciousness." They are in the form of extremely free transcriptions which respect the thematic material and the original structure of the works on which they are based. However, this structure is considerably amplified by the typically Schoenbergian contrapuntal workmanship and technique of variation. Furthermore, the melodic and harmonic structure is enriched with chromaticism un-

---

[1] The fact that this attempt remains isolated, and that the row of this piece does not contain twelve tones, seems to me to obviate the necessity for its further discussion. Although this chorus is undeniably successful in every way, it does not seem to have influenced the evolution of the problems which concern us at present.

[2] Pre-classic Viennese composer (1717–1750).

known to the period of the original works, and with obvious applications of certain principles of the twelve-tone row. Many people find these works sacrilegious. I think that they represent a phenomenon analogous to that produced when a great painter executes a picture modelled on a work of an earlier artist. In every way, Schoenberg has here the opportunity to proceed to acquisitions of instrumental style as important as those of his earlier works. In the first of these two pieces, the method of writing for 'cello is completely changed. The second work is the first attempt to juxtapose string quartet and full orchestra; the way in which Schoenberg proceeds to solve this difficult problem of tonal equilibrium in a hitherto untried combination proves that this new phase of his evolution is as legitimate, as valid, and as important as all the preceding phases.

However, though one may truly speak of a new tonal consciousness in Schoenberg's music, these two pieces are still only transcriptions. We have not yet seen a tonal project which owes nothing to outside stimulation. Such a project is now manifested in the *Suite for Strings* (1934), Schoenberg's first "American" work.

Some have claimed that this piece was only an act of defiance, Schoenberg's attempt to shock the Americans who thought that he could not compose "just like everybody else." The absurdity of this idea must be obvious after what we have said about the problems which confronted Schoenberg during these years. Evidently, there is some more profound reason for this work. Let us look at the score. What strikes us first is its intense seriousness. The adoption of the "pre-classic" form of the suite (let us not forget that this already took place in Op. 25 and 29) does not remind us, here, of the neo-classical *pastiche*. On the contrary, Schoenberg's style is manifest in every particular: strict counterpoint, "chromatic" harmony, very elaborate forms, daring treatment of the instruments. There are five movements: an Overture (which contains a very strict fugue), an Adagio (where it is not infrequent to hear passages of sumptuous counterpoint and harmony—in eight real parts), a Minuet (with a very cleverly constructed Trio), a Gavotte with Trio and Coda, and a Gigue.

The most striking characteristic of this work seems to be its very rich harmony. The most complex tonal relationships are constantly in use; their coherence is primarily achieved by the systematic use of artificial and chromatically obtained dominants, which thus incorporate the total resources of chromaticism into the principal tonality.

The second tonal work is the second *Kammersymphonie*, Op. 38 (1940). I shall not discuss this work for two reasons, firstly because I do not know it (the score still being unpublished) and secondly because it is a very old work, which, although nearly finished in 1911, was nevertheless abandoned at that time. (It is probable that Schoenberg remodelled it somewhat.)[3]

On the other hand, the *Kol Nidre*, Op. 39, demands further attention. This work, commissioned by a Jewish organization, uses a Jewish liturgical theme. Here we find many of the tone-row principles incorporated into a freely handled tonality. All possible aggregations of the total resources of chromaticism are tried. The motives appear in all their variations according to the tone-row principles. The contrapuntal texture is remarkably dense.

[3] This second *Kammersymphonie* was begun simultaneously with the first (Op. 9) in 1906. After having carried on both compositions at the same rate for a while, Schoenberg finished Op. 9 only. The other symphony was resumed in 1908, abandoned and taken up once more in 1911. Apparently it then lacked only the coda. Everyone who knew the manuscript deplored the abandonment of a work which apparently contained some of Schoenberg's most remarkable passages.

Since I wrote these lines I have been able to become acquainted with this work and I should therefore like to add a few observations. Harmonically, melodically, structurally, and instrumentally, the Second *Kammersymphonie* poses problems analogous to those already discussed with reference to Op. 9 and other works of the same period. If, at first glance, the amazing invention of the fourth-chord seems to lend to the first symphony a boldness of approach which is not found in the second, it would be unfair not to take cognizance of numerous innovations in the later work, which, though not so obvious as in the earlier one, are no less radical for all that. This is already evident in the form of the second symphony, which consists of an Adagio (recognizably in a skilful and involved *Lied* form) and a sort of very fast Scherzo, which ends with a slow coda in which varied elements of the first movement reappear. This bipartite structure is quite new. Furthermore, we see here a broadening of tonal functions which goes even further in certain respects, perhaps, than that which took place in Op. 9. This broadening of tonal functions gives rise to a specifically melodic motive of two successive fourths separated by a half-tone (descending: E flat–B flat–A–E natural). Such progressions are typical of certain works in which tonality is suspended. Cf. Ex. 40 and the accompanying footnote, as well as Ex. 59b. A more thorough study of this form in its structural significance is the subject of one of my coming articles (to be published in No. 4 of *Polyphonie*, which will be devoted to Schoenberg).

The coherence of all these elements is here caused less by chromaticism (chromatic dominants, etc.) than by the functional roles, like those of the tone-row in a composition according to its principles, which the principal motives play. The presence of chords like that of Example 27a is explicable only in the light of the motives 27b and 27c.

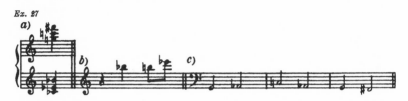

Ex. 27

31. *The series of pure twelve-tone works.*—Between the *Suite for Strings* and the *Kol Nidre* come the Violin Concerto, Op. 36, and the Fourth String Quartet, Op. 37 (both 1936). I do not think I am exaggerating when I say that these two works are the culmination of Schoenberg's twelve-tone style. All the qualities which we noted in the last "European" works are here brought to so high a pitch of perfection that it would seemingly be impossible for Schoenberg to continue any further along these lines. I discussed these works in my other book and analyzed some passages from them.[4] From this analysis there results 1) the definite establishment of certain fixed harmonic principles of the twelve-tone technique, and 2) the equally definite establishment of certain means of articulation which properly belong to the twelve-tone system, and which make possible a musical architecture that owes virtually nothing to the "classical" formal schemes. Our minds may still be constrained to search for—and find—superficial elements of such schemes, but in reality these are now powerless to give us a clear idea of the architectonic principles which operate in these two compositions. Thus Op. 36, which uses the traditional divisions, two fast movements surrounding a slow movement (movements which resemble the "sonata allegro form"—I—the ABA form—II—and the Rondo—III), really owes its precise articulation to the architectonic use of various treatments of its

[4] See Part IV of this book, §68, Ex. 73, for an example from the Fourth Quartet.

basic twelve-tone series (all forms). Certainly, the spirit of the violin concerto is reactivated here in its most traditional meaning—as witness the amazing richness of the solo part, its cadenzas, etc.—but the very way in which this instrumental form is treated here again emphasizes that Schoenberg's technique is the culmination of certain tendencies implicit in all the music of the past.

Let us approach this question more closely. The very form of the concerto, aside from certain other factors which necessitated it, was created essentially to set off the virtuosity of one or more solo instruments against a background of many instruments. In the works of the great masters of the past, virtuosity was never sought *for itself alone,* but was always to be endowed with a constructive and functional meaning. However, even with the best of these composers, this project could not always be carried into effect, on account of the very nature of the tonal technique. Although we often find, in classical concerti, passages derived from genuine motives and accompanied by structurally appropriate harmony, we also find many passages which are, so to speak, *empty* because they have no real functional relationship with the rest of the musical architecture.[5]

Now it is evident that the twelve-tone technique, by its very structure, renders impossible *a priori* [6] such an absence of function, since every figure, whatever it may be, comes from the structural functions of the intervals of the row.

In this sense the Violin Concerto (as, later, the Piano Concerto) appears to me as one of the most highly perfected works— and, in some respects, as the culmination—of the grand tradition of the concerto, which has produced so many masterpieces ever since the seventeenth century.

In order to give a concrete illustration of what we have just said about the essentially functional role of virtuosity in the concerto, I should like to comment briefly on the few measures

[5] I am obviously exaggerating on purpose. I cannot give a general discussion of this subject without simplifying it a little; but I think that the reader will understand my true meaning.

[6] I say *a priori*, although this technique obviously cannot guarantee the composition of good music. A bad twelve-tone composer will write empty passages, but they will be empty only *a posteriori* with respect to the technique used.

of Example 28. This passage appears shortly after the violin cadenza and shortly before the stretto which closes the movement. It constitutes a marked cesura within the movement, and serves as a harmonic preparation for the final cadence. Architectonically, the stress which is required at this point can be obtained only by an extremely involved elaboration of many harmonies. This is exactly what takes place here. A glance at our example shows that it consists of successions and superpositions of various chords; the superpositions produce chords of six or eight different tones. The violin, in order to participate in these chord-progressions, calls upon previously untapped resources of the technique of triple and quadruple stops.[7] And yet, the fantastic virtuosity demanded here is not an end in itself, but is required by the functions of the tone-row. Further analysis will elucidate this.

The first four chords of the violin break up the form R6 into four equal parts of three tones each [8] (cf. Ex. 28b) . Simultaneously, in the orchestra, RI 11 is broken up in exactly the same way (cf. Ex. 28c) . The violin now plays two triplets, which divide O9 into two equal parts (cf. Ex. 28d) ; to this, the orchestra adds I2, likewise divided into two equal parts (cf. Ex. 28e) . Two new triplets in the violin (measure 242) take up this same form I2, and divide it into two equal parts, as before; but this time, through a subtle device of repeating some of the tones from one chord to the next, chords of three and four tones are made possible (second beat of the measure) . These three- and four-voiced chords, which persist until the end of the passage, give the harmony its necessary weight. The violin now breaks up O1 (cf. Ex. 28f) into three quadruple-stops [9] (last two chords of 242, first chord of 243) and continues to treat I6 (cf. Ex. 28g) in the same manner (last three chords of 243) . Here, the orchestra presents these three four-voiced chords of I6 (A B C) in the order B C A, thus producing eight-voiced chords with the quadruple-stops of the violin. The violin continues (244) with O1, which is also used in the orchestra.

---

[7] Schoenberg said that this concerto called for a new type of six-fingered violinist. Cf. Dika Newlin, *Bruckner—Mahler—Schoenberg*, p. 187. (King's Crown Press, New York, 1947.)

[8] See my *Introduction to Twelve-Tone Music.*

[9] *Ibid.*

Ex. 28

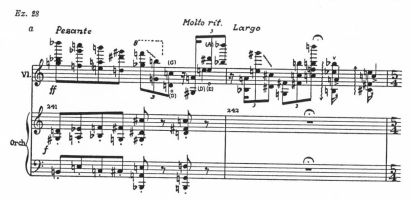

It goes without saying that such an elaboration of harmonic functions according to the strictest laws of twelve-tone composition automatically excludes all empty virtuosity, while, at the same time, the adequate realization of the harmonic conception is dependent upon the juxtaposition of the two basic elements of concerto form—soloist and orchestra.

The Quartet, Op. 37, is, like Schoenberg's three earlier quartets, in four movements: an Allegro vaguely reminiscent of sonata form, a *Commodo* which is a kind of minuet, an Adagio of novel form which includes two recitatives played by all four instruments in unison, and a final Allegro written in a complex form which can be related to that of the Rondo.

It is fruitful to study the two abovementioned recitatives, not only in order to observe the instrumental style, but also in order to see the differences in the two appearances of this figure, which, like two pillars, firmly uphold the form of the movement. It will be noted that, from the point of view of the tone-row, the second recitative is the inversion of the first.

Ex. 29

Doubtless one might already speak, in the Third Quartet, of a culmination of the quartet form comparable to that culmination of the concerto form which we have found in Op. 36. But Op. 30 exhibits, perhaps, a certain intentional purity of style which might be interpreted as a reaction against the impurity of string-quartet writing in the twentieth century (orchestral atmosphere, harmonic style instead of contrapuntal style, useless "effects," and so on). In this sense, Op. 30 succeeded in restoring the purity of

Ex. 30

the string quartet; but Op. 37 is even more astonishing in this respect, because of its greater freedom. It almost seems as if this work—and God knows, it is strictly enough constructed!—had been written without the slightest intentional systematization. It is a flood of the most limpid music, a succession of melodies each more beautiful than the next, of rich and varied harmonies and rhythms—all in all, a musical discourse of the most exceptional quality. This is, perhaps, the culminating point of Schoenberg's chamber music. There is not a single figure, no matter how episodic it might be, which does not have its precise function in the musical structure. It goes without saying that all this is explicitly made possible through the use of the new technique, for tonal technique could not always fulfill those needs for the satisfaction of which the form of the string quartet was expressly created.

The perfection attained in Op. 37 is of so high an order that it seems almost impossible at the present time to make any new contributions to the string quartet.[10]

Two further examples, taken from the third and fourth movements respectively, display the independence and flexibility of the voice-leading, as well as the richness and clarity of the resultant polyphony (Example 30).

32. *The Variations on a Recitative for Organ, the Ode to Napoleon, the Piano Concerto, the Variations for Band, and the String Trio.*—Our study of Schoenberg's works will close with these five compositions (Op. 40, 41, 42, 43, and 45), written respectively in 1941, 1942, 1943, 1944, and 1946. Two tonal works, the variations for organ and those for band, attack the problems which had already been approached by Schoenberg in the *Suite for Strings* and the *Kol Nidre.* Schoenberg is primarily concerned with drawing the utmost consequences from the idea of a tonality expanded to its furthest limits (that *monotonality* which we discussed above). During these last years, Schoenberg seems to have become increasingly aware of this idea. His attitude towards tonality is of a hitherto undreamed-of radicalism; therefore, his new tonal works appear to be much more daring than the preceding twelve-tone compositions. The most distant, unheard-of tonal relationships are established; there is a systematic effort not to let a single possibility of such tonal relationship go unused. Schoenberg himself considers these works as backward glances at the musical language of the past, which, before it is entirely *surpassed,* must undergo a final consolidation. Such a consolidation serves as a

---

[10] Webern alone appears to have succeeded in doing so. Cf. Part IV of this book.

sort of bridge between his last tonal works before the suspension of tonality (e.g. the two *Kammersymphonien*) and the works which followed that great *leap* into the unknown (e.g., the two dramatic works Op. 17 and 18). In addition, these works bind the tonal system to the twelve-tone technique, which enriches tonality with innumerable new elements. There is nothing new in this attitude on the part of a composer given to innovations. Bach, composing his English and French Suites in addition to the *Well-Tempered Clavier*, Mozart and Beethoven, writing in the "archaic" form of the fugue even as they composed their symphonies and sonatas—these men had the same attitude towards *their* musical past, the resources of which they experimented with for the last time. Schoenberg is entirely aware of all this, and once more we cannot help admiring the lucidity and the honesty of a musician whose mind is ceaselessly preoccupied with all the problems of contemporary polyphony.

Since my knowledge of the *Variations for Band* is rather superficial, I shall not discuss them here. However, I should like to say a few words about the *Variations on a Recitative for Organ*.

The very idea of composing variations on a recitative may appear surprising. The recitative is, in its very essence, not only a so-called "free" form, but above all an "open" form, often entirely lacking in that firm structure which is required by a theme suitable for variations. But Schoenberg's mind gives no quarter to such theoretical abstractions. At the end of his *Structural Functions of the Harmony* he says, "It is difficult to believe that the sense of form, balance and logic of those masters who have produced the great symphonies should have been renounced in controlling their dramatic structures." In fact, a master of the art of composition whose principal characteristic is the invention and presentation of ideas with the maximum of precision and clarity will necessarily invent in this way no matter what *genre* he composes in. Therefore, a recitative will have to be as logical and coherent as any other musical form, and this will justify its use as a theme for variations.

The above statement is clearly proved by the composition of Schoenberg which concerns us here. The recitative which he has chosen (Ex. 31) is of the loosest possible construction. The series of little motives on which it is built seems to be without any order or discipline. And yet, a more detailed examination clearly shows a carefully constructed curve which moves within the range of a major seventh. Thus, the outer tones of this seventh, D and C sharp, acquire a special value which is distinctly emphasized.[11] In addition, subtle relationships among the various motives appear; it is evident that much use will be made of these relationships in the course of the variations.

Ex. 81

After the tenth variation, there is a cadenza, which is, as one would expect, of a free and improvisatory character, but which still preserves the functional structures established at the beginning of the work. There follows a fugue of significant dimensions, the structure of which is entirely new. This novelty consists primarily in the use of entrances in contrary motion (the D being considered as the central point). I should also like to call attention to the fact that the motive of measure 4 of the recitative

---

[11] Note that the melody includes all the tones between these two points. Thus, the use of the total resources of chromaticism is immediately seen to be one of the fundamental principles of this work.

(NB) frequently appears, in numerous variants, throughout the work; it is also found in the fugue, where, in the form of Ex. 31b, it serves as a countersubject to the theme of the fugue (which is built on the first three measures of the recitative). The diminution of this countersubject (Ex. 31c) plays an important part in the contrasting sections of the fugue. Finally, a long cadence leads to the powerful close, in D major, which is reached through unmitigated juxtapositions of the most distant tonal regions.

In contrast to Op. 40, which shows a principal tonality, the *Ode to Napoleon* seems to oscillate perpetually among all possible tonalities, and, though it ends in E flat major, it is impossible to say that this tonality plays a preponderant part in the entire composition. Here, then, is revealed a new tonal principle, which surely fulfills Schoenberg's original plan.

Ex. 32

The work is entirely free in its use of the twelve-tone system. In fact, there is not a single place where the row appears as such, but its functional action is felt in every measure because of the functional role assigned to certain melodic and harmonic intervals (which produces coherence according to tone-row principles) and also because of the constant use of the total resources of chromaticism. The important intervals are those which make up the first chord of the piece, F–G sharp–C sharp–E: a second or seventh (F–E), a major third or minor sixth (F–C sharp and E–G sharp), a minor third or major sixth (F–G sharp and C sharp–E), and a fifth or fourth (C sharp–G sharp). Example 32 shows how these two last-named intervals, together with the minor sixth, are elaborated with the total resources of chromaticism.

The first violin and 'cello have the fifth G–D, the piano the fifth A–E, and the second violin and viola, respectively, the fourths F sharp–B and B flat–E flat, the superposition of which produces sixths; the piano plays, also in parallel sixths, the fourths G sharp–C sharp and C–F. The whole structure makes strict use of all twelve tones of the chromatic scale.

On the other hand, the first chord, which incorporates two triads, one major and the other minor (F–G sharp [A flat]–C sharp [D flat] and G sharp–C sharp–E), inspires Schoenberg to the frequent use of superimposed triads or other similar aggregations; however, this does not result in any so-called "polytonality."

The twelve-tone row which, in my opinion, comes nearest to explaining all the forms of this work is E–F–D flat–C–G sharp–A–B–B flat–D–E flat–G natural–F sharp. (This form may, for example, be deduced from measures 37–38.) It has the following characteristics: 1) In itself it contains all the typical forms of tone-row variation (if it is divided into four fragments of three tones each, it is seen to consist of: a) O [first three notes]; b) RI [second fragment]; c) I [third fragment]; d) R [fourth fragment]); 2) if we divide the row into two equal halves, A and B, we find: a) that B is the inversion of A; b) that R of B is identical to O of A, and vice versa; c) that A and B produce the same chord; 3) the retrograde row is identical with its original form.

The free handling of the chords A and B permits the row to produce all sorts of different figures. If we group the notes of the chord A in the order A–C–F–G sharp–C sharp–E, and spread them out horizontally, we find many characteristic aggregations of the work (among others, the first chord).

I should also like to draw attention to the final cadence, in E flat major, which appears to me to be a highly evolved form of the classic I–V–I scheme. The last five chords (built up according to precise tone-row functions) may be analyzed as follows (I reduce these chords to the system of superposition in thirds, and so do not consider the positions which they actually occupy in the music): the first chord is I (E flat–G–B natural–D–F sharp), i.e., a ninth chord with *major third* and augmented fifth; the second chord is still I (E flat–G flat–B flat–B natural), i.e., a chord with *minor third* and two fifths, one perfect and the other augmented; the third chord (E flat–B natural–D) is again I— this time *without third* but with augmented fifth and added seventh. The fourth chord is V (B flat–D–F sharp–A flat–C sharp– E flat), i.e., an eleventh chord with augmented fifth and ninth. The fifth chord is I in its natural form.[12]

Has Schoenberg completely resolved the problems of the *Ode to Napoleon* or does he intend to reattack them later? In any case, the Piano Concerto returns to a more nearly "normal" twelve-tone style. Since I analyzed certain aspects of this score in my *Introduction to Twelve-Tone Music*, I shall say here only that everything said about the culmination of the concerto form in Schoenberg applies to this work as well, and that its structure is grandiose and bold in the reforms which it introduces.[13]

In addition, one of the most remarkable traits of this concerto is its extreme thematic economy. While in some of his previous works Schoenberg, starting from the fundamental unity guaranteed by the use of the tone-row, seemed to want to establish as varied a superstructure of motives and themes as possible, the thematic technique of Op. 42 shows his desire to limit himself to a very small number of figures. Thus, the *Kopfmotiv* of the first theme, Ex. 33a, plays a preponderant role throughout the work. Its inversion forms the characteristic upbeat of the principal theme of the last movement, Ex. 33b. In the stretto, the original form of the motive returns in the variant of Ex. 33c; and, finally, the last measures are dominated by the superposition of the two forms, Ex. 33d. The idea of "monothematism" has never been carried so far before.

Finally, the String Trio, Op. 45, introduces important inno-

---

[12] A more thorough study of the *Ode to Napoleon* will appear in the second volume of my work *Meanings of Contemporary Musicians*, about to be published (Savel Edition, Paris).

[13] See the analysis of Ex. 85, taken from the Piano Concerto. The reader may also consult the remarks on the concerto in Dika Newlin's article "Schoenberg in America," which will appear in *Polyphonie*, No. 4.

vations in every respect. The instrumental style of this work (the detailed analysis of which will be the subject of a separate study) is of a variety, density, and difficulty which even Schoenberg had not previously achieved. From the twelve-tone viewpoint, the Trio represents a sort of synthesis of the procedures of the *Ode to Napoleon* and the Piano Concerto (changing the position of the same chord, etc.) ; but it is different in that it never evokes any tonal functions. It may even be said that, with respect to this last

Ex. 33

problem, Schoenberg has transcended the tonal world further than ever before—even in his strictest twelve-tone works. But we cannot sufficiently emphasize the extraordinary freedom and ease with which these marvelous pages appear to have been composed. The very dates of composition of this dense and complex work— August 20–September 23, 1946—furnish eloquent proof of this. In spite of this liberty, we find passages of the strictest counterpoint, in which the independent and flexible individual lines, as well as the vertical aggregations produced by the combination of these lines, compose a musical language of great beauty.

When, in addition to all this, we find that the form is completely liberated from all *a priori* schemes, and that it is completely coherent, we may deduce that the Trio, Op. 45 is perhaps the most perfect, finished, and beautiful work ever to come from the pen of Arnold Schoenberg.

33. *The historic role of Schoenberg.*—Thus ends our study of the work of Schoenberg—a work which, I believe, has been the source of all contemporary polyphonic problems. I firmly believe that it is a work of total renewal, founded on a masterly reactivation of all previous polyphony which serves as a basis for the numberless acquisitions of Schoenberg's music—acquisitions which, in their turn, will constitute a firm basis for all the acquisitions of the future. And I am not alone in believing this.

In a homage to Schoenberg,[14] Alban Berg, citing and paraphrasing Riemann, gives us the following *Credo*:

. . . one of the greatest masters of all time, one of those who can never be surpassed because they embody equally the musical feeling

---

[14] *Credo*, in *Die Musik*, Berlin, January, 1930.

and the musical knowledge of an epoch; a master who owes his deeper meaning and his unparalleled greatness to the confluence in him of the styles of two different eras, so that he stands between the two as a mighty landmark, looming gigantic over two worlds. He belongs equally to the earlier

period of polyphonic music, of the contrapuntal and "imitative" style, and to the period of harmonic music,	period of harmonic style and to the period, which reopens with him, of polyphonic music, of contrapuntal and "imitative" style

as well as to that system which, now constituted for the first time, replaces

ancient modes with modern keys.	major and minor keys with the twelve-tone series.

He lives in an era of transition, that is, at a time when the old style has not yet disappeared but the new style is still in the earlier stages of its development and presents an unfinished appearance. His genius unites the characteristics of both styles. . . . His inexhaustible fund of melody is so fundamentally sound, his rhythm is so varied and pulsing with life, his harmony is so esoteric and daring and yet so clear and transparent that his works must remain not only the object of admiration, but of the most assiduous study and the most constant emulation.

     (Riemann on Bach) | (Alban Berg on Schoenberg)

PART III

ALBAN BERG

The Awareness of the Past in Contemporary Music

"To live is to defend a form."
(Hölderlin)

CHAPTER VII

The Work of Alban Berg

34. *Adolescence. The "Sieben frühe Lieder."*—Alban Berg was
born in Vienna on February 9, 1885,[1] into a well-to-do family of
business people. From his fourteenth year onward he displayed
what is commonly called a true vocation for music; in this he was
stimulated by the excellent piano-playing of his sister Smaragda
(two years younger) and the singing of his brother Charley (three
years older). The death of their father (1900) left the family in a
rather precarious financial situation, but, thanks to the help of a
rich relative, Alban was enabled to continue his secondary studies.
From this period date his first compositions (three songs). On
July 23, 1900, occurred his first attack of asthma, from which he
suffered chronically for the rest of his life. Up till 1902, he composed more than thirty songs and duets. He had a passionate love
for literature; but, in June, 1903, he failed in his baccalaureate
examination because of a poor theme in German. However, his
letters of this period bear witness to his prodigious skill in the art
of letter-writing and to his well-rounded culture. His favorite
author was Ibsen. In September, as the result of an unhappy love-
affair, he tried to commit suicide.

In 1904, he passed his baccalaureate examination. He wrote
many songs during that summer—at this time his favorite composer was Mahler—and he also wrote letters in the style of Peter
Altenberg.[2] In October, he was obliged to accept the post of a
government clerk (which he abandoned two years later). Shortly
after this occurred the most significant event of this period of his
life—the meeting with Schoenberg.

[1] I owe most of the biographical details to the book of Willi Reich, *Alban Berg*
(Herbert Reichner Verlag, Vienna, 1937).

[2] Viennese poet whose "postal cards" served Berg as texts.

Charley Berg had paid a clandestine visit to Schoenberg in order to show him his brother's compositions. After having perused these compositions, Schoenberg invited Alban to visit him, and consented to give him lessons.

Berg's apprenticeship was to last six years. His first recognized works date from this period. The most impotant of these are the songs later collected under the title *Sieben frühe Lieder* (*Seven Early Songs*). They date from 1905 to 1908. No. 5 and No. 3 were written respectively in the summer and winter of 1905, No. 6 in the fall of 1906, No. 4 at the beginning of 1907, and Nos. 1, 2, and 7 in the spring of 1908.

These songs are composed in a number of different styles. Although some of them (e.g. No. 3) come from the intense romanticism of Schumann, No. 6 is already scented with the heavy post-romantic perfume of the four songs, Op. 2; likewise, No. 1, with its whole-tone chords, is definitely post-Wagnerian, and even impressionistic. The influence of Schoenberg (especially of the *Kammersymphonie*), is particularly evident in Nos. 4 and 7, which may be considered as preparatory studies for the Sonata, Op. 1. In spite of these stylistic differences, it is possible to affirm that all the songs in this group present, in one way or another, the fundamental problems of the musical language of that time, as they appeared to genuine composers. Since, in the preceding part of this book, we have emphasized many details of these problems, it will now be sufficient to make a rapid sketch of their presentation in Berg's first works.

Thus, in the first song we immediately find such forms as the following in the piano part:

Ex. 34

These aggregations are composed of augmented-fifth chords (produced by the whole-tone scale), which, in the present case, expose all the notes of the chromatic scale. In addition, we note here Berg's preoccupation with counterpoint; thus, the last of these songs begins with a kind of *stretto* dominated by the following motive,

Ex. 35

which adumbrates the basic motive of the piano sonata, and the intervals of which are typically Schoenbergian.

In connection with these songs, it is significant that, in 1928, Alban Berg, now a full-fledged master, set himself to orchestrate this work of his youth. This orchestration is extremely interesting, for it pointedly underlines many important architectonic and compositional characteristics which were merely implicit in the original version. Thus, the contrapuntal character of the last song is brought into relief by the addition, in measures 7–10, of two solo violins which, in a canon with the bass (where the motive of Ex. 35 is heard), play an inversion of the initial form. But it is in still another realm that this orchestral underlining of the compositional characteristics of these songs becomes especially obvious. This music shows Berg becoming aware, for the first time, of Schoenberg's technique of variation. But this technique is rather timidly used. Indeed, there are hardly any literal repetitions, and the musical speech certainly results from the variation of basic motives, but the piano version of the songs does not succeed in giving us a very clear picture of all this. However, the orchestral score reveals everything. Not only is the variation of the repetitions brought into sharp relief, since the orchestration of each repetition is completely different from that of the original statement, but also the subtlety of the transition from one motive to another, the "liquidation of motivic remains," the unity and variety of the musical discourse—all these things are especially underlined by the instrumentation.

In orchestrating and publishing the *Sieben frühe Lieder* more than twenty years after their composition, Berg has brought to us, with the clearest possible explanations, his first experiments, wherein his lucidity of thought was already manifest.

35. *Sequel to Berg's apprenticeship.*—(A). *The Piano Sonata, Op. 1.*—At the end of July, 1907, Berg wrote to a childhood friend:

Today I finished my studies in counterpoint with Schoenberg; and I am very happy to know (I found it out quite by chance) that my work has merited his satisfaction. Next fall we shall begin "composition." During the summer I am supposed to do some very concentrated work: partly composition pure and simple (right now I am doing a piano sonata, just for myself) and partly contrapuntal exercises (six- and eight-part choruses, and a fugue with three subjects for string quintet with piano accompaniment). All this gives me great pleasure and it is evidently quite necessary, for I'd never get anywhere without it. Indeed, thanks to Schoenberg's tremendous knowledge, one gains a marvelous perspective of all musical literature, and one acquires a sound critical judgment. This is a good thing, for, given the number of works composed in our time—and look at what is prized by press and public!—taste is all too easily corrupted. Anything really good is not recognized till too late—and if it is recognized sooner, it is only because it becomes fashionable.

It is easy to see why I consider these lines significant (allusions to the importance of counterpoint, to Schoenberg's "perspective" of "all musical literature"—reactivation!—etc.).

The abovementioned fugue was, along with three of the *Sieben frühe Lieder*, to figure in the first public performance of Berg's music (November 7, 1907). It was not published, and the manuscript is apparently lost.

In the course of the summer of 1908 the Sonata, Op. 1, was to be completed.[3] Here Berg is completely preoccupied with the

[3] Berg had previously composed another work (also unpublished), *Theme, Twelve Variations, and Finale* for piano, which was played November 8, 1908 (at the same time as the première of Webern's *Passacaglia*, Op. 1, conducted by the composer). Some of the criticisms were as follows:

"After eight promising measures, the variations are lost in a labyrinth of indescribable modulations."

"Twelve variations on no theme."

"Berg's variations, refined and rich in melodic invention and remarkable in piano style, display a great talent for composition. Technically he seems to have learned much from Brahms."

The allusion to Brahms is justified, for these variations, the manuscript of which has been preserved, prove to be completely Brahmsian in conception.

musical problems raised by the genius of Schoenberg. The form, with its ironclad strictness and its feeling for architectonic economy, is a masterly solution of the essential problem of musical composition—how to invent numerous sound-forms and reduce them all to a single unifying principle. Berg accepts the model of the *Kammersymphonie*, which, two years earlier, had achieved a successful *tour de force* in this respect; but, in spite of this influence, the various manifestations of which we shall soon observe, we find here a musical temperament which is already sure of itself and which knows how to adapt its master's acquisitions to its own needs.

The Sonata consists of a single movement—exposition, elaboration, recapitulation. However, it may be said that the differences in character among the different sections thus articulated are rather pronounced, so that both the *Scherzando* and the *Adagio* are incorporated into the musical structure. This, together with the way in which each section is developed out of the preceding one according to principles of "perpetual variation," is the clearest demonstration of the influence of Schoenberg's Op. 9. Certainly, there are even some literal borrowings from that work; thus, the *Kopfmotiv* of the first theme of the sonata uses the intervals of the *Kopfmotiv* of the second theme of the *Kammersymphonie*, and the sixteenth-note figure of the second theme of the sonata is taken practically note for note from the transition of Schoenberg's model. But this is really not very important; of greater significance, it appears to me, is the use made by Berg (again following his master's example) of certain neutral material, aggregations of whole-tones and of fourths.[4] However, in the way in which he uses this material we see one of his most personal characteristics, which distinguishes him from his master.

Schoenberg's fourths are invented *for their own sake*. They are exposed without ambiguity, with all the assurance of a purely harmonic plan masterfully put into effect. Not so with Berg. In measure 26 of the sonata, the fourth-chord F sharp–B–E appears as I of B minor (the E being considered as a suspension to D).

---

[4] On the importance of these neutral elements, cf. Chapter I, *Introduction to Twelve-Tone Music*.

Then, almost unnoticeably, by means of transpositions and chromatic movement, the fourth-chord becomes emancipated little by little, and finally appears in measure 28—though only for a moment—in its pure form, as an aggregation of five notes superimposed in perfect fourths. But this chord undergoes an immediate chromatic transformation into an artificial dominant of A major. Thus, the fourth-chord is completely absorbed into the tonal structure.

This attitude entirely defines the particular role which Berg's genius was to play in the Schoenbergian universe. What principally impresses him in the innovations of his master is the relationship between these innovations and the past. It is not timidity or lack of daring which causes Berg to act in this way—we shall see what bold strokes he could bring off. Rather, it is a matter of the retroactive consolidation of Schoenberg's discoveries, a consolidation which often renders explicit those details which were merely implicit in the Schoenbergian reactivation. Schoenberg comes to the new chords through his purely harmonic plan, the ineluctable consequence of the evolution of polyphony. Berg reveals the very process by which this evolution produces such a plan. "Such was the relation between the master and the pupil, even after the pupil had long been a master in his own right." [5]

In fact, Berg's debt to Schoenberg really consists of certain principles to which we have already drawn attention, and which we must now define more precisely. Let us look at the first theme of the Piano Sonata.

The antecedent constitutes a cadence to the tonic. The harmony is based upon the total resources of chromaticism (only the F natural is not used, but it appears at the beginning of the consequent), controlled with complete awareness of the functions

---

[5] Theodor Wiesengrund-Adorno, in *Alban Berg* by Willi Reich (*loc. cit.*). (I owe many of my present observations to the excellent analyses by Adorno, Reich, Křenek, and Berg himself which are included in that book.) We shall return to the specific role of Berg in the next section of this work, in order to show how the role of Webern is diametrically opposed to it although its essence, if I may say so, is the same.

of the degrees. The scheme is as follows: II–II (Neapolitan sixth) –
I–IV–V–I.[6]

In using such subtleties, which imply the greatest freedom
within the strictest limitations, Berg shows how deeply he is imbued not only with the harmony taught by his master but also
with the inner meaning of the polyphony of his time.

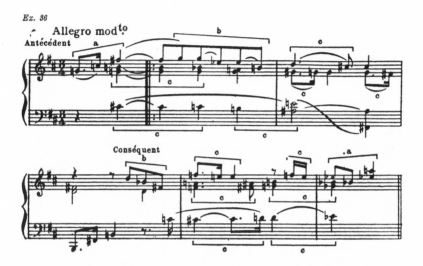

Ex. 36

Melodically, this theme is elaborated from the three motives
(a, b, and c) of the antecedent. The consequent uses first b
(treated as a *remainder*) and then c. C is in turn used as a
remainder, and then comes a variant of a (the vertical superposition of B flat–E flat–A being identical with that which results
from a). Our annotations on Example 36 show the persistence of
these motives and their variants in every strand of the polyphonic
web.

It may then be said that the entire sonata comes from the
material of the beginning or from this initial idea. Example 37

---

[6] In detail: the first chord is II, with suspension on the F sharp (lower appog-
giatura of G), the second chord is the Neapolitan sixth in root position with added
seventh, the third chord is an altered I (B–D sharp–A, with the G acting either as
F double sharp or as a pedal-point), which acts as an artificial dominant to an altered
IV; then the whole closes with V–I.

reproduces the beginning of the second theme (a) and the principal figure of the group of closing themes (b). Here, too, we
observe the presence of the same motives. In this sense, it seems
that Berg's keen awareness of the principal polyphonic problems
of his time can no longer remain in doubt.[7]

Ex. 37

36. *Sequel to Berg's apprenticeship.— (B) .—The songs, Op. 2, and
the quartet, Op. 3.*—The four songs with piano accompaniment,
Op. 2, date from the beginning of 1909. In this work, an important
step is taken, for the first three songs are Berg's last tonal pieces;
in the fourth song, he consciously breaks the bonds of tonality for
the first time. After the effort demanded by the sonata, these songs
appear to represent a moment of relaxation—which does not mean
that they do not raise certain fundamental problems.

The first is primarily harmonic. Here the scope of the procedures noted in the previous work is widened.

In the second, we are confronted with an extremely interesting
piece of polyphonic workmanship. The vocal part begins with a
very expressive melody which seems to be accompanied only by
simple chords. The piano takes up a fragment of this vocal part
and now creates a diversion by elaborating this fragment in imi-
tative style. The voice returns, and is now based on the top part
of the opening chords, while the piano continues to elaborate the
abovementioned fragment. The entire last section of the piece is
governed by the superposition of these two elements.

The third song, though brief and concise, is full of contrasts.
Curiously, it begins in C flat major and ends in E flat major, thus
revealing and expressing the relationship between a major key and
its subdominant minor region. As we noted in Part I of this book,

[7] The thorough analysis of Op. 1 reveals not only a profound preoccupation with
counterpoint (constant superposition of different thematic elements) but also certain
adumbrations of the tone-row technique. (Cf. Chapter I of my *Introduction to Twelve-
Tone Music.*)

this relationship made one of the most important contributions to the incorporation of the total resources of chromaticism into any one given tonality. Thus we see how the "reconstitution" of the historic process synthesized in Schoenberg's discoveries takes place in the work of Berg.[8]

Thus, the last song is the first composition of Berg in which the tonal system is suspended. Berg, visibly inspired by the example of Schoenberg's *Erwartung* (even the text of this song suggests that of the monodrama), avoids repetitions and the elaboration of thematic material. What is more, we perceive here the awakening of Berg's dramatic genius. What about that *glissando*, an effect as yet unheard in the realm of song, really out of bounds in that style? What about that very low B flat, a striking effect which lasts too long to remain part of the given form? These are *dramatic gestures*, taken from opera, which break the form of the song, according to that basic law of opera which demands that form must constantly be surpassed in order to be realized.[9]

Finally, let us note the last chord of the work,

Ex. 38

which is only an inversion of the second chord of our Example 1, taken from Schoenberg's Op. 2. Once more, Berg's activity forges a bond between past and present, clearly pointing out, in his first "post-tonal" work, the road which leads from the very first works of his master to the suspension of the old order.

In the spring of 1910, Berg finished his String Quartet, Op. 3. This was the last work which he was to write under the direct supervision of Schoenberg. All the problems of the Piano Sonata

---

[8] Let us also note in this song the first manifestation of the musical symbolism of the alphabet, which Berg believed in all his life to the point of superstition. At the point where the text speaks of a "white hand in a fairy-tale" are heard the notes A–B flat–B natural (in German A–B–H), the initials of Berg and his wife: Alban—Berg—Helene.

[9] Cf. Chapter VIII.

are here taken up anew, more profoundly examined, and solved on a grander scale. Evidently the work is largely derived from Schoenberg's Second Quartet, Op. 10, but altogether it emphasizes certain typical traits of Berg's personality more than do the previous works.

Following the analysis of Wiesengrund-Adorno, I showed, in my other book, how many elements of this quartet tended toward the establishment of certain fundamental principles of the tone-row technique. Rather than return to this analysis here I shall limit myself to the description of certain more general phenomena.

In the first place, it is necessary to emphasize that this is Berg's first approach to chamber music proper—a form the importance of which we know—and that he begins with what we may call its *ideal form*, the string quartet. The authenticity of Berg's feeling for composition is manifest in the fact that the form which he chooses is not an excuse for the expression of hedonism, but is indispensable for the expression of a contrapuntal style more advanced than any which he had yet attempted.

The work consists of two movements. The first is sonata-like, the second rondo-like; but the technique of variation already applied in Op. 1 is used so strictly here that we may call the whole work one long development section. In this sense, Berg does not dress up old forms in new clothes; he does not disguise the sonata form or the rondo form with "modernistic" chromatic trimmings, as, for example, Reger often does; but he tries to reactivate the original meaning of these forms, and to elaborate them by means of Schoenberg's architectonic principles, which he learned to use in his piano sonata. Berg will believe in these principles his whole life long, with a sort of fanaticism which will never permit him to abandon the large instrumental forms, even when Schoenberg and Webern are consecrating themselves exclusively to miniatures and to vocal music.[10] Viewed from this angle, the quartet Op. 3 comes close to the realization of that principle which was abandoned with the suspension of tonality and which was to be revived twenty years later, with the twelve-tone technique. But there is no "prophecy" on Berg's part. On the contrary, his merit is that,

[10] Cf. Chapter I, *Introduction to Twelve-Tone Music.*

even when his master and his colleague were following other paths, he tried to maintain an ideal which might appear obsolete, but which, because of its fundamentally traditional meaning, was bound to present itself sooner or later to the compositional consciousness of every true musician. In this way, Berg once more proves faithful to his mission, which is to relate to the past each new phase of the future of the Schoenbergian universe.

In the work which concerns us, there are no real themes. The technique of variation, which uses the smallest fragments, here takes root in the absolute minimum, the chromatic half-step. It is this interval which, generally speaking, dominates the melody. Most of the motives are based on this interval or on its progressive enlargement. Example 39 (a and b) which reproduces the beginnings of both movements, clearly shows this state of affairs.[11]

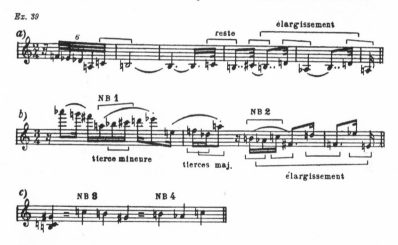

The harmony, for its part, is no longer a succession of artificial dominants as in Op. 1. Completely emancipated from tonal functions, it is derived from counterpoint, and also from the vertical presentation of certain intervals of the melody. Example 39c shows us such an element of unification between melody and harmony. In fact, the motive NB¹ of Example 39b is harmonized with the chord of Example 39c. This chord may be deployed horizontally— NB³—as the inversion of NB¹. On the other hand, a different

[11] The use of similar devices is later to be noted in the *Lyric Suite.*

arrangement of these tones, NB⁴, is equivalent to the motive NB₂ of Example 39c.

All this shows us that, with his Quartet Op. 3, Berg has attained a mature comprehension of the fundamental problems of the polyphony of his time.

37. *Berg's first independent works.*—1910 is an important year in Berg's life. His studies with Schoenberg are finished at the beginning of the summer. Two significant events are 1) a lecture of Karl Kraus on Wedekind, which will eventually inspire the choice of Wedekind's two tragedies as the libretto for the opera *Lulu,* and 2) an interview with Mahler before his departure for America.

On April 24, 1911, Op. 1 and Op. 3 receive their first performance.[12] Berg is married on May 3. During this year, he is also commissioned to make the piano reduction of Franz Schreker's opera *Der ferne Klang.*

It is at the beginning of 1912 that Berg finishes his *Five Orchestral Songs on Postcard Texts of Peter Altenberg,*[13] Op. 4, his first independently composed work. In these songs, Berg's vocation as dramatist becomes entirely obvious for the first time. This may be seen in the many "extravagances" of the score: the choice of frequently "raving" texts; the small dimensions (considering Berg's temperament!) of the various numbers—the longest has fifty-five measures, the shortest eleven; the contrast of these small proportions with the size of the orchestra (three-fold woodwinds, four horns, three trumpets, four trombones, tuba, celesta, harp, piano, harmonium, many percussion instruments and strings). Furthermore, the most extreme instrumental and vocal effects abound: trills and roulades in the voice, all kinds of *glissandi* in the instruments (trombone *glissandi* and *glissandi* of the strings in harmonics), tuning down of the tympani during a roll, tremolo on

---

[12] A single newspaper review: "Under the pretext of writing something called a *String Quartet,* this form has been severely manhandled, courtesy of Mr. Alban Berg. However, this same Mr. Berg has written a piano piece (daringly entitled *Sonata for Piano*) which gives proof of *traces* [italics in the original] of talent and feeling for music."

[13] These "scandalous" texts were actually written by the poet Altenberg on postcards, which he then sent to his friends and enemies.

the tam-tam, etc. All this indicates that desire to broaden the instrumental means which generally characterize the polyphonic development of that period; but it also shows that the form of the song is only a temporary pretext in Berg's Op. 4, and that the future composer of *Wozzeck* and *Lulu* makes his dramatic gestures in the midst of the crumbling ruins of that form.

And nevertheless, at every point in this score—chaotic at first glance—we feel the presence of the conscious architect, who never repudiates his earlier works. Everywhere we recognize the technique of variation and fragmentation which we have previously studied. The fifth song [14] is in the form of a well-constructed strict passacaglia, and adumbrates that incorporation of instrumental forms into vocal and dramatic music which takes place in *Wozzeck*.

This work contains a number of more specific traits characteristic of the later Berg. The second song, for example, presents at one point the following motive, which, twenty years later, becomes one of the principal motives of *Lulu:* [15]

Ex. 40
a)

A little later, this motive is transformed into a new figure in fourths, which is related to the most typical *Wozzeck* figurations:

b)

Even more interesting are certain direct allusions to the future twelve-tone technique. The third song begins and ends with a twelve-tone chord, that is, with the total resources of chromati-

---

[14] Published with piano accompaniment in the magazine *Menschen* (Dresden, 1921).

[15] It is interesting that the same motive is considerably exploited in the third piece of Webern's Op. 7, which dates from approximately the same period (1910).

cism presented in vertical form; [16] and, in the fifth song, the first
counterpoint to the ground-bass unfolds a twelve-tone row, that
is, the total resources of chromaticism presented in horizontal
form:

Two songs of Op. 4 were performed on March 31, 1913, on the
famous occasion which we described in Part II of this book.[17] As
we know, they caused a riot. Since then, unperformed and unpublished, they have fallen—after their frightening first appearance—into an abyss of oblivion from which no one has yet thought
of rescuing them.[17a]

The *Four Pieces for Clarinet and Piano*, Op. 5, were composed
during the summer of 1913. This is the first published work of
Berg to bear a dedication to Schoenberg. The earlier works rendered homage to Schoenberg through their crystallization of his
teachings; now, for the first time, the young master addresses himself freely to his friend in an act of heartfelt recognition. Op. 5
is also intended as a homage to the spirit of the miniature form,
which was inaugurated with Schoenberg's Op. 19, and which Berg
uses here for the first and last time in his life.

We have seen (and will see even more clearly in connection
with Webern) that the miniature form was created so that the
musical discourse might evolve without ever repeating itself in
any way. This is perfectly exemplified by the four pieces which
concern us now. We might, of course, consider that these pieces
were derived from the four traditional sonata movements—the
first being a sonata Allegro, the second an Adagio, the third a
Scherzo, and the fourth a Rondo. This is because Berg's extremely
traditional mind is always capable of rediscovering, or rather of

---

[16] This chord is treated like the famous "Changing Chord" in Schoenberg's Op. 16
No. 3. The influence of Schoenberg's Op. 16 on Berg's Op. 4 is perceptible throughout.

[17] Cf. Chapter IV, note 14.

[17a] For further details see my preface to the score of Op. 4. (Edition Dynamo,
Liège.)

recreating, the most fundamental laws of architectonic equilibrium in the midst of any and all innovations. However, I should like to use two short examples to show how subtly Berg manages to preserve and to overthrow, at one and the same time, the formal schemes inherited from tradition.

Ex. 41

In the first example, taken from the first piece, the antecedent of the first theme is played by the clarinet alone (Ex. 41a). The consequent is accompanied by a counterpoint in the piano. The recapitulation of this theme is limited to the varied antecedent, exposed in the piano (Ex. 41b), to which the clarinet immediately adds a variant (with enlarged intervals) of the preceding counterpoint; in addition, there appears, in the bass of the piano, a new counterpoint.

The following example comes from the last piece.

Ex. 42

The "theme" of the Rondo consists of a repeated syncopated chord in the piano, over which the clarinet plays a chromatic motive (Ex. 42a). The recapitulation occurs as follows: the repeated chords reappear in the piano (in a different rhythm this time), and the clarinet plays a curtailed version (using only the first and last notes) of the chromatic motive, in contrary motion. Furthermore, although the first appearance of the "theme" included a consequent which was a mere variation of the chromatic motive in question (which became, in a different rhythm, C sharp–C–B–B flat), this antecedent disappears from the recapitulation, and the clarinet merely plays the motive b three times, each time in a different rhythm.

All this bespeaks the kind of musical workmanship which could be perfected only within the limitations of the miniature form; here, then, we have the most "modern" aspect of Berg's musical consciousness. However, the results here achieved by means of this form throw still more light on the specific role of Berg which we have already stressed. Indeed, quite aside from the fact that the pieces of Op. 5 are definitely longer than the corresponding pieces of Schoenberg or Webern, we must note that, while the latter composers try to build in the grand style with the fewest possible notes in the shortest possible time (for example, Webern, in the words of Schoenberg, "writes a whole novel with one sigh"), Berg primarily tries to *shorten* his pieces. Thus, Webern's pieces do not seem short musically, while Berg's pieces emphasize the fact that they last only a moment. With Webern, it is an *inner process*—the extension *from within* of the *minimum of material* which is capable of all conceivable extensions; with Berg, it is an *outer process* (without any pejorative implications!) —the compression *from the outside* of the *maximum of material* often furnished to us by tradition in an "overstuffed" form.

For September 13, 1914 (Schoenberg's fortieth birthday) Berg is planning an important orchestral work, which he would like to dedicate to his master and friend. At first he works (1913) on a symphony, but he abandons this in favor of the *Three Orchestral Pieces*, Op. 6. Only the last piece is finished in time; the two others will be completed at the end of 1914. In some respects (especially orchestration) these pieces appear as a continuation of the songs, Op. 4; in other respects, they display the evolution of many elements in Op. 3 and Op. 5. But, actually, this new work marks a cesura in Berg's creation. Not only does he get a firm grip on the large form, which he will never let go, not only does he develop a more radical and *constructive* [18] contrapuntal style, but he also becomes completely aware of the musical past, which henceforth never ceases to condition his entire ulterior development. This is manifest in a curious circumstance: Berg's new score, without sacrificing in any way the slightest acquisition of the Schoenbergian

[18] Since the structure of each piece is now primarily based on this counterpoint.

universe, shows definite relationships to earlier and quite different worlds of sound, those of Mahler and Debussy. With these *Three Orchestral Pieces*, the school of Schoenberg joins the rest of the contemporary movement; or, rather, the subjective movement of Schoenberg's school culminates in that stylistic moment which, objectified, is the genuine and legitimate consequence of the past and the historical present. No longer can this school appear as an esoteric sect speaking a secret language; its work is now seen to be the highest expression of musical knowledge. In it are consummated those tendencies which the other powerful contemporary forces merely touched upon. It was Berg's feat to establish the bond between the language of Schoenberg and that of the past; for he could consolidate the most recent events by testing them against what had gone before. And this line of retrospect may be projected into Berg's own future. In this he differs from the apparent "neo-classicists," who merely tried to warm up a few musical left-overs; for the will to create in large form (which causes the resemblances between Berg and, for example, Mahler) is actually brought about by Schoenberg's re-examination of large form between Op. 19 and *Pierrot Lunaire*. Therefore, Berg's most Mahlerian score becomes at the same time his most complicated work.

Prelude, Dance, March: with their constant use of the total resources of chromaticism, with their complex and unceasing counterpoint, with their technique of perpetual variation and their extreme means of orchestration, these three pieces constitute one of the highest accomplishments of "pre-tone-row" polyphony.

38. *Berg's first awareness of the tone-row.*—In May, 1914, Berg attends a performance of the fragments of Büchner's play *Wozzeck*. A little later he conceives the idea of using this work for an opera. But he is drafted in August, 1915, and remains in service till the end of the war (since he is declared unfit for active military service, he is attached to the Ministry of War). After completing the libretto of *Wozzeck* during the summer of 1917, Berg begins

the composition with Act II, Scene 2. The work is completed in
the fall of 1920, the orchestration in April, 1921.[19]

After *Wozzeck,* Berg's activity returns to the field of chamber
music, from which he had absented himself for more than ten years
(ever since Op. 5).

Between 1923 and 1925, he composed his *Chamber Concerto*
for violin, piano, and thirteen winds (piccolo, flute, oboe, English
horn, piccolo clarinet, clarinet, bass clarinet, bassoon, double-
bassoon, two horns, trumpet, and trombone). The work is dedicated to Schoenberg for his fiftieth birthday. It even begins with
a sort of musical dedication which unites the names of Schoenberg, Webern, and Berg. The piano plays the notes corresponding
to the capitalized letters in the name of ArnolD SCHönBErG, the
violin continues with the notes of A. wEBErn, and the horn con-
cludes with those of AlBAn BErG.

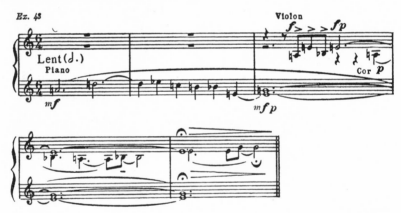

Ex. 43

The motives thus obtained play an important part throughout
the work.

[19] Since the next chapter is devoted especially to Berg's operas we shall not
emphasize this subject here; but let us mention a few details in connection with
Wozzeck. The work was at first published on a subscription basis, in the form of a
vocal score with piano accompaniment. This plan was principally initiated by Alma
Maria Mahler, the widow of the composer. The appearance of *Wozzeck* at first attracted
no attention. However, a eulogizing review appeared, in April, 1923, in the magazine
Die Musik (Berlin); this, in addition to Scherchen's performance (Frankfurt, June 11,
1924) of a concert suite of selections from the opera—an idea which he had suggested—
finally interested an increasing number of musicians. Thanks to the initiative of Erich
Kleiber, the world première took place at the Berlin Opera on December 14, 1925, under

The concerto is analyzed by Berg himself, in a letter which he sent to Schoenberg, along with the score, on February 25, 1925.[20] Since I have already used this analysis in my other book I shall reproduce only its most essential elements here.

The first movement is entitled *Thema scherzoso con variazioni.* The theme itself is an extended form of thirty measures, divided into three distinct sections. The first time, it is exposed in the orchestra alone. The first variation (which Berg considers as a first reprise) is a piano solo. The theme reappears in its original form, but the variation consists in a change of style; the piano adapts the previously heard material to its specifically *virtuoso* style. The second variation (like all the other variations) is played by the piano with the instrumental group. It presents the notes of the theme in their retrograde order. The third and fourth variations present the inversion and the retrograde inversion, respectively; thus, Berg considers the group formed by variations II, III, and IV as the development section of this "sonata form." The last variation (variation V) acts as the recapitulation (really a second reprise), for it brings back the theme in its original form. However, since this original form is exposed in a new way by the piano and winds, with all sorts of contrapuntal combinations (canons, etc.), this last variation also acquires the function of a coda.

The same preoccupation with the tone-row is seen in the second movement.[21] Again, it exposes a long section (120 measures)

---

his direction. The work was performed ten times there during that season—twenty-one times in all, up till 1932. The next performances, both of which Berg attended, were in Prague (November, 1926) and Leningrad (1927). But the real success of the opera begins with its "première" in a little German provincial city: *Oldenburg* (March 5, 1929). There rapidly followed performances in the following cities (listed in chronological order): *Essen, Aix-la-Chapelle, Vienna, Düsseldorf, Königsberg,* Lübeck, Liège, Amsterdam, Cologne, *Gera,* Brunswick, Rotterdam, *Darmstadt,* Philadelphia, *Frankfurt am Main, Freiburg im Breisgau,* Wuppertal, *Leipzig, Zurich,* New York, Chemnitz, *Brussels,* Mannheim, Bremen, London. (The italicized names of cities indicate Berg's presence at the "premières" there. In most cases he introduced the work with an important lecture.) Until the end of 1936, *Wozzeck* was performed a total of 166 times in 29 different cities; the work was sung in German, Czech, Russian, French, and English. In 1934, the Library of Congress bought the three volumes of the manuscript of the score.

[20] This letter, reproduced in numerous musical magazines, was first published in *Pult und Taktstock* in 1925.

[21] The reader is now so familiar with these questions that I need not go further into the matter. For the twelve-tone aspects of this work (which fulfill the idea of the tone-row) see Chapter II of my *Introduction.*

which is divided into three parts, A^1–B–A^2. A^2 is the inversion of A^1. The recapitulation of this whole section is retrograde, so that, in the four appearances of A, we have all possible tone-row variants.[22]

Finally, the third movement, which begins with a cadenza of the two soloists, marks the culmination of Berg's preoccupation with counterpoint and "economy." In fact, it uses no new material, but merely works with contrapuntal superposition of all the elements of the two preceding movements. This superposition of the first two movements and the variation of all their constituent elements in every possible way (change of register, altered rhythm, etc.) give this movement a highly novel and original tone.

It is in the *Lyric Suite* for string quartet (1925–26) that Berg uses the twelve-tone technique for the first time. The work entirely justifies its title of *Lyric Suite*; for, in contrast to the symphonic spirit which imbues almost all other string quartets, this one, despite its solid structure and masterly art of variation, presents itself to us in a dramatic form, so that some have even seen in it a sort of "latent opera"—an accompaniment to an invisible opera. This is indicated by the rise in dramatic intensity expressed in the tempo indications and dynamic markings of the successive movements.

The carefree *Allegro giovale* is followed by a tender *Andante amoroso*; then comes a very characteristic piece, the *Allegro misterioso* (restrained at first, but more "explosive" in its middle section, the *Trio estatico*). Then, with the powerful song of the *Adagio Appassionato*, we reach the culminating point of the lyricism of the work. The outer circumference is reached in the *Presto delirando*, with its more restrained middle section, *Tenebroso*. Finally, the *Largo desolato* is extinguished in despair.

This scheme clearly indicates the progress of dramatic intensity alongside that of the tempo. On the one hand, faster and faster tempi (Allegretto, Allegro, Presto); on the other hand, slower and slower ones (Andante, Adagio, Largo).

Architectonically, the work shows a close-knit construction

---

[22] A^3, the retrograde form of A^2, thus becomes RI, and A^4, the retrograde form of A^1, becomes R. Also, the recapitulation of B is a perfect mirror-image.

insofar as the different movements are interconnected in a very special way. Thus, the basic idea or theme of one movement always reappears in the next.[23] Furthermore, the partial application of the twelve-tone technique (which is used in exactly half of the work) and the closely related preoccupation with the tone-row [24] impart to the *Lyric Suite* an exemplary solidity of structure, wealth of ideas, and "economy" of polyphony.

The first movement, entirely written in the twelve-tone technique, is a sonata movement without development. Thus the recapitulation follows directly upon the exposition; but, because of the highly advanced twelve-tone technique of variation, *everything* in this movement is developmental.

The second movement is a rondo with three themes. Its second theme is a variant of the second theme of the first movement, thus carrying out the interconnecting plan of the whole work. This movement is not twelve-tone, but at one point the viola unfolds a figure which proves to be a variant of the basic twelve-tone row of the first movement (connection with what precedes), and which, in this new form, serves as a basis for the twelve-tone sections of the third movement (connection with what follows).

The third movement is in the form of a Scherzo. Its principal sections, the exposition and the retrograde recapitulation of the Scherzo, are twelve-tone. On the other hand, the *Trio estatico* exposes all of the materials which are used, in a different order, for the following movement.

The fourth movement (not twelve-tone) may be considered the central development section of the whole Suite, for its extremely contrapuntal style elaborates, from the very beginning— in *stretto* fashion—the basic thematic materials.[25] We know that

[23] In this respect Berg is absolutely faithful to the idea of thematic unity elaborated in Schoenberg's Op. 5, 7, 9, and 10. This principle, used in all Berg's works, once more proves his desire to establish a living link between past and present.

[24] The statement made in the previous footnote may be repeated here, and Berg's first use of the new technique may be compared to his first use of fourth-chords in Op. 1. Indeed, just as Schoenberg's harmonic acquisition of fourth-chords was traditionally consolidated, in a tonal manner, by Berg, the "traditional process" of the creation of the twelve-tone technique is repeated in the *Lyric Suite*.

[25] Here, too, occurs the citation of a motive from Zemlinsky's *Lyric Symphony*. Berg's work, which owes its title to that of Zemlinsky, is dedicated to him.

it is built on the elements of the *Trio estatico*, but in its turn
it will furnish an element of basic importance—the viola melody
of the *Molto tranquillo* section, which appears to be nothing but
a simple accompaniment—to the next movement.

The fifth movement is a Scherzo with two Trios. Here it is the
Trios which are twelve-tone. They are based on a variant of the
twelve-tone series of the third movement, which, in this new form,
is used for the last movement.

The sixth movement, entirely twelve-tone, is very free in form.
Its principal element is a syncopated rhythm. Besides the twelve-
tone series, there are many other elements which bind it to the
preceding movements—especially a secondary motive of the first
movement, which closes the circle.

Before leaving this work I should like to give two quotations
from it, which seem to me significant in a number of respects.

The first is taken from the *Presto delirando*, and therefore is
not twelve-tone. However, the use of certain elements which inevitably lead to the twelve-tone technique is highly characteristic.
The piece begins with the unfoldment of the total resources of
chromaticism (a), and this material is functionally elaborated in
the coda of the movement, from which I extract one passage (b).

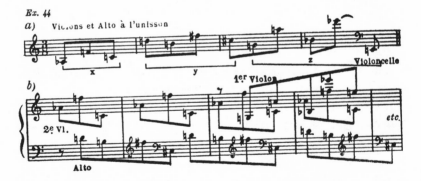

Here we see the superposition of fragments (x, y, z—x in the
second violin, y in the viola, and z in the first violin) of the beginning. It is interesting to note, as well, the application of one
of Schoenberg's typical rhythmic procedures. The rhythmic unfoldment occurs in equal eighth-notes; but, since the three motives

are of unequal length, their individual accentuations give rise to a very special kind of polyrhythm. The motive x, consisting of three eighth-notes, continuously unfolds (since the ⅜ time-signature remains unchanged) in dactylic meter. The motive y, because of its structure of four eighth-notes, is continually changing its accent. Its first appearance combines the anapest with the trochee (a strong beat preceded by two weak beats and followed by a weak beat); its second appearance combines the iamb with the dactyl (a weak beat which precedes a strong beat followed by two weak beats); its third appearance combines the dactyl with the iamb, etc. In the same way, the motive z varies constantly.

Our second example is taken from the beginning of the *Allegro misterioso*. Here we see how subtly Berg handles the twelve-tone technique, and how this technique permits and engenders the most effective devices for producing variety and coherence in the music.

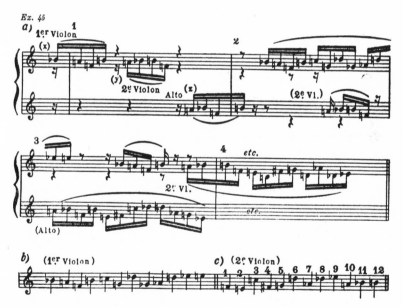

Ex. 45

The movement begins with the exposition (a) of the three motives x, y, and z—similar insofar as they are made up of the same notes, different insofar as they are varied rhythmically and insofar as their constituent tones appear each time in a different order. The tone-row forms from which these motives are derived (and the complete unfoldment of which occurs in the following passages of each instrument) are as follows: the first violin plays O, pure and simple (b); the second violin transposes it a fourth down or a fifth up, and plays this transposition beginning with the tenth tone and ending with the ninth (c); the viola transposes it once more, beginning with the fourth tone and ending with the third (d). Later, the first entry of the 'cello exposes the three motives consecutively and organizes them into a theme (e).

Thus in the *Lyric Suite* the genius of Berg becomes definitely aware of that culmination of contemporary polyphony which is the twelve-tone technique.[26]

39. *The last works of Berg; his death.*—After the completion of the *Lyric Suite*, Berg is preoccupied with plans for a new opera. On January 30, 1928, he pays a visit at Rapallo to Gerhart Hauptmann, whose *Und Pippa tanzt* interests him; but, during the spring of that year, he definitely decides on *Lulu*, the libretto of which he constructs himself, combining Wedekind's tragedies *Erdgeist* (*Earth-Spirit*) and *Die Büchse der Pandora* (*Pandora's Box*). This work, which we shall study in the next chapter, was to occupy Berg until his death. However, its composition and orchestration were to be interrupted several times—first by work on the concert aria *Der Wein*, later by the Violin Concerto.[27] The

---

[26] This awareness of the twelve-tone world gave rise to still another work, completed during the summer of 1926. An unpublished song of Berg, composed in 1907, was rewritten in the twelve-tone system. Both versions were dedicated to Emil Hertzka, director of the Universal-Edition (for the twenty-fifth anniversary of that organization), who had done much to help our three musicians. These two songs appeared in *Die Musik* (Berlin, February, 1930) to illustrate an article on Berg by Willi Reich.

[27] Let us mention some other works completed between 1928 and 1935: the above-mentioned orchestration of the *Sieben frühe Lieder*, the transcription for string orchestra of the three central movements (2–4) of the *Lyric Suite*, the transcription for violin, clarinet, and piano of the second movement of the *Chamber Concerto* (February, 1935), and a concert suite, the *Lulu Symphony*, taken from the opera *Lulu* (summer of 1934).

actual composition of *Lulu* was finished in April, 1934. Berg immediately threw himself into the task of orchestration with feverish haste. This work was to be interrupted in the spring of 1935 by the commission for a violin concerto offered to Berg by the American violinist Louis Krasner. After the completion of this concerto in less than two months, Berg returned to the orchestration of *Lulu*. He was not to finish it; only the first two acts and some important parts of the third [28] were orchestrated. The work, which was performed in this incomplete form in Zurich in 1937, was dedicated to Schoenberg for his sixtieth birthday. Lulu's aria in the second act (which figures in the concert suite) was dedicated to Anton Webern, for his fiftieth birthday.

It was in the spring of 1929 that the singer Ružena Herlinger induced Berg to write a concert aria for soprano and orchestra. He interrupted his work on *Lulu*, and based his aria, *Der Wein*, on three poems of Baudelaire, which may be sung in the original or in the amazing German translation of Stefan George. The composition was finished on July 23, 1929, and the orchestration was completed a month later.

This work presents us with a first glimpse of the world of *Lulu*. In fact, the sonority of the orchestra, which makes considerable use of the piano and the saxophone, already has that transparency which will characterize the purely dramatic expression of the sonority of Berg's second opera. The very form, which at once surpasses and sublimates that of the three-part song, displays, not only dramatic expansion, but also that thematic unity which is the fundamental principle of every musical structure—qualities the particularly Bergian nature of which needs no further emphasis.

The work follows the general scheme of the A–B–A form. The first part, A, takes the form of a sonata exposition:

Orchestral introduction—1–14.
First theme, divided into two parts—
    a) 15–23, b) 24–30.
Transition—31–38.

---

[28] Especially those used in the *Lulu Symphony*.

Second theme (Tango) [29]—39–63.
Closing group—64–87.
The second part, B, adopts the form of the Scherzo:
Scherzo—88–96.
Trio—97–122.
Recapitulation of the Scherzo—123–141.

An orchestral intermezzo, 142–172, leads to the third section,
a much-varied recapitulation of the first section:
First theme—173–178.
Transition—179–180.
Second theme (Tango) —181–195.
Closing group—196–201.
Coda—202–208.
Orchestral epilogue—209–216.

Der Wein is also interesting because the twelve-tone system
is there handled for the first time in such a way as to create the
possibility of tonal functions within the total resources of chromaticism. This problem, which we have already had occasion to
discuss, becomes still more acute in *Lulu* and especially in the
Violin Concerto.[30]

I should like, with the help of two examples, to call attention
to certain principles of architectonic economy in *Der Wein*.

The first example shows the only two genuinely thematic appearances of the entire twelve-tone row. Example 46a is the first
entrance of the vocal part, while Example 46b reproduces the
principal motive of the orchestral epilogue, stated in the bass.

Ex. 46

a)

(*Lent*) Chant

---

[29] The Tango is one of those elements which break the bounds of the simple
concert aria. Such excursions into dance music are even more evident in *Lulu*.

[30] It is not surprising, given Berg's specific mission in the Schoenbergian universe,
that he was attracted by the "tonal possibilities" of the new technique from his second
twelve-tone work onwards. Is this not the most radical way of creating a firm bond
between Schoenberg's work and the past?

These are the two pillars of the unity of the work—a unity to which they contribute in spite of their differences in rhythm, register, and means of presentation.

The second example shows us how carefully and subtly Berg creates the diversity and coherence of his forms; Schoenberg's instruction turned his mind irrevocably in the direction of this compositional attitude, which, in this passage, leads to the invention of new rhythmic possibilities.[31]

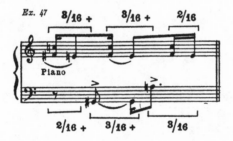

This is the beginning of the Tango, the rhythm of which is here very cunningly constructed. The right hand divides this rhythm into metrical patterns of 3/16+3/16+2/16, while the left hand presents the same patterns in exactly the reverse order: 2/16+3/16+3/16. Thus, the two forms embody, at one and the same time, the greatest diversity and the most perfect unity.

In the spring of 1935, Berg interrupts the orchestration of *Lulu* to write the Violin Concerto, the composition and orchestration of which are completed on July 23 and August 11 respectively. The work is dedicated to Louis Krasner, who commissioned it, and "to the memory of an angel" (Manon Gropius, the daughter of Alma Maria Mahler). It may be considered as a *Requiem* for

---

[31] I owe my knowledge of the present instance to the analytical perspicacity of Wiesengrund-Adorno. Many of the keenest observations on Berg's music are to be found in the brilliant analyses of this remarkable connoisseur of the music which concerns us.

Berg himself; the text of the Bach chorale which is used at the end of the last movement is quite explicit in this respect.[32]

Like the preceding works, this concerto is constructed according to a firmly grounded form, which amalgamates the traditional thematic unities with the most advanced formal innovations. The formal scheme of the two movements is as follows:

First movement: I. Andante. Three-part form: ten measures of introduction, then,

A—11–37.
B—38–83.
A—84–103.

The last four measures form a subtle transition to
II. Allegretto. Scherzo form.

A—104–136.
B (Trio I)—137–154.
C (Trio II)—155–166.
B—167–172.
A—173–257.

Second movement: I. Allegro. Three-part form.

A—1–43.
(Cadenza) B—44–95.
A—96–135.

The last ten measures act as a transition to
II. Adagio.

Chorale—136–157.
First variation—158–177.
Second variation—178–197.
Reminiscence of the first movement—198–213.
Coda—214–236.

Needless to say, the different repetitions are radically varied, and the most subtle connections are established between diverse

---

[32] The beginning of this text is as follows: "Es ist genug! Herr, wenn es Dir gefällt, so spanne mich doch aus!" It is possible that Bach, dictating the chorale *Vor deinem Thron tret' ich hiemit* on his deathbed—Brahms, composing his last work, the organ fantasy on the chorale *O Welt ich muss dich lassen*—Mahler, writing *Das Lied von der Erde*—that all these artists were bidding farewell to life. It is impossible to say whether Berg foresaw his imminent death. The text of the chorale, as well as the amazing speed (in view of his usual slow work) with which the concerto was finished, seem to indicate that he did.

sections and periods. Furthermore, Berg's concern with counterpoint is manifest, especially in the variations of the chorale. The very use of this form (also found in *Lulu*) is highly significant. The harmonization and the variation of the chorale are among the most strictly traditional elements of Schoenberg's teaching. There is no doubt that young Berg, during his apprenticeship, had to devote many arduous hours to the study of these forms, the most meticulous and perfected realization of which was required by Schoenberg. So it is not surprising that Berg, having attained the height of mastery, again approaches, traditionally as well as radically, those forms which link the Schoenbergian universe with the previously evolved world of music.

This link is also found in the restoration of certain tonal functions within the total resources of chromaticism. Here we have, next to Schoenberg's *Ode to Napoleon,* the most extreme example of this process. (I have discussed it in my other book and so recall only the essential details here.)

From the point of view.of tonality, the concerto is perpetually oscillating between B flat major and G minor. The functions of these two keys are, first of all, realized by the very structure of the twelve-tone row:

Ex. 48

This structure permits all sorts of *tonal* combinations, and allows the inclusion of the beginning and end of the Bach chorale. In fact, the last four notes of the row are identical with the first four notes of the chorale,

while the last four notes of the chorale

are identical with the inversion of the segment 8 9 10 11 of the row. Hence it comes about that certain treatments of this row permit the elaboration of many "classical" tonal functions (such as the tonic-dominant type of progression).

Ex. 49
a)

On the other hand, it is evident that combinations very different from those of tonality result with equal frequency, but, thanks to the twelve-tone row technique, form a coherent part of the total harmonic structure:

b)

c)

After composing the Violin Concerto, Berg expected to finish his second opera quickly. He was living in poor circumstances and hoped that a performance of *Lulu* would materially better his financial situation. He was planning many new works: a third string quartet, a chamber-music composition with piano, a symphony, a piece written especially for the radio. But, when he was asked to take part in the ISCM festival at Prague in September, 1935, he had to decline because of an abscess on his back, apparently caused by an insect-bite. The abscess was treated, but Berg still felt quite ill. On November 12 he left his country house (where he had worked in complete isolation during the last years) for Vienna, where he took active part in the preparation of the

Viennese première of the *Lulu Symphony*. He managed to hold out by secretly taking innumerable aspirin tablets. Although already suffering from the high fever of furunculosis, he still supervised the piano reduction of the Violin Concerto on December 14. On December 16, the pain left him—the abscess, bursting internally, caused general blood-poisoning. On the 17th he was taken to the hospital and operated on immediately, but the source of infection could not be located. A blood transfusion brought only superficial improvement. Berg—unaware of the seriousness of his condition or trying not to alarm his wife and friends—endured all this with amazing patience and good humor. He asked to see the blood donor so that he could thank him personally. After the donor, a typical young Viennese, had left, Berg turned to one of his friends and said, with an indescribable expression, "Just so I don't turn into an operetta composer!"

December 22 was the beginning of the end. Berg's heart, fortified by strong remedies throughout his entire illness, began to fail. His death-agony began. On the morning of the 23rd, he said very quietly, "This will be a decisive day." In his delirium he seemed to dream of nothing but his opera. He died on December 24, about one o'clock in the morning. A peaceful and tranquil expression soon obliterated the lines of suffering on his face.

CHAPTER VIII

Alban Berg and the Essence of Opera

40. *Schoenberg's criticism of post-Wagnerian opera: Berg's dramatic preoccupations.*—"A symphony for large orchestra accompanied by a solo voice." In these ironic terms Schoenberg describes the post-Wagnerian opera. Opera had, in fact, followed the symphonic tendencies of Wagner; but, while Wagner had succeeded in preserving the dramatic structure, this structure is completely undermined in the works of most of his successors. Wagner, the true musical dramatist, had achieved a precise organization of his musical speech in spite of his ultra-violent reaction against the old "number opera" and his ideas of "endless melody." Even in *Tristan,* the "paroxysm" of the system, we find numerous "pieces" which are perfectly complete in themselves—the love duet, the interpolated "arias" of Brangäne, King Mark's recitatives, Isolde's Love-Death, etc. This does not detract in any way from the symphonic unity of the whole. But Wagner's epigones saw only the most deceptive side of the work of their great predecessor; concentrating entirely on the so-called "symphonic" aspect of the *Gesamtkunstwerk,* they forgot the dramatic essence of opera, and thus deprived it of all musical value. This theory will explain itself further as we pursue our study of Berg's operas.

However, Schoenberg's irony is particularly directed at another equally important aspect of post-Wagnerian opera. In this opera, the voice is killed. We know that one of the principal elements in the original conception of opera was that *altro modo di cantare che l'ordinario.* Although the elaboration of the recitative in the Florentine opera was unsuccessful because it lacked a solid musical basis, Monteverdi's powerful genius successfully introduced many new vocal styles into opera. Here we touch upon the crucial prob-

168

lem of dramatic music; and it is this problem which is principally neglected by the post-Wagnerian opera. Wagner had already contented himself, for the most part, with the perpetual use—almost to the exclusion of any other form of singing—of the *arioso* style. His successors go farther still; even the *arioso* is drowned in the orchestral floods.

This was more or less the condition of the opera [1] at the moment when Berg began his first dramatic work.[2]

He, an authentic musician, could approach the opera only in the most authentic fashion. Several years after the completion of his first opera, when it had already been performed on many stages, he had occasion to define his operatic intentions in a number of articles and interviews. Here are several lines taken from his answer to a questionnaire on this subject: [3]

"One must write such good music that good theater results in spite of it," and, later, along the same lines, "When I decided to write an opera, I had no other plan . . . than to render unto the theater what was the theater's—that is, to build the music in such a way that it would never deviate from its function of serving the drama."

Although these few remarks explain Berg's dramatic intentions, we see a little further on in the same article that the composer has no intention of relegating music to a position of secondary importance. On the contrary, it is only through its deep concern with the drama that operatic music really becomes "pure music."

"The necessity of making a choice for my libretto, among Büchner's twenty-six loosely constructed and sometimes fragmentary scenes, while avoiding repetition insofar as they did not lend themselves to musical variation; the necessity of pulling these scenes together and juxtaposing them so that they could be grouped into several

[1] It goes without saying that Debussy's *Pelléas et Mélisande,* as well as Schoenberg's *Erwartung* and *Die glückliche Hand,* are exceptions to this statement. These works, especially Schoenberg's, profoundly influenced Berg's operas.

[2] Let us recall that Berg decided to compose an opera when he saw a performance of Büchner's *Wozzeck* in the spring of 1914. He worked on the adaptation of the text between 1915 and 1917. The actual composition occupied him between 1917 and 1921. Let us also note that Berg undertook this work when he was thirty-two, having already acquired a solid technique in all forms of musical composition.

[3] *Neue Musik-Zeitung,* Stuttgart, 1928.

acts—all this, whether I liked it or not, confronted me with a problem which was rather musical than literary; a problem, that is to say, which could be solved only by the laws of musical architecture, not by those of dramaturgy."

As to the other essential problem of opera—the voice—a short article called *The Voice in Opera* [4] gives us a masterly summary of Berg's attitude. In the opera, it is necessary to use all the possibilities of the human voice, "from *recitative* to *parlando*, from *cantilena* to *coloratura*. Thus, the *bel canto*, too, may unfold."

Later, Berg states that there are not more than a dozen measures of recitative all told in his *Wozzeck*; on the other hand, he feels that he has bridged this gap with the "rhythmic declamation" invented by Schoenberg in *Die glückliche Hand* and *Pierrot Lunaire*. "This manner of treating the voice, which includes possibilities of musical articulation unknown to the recitative, furnishes a means of artistic enrichment for opera, and draws upon the purest sources of music." [5]

This remark strikes to the very heart of dramatic music. The recitative is the last survival of an "impure" mode of thought. If it was able to maintain itself for three centuries, that is only because dramatic necessity sometimes demands spoken language to elucidate the action, and because no more strictly musical means of carrying out this function had been discovered before Schoenberg and Alban Berg.

Finally, when Berg states that the use of rhythmic declamation creates the possibilities of incorporating such declamation into "solos, duos, trios, small and large ensembles, male and female choruses, mixed choruses, *a cappella* singing, and accompanied singing," he deduces that "these are the possibilities which predestine opera, *more than any other musical form, to the service of the human voice. . . .*" (The italics are mine.)

In informing us of the basic principles which guided him in the conception of his first opera, Berg reveals to us the authenticity of his dramatic genius. We shall understand it still more clearly if we make a more profound study of *Wozzeck* and *Lulu*.

[4] *Gesang*, 1929.
[5] Cf. Part II of this book (Chapter IV, footnote 5, § 20).

41. *Wozzeck.*—The twenty-six scenes of Büchner's *Wozzeck* are reduced to fifteen in Berg's opera. Their distribution in three acts revives the traditional dramatic scheme: exposition, development, catastrophe. After dramatic unity had thus been created, the same process had to be applied to the musical structure, without the help of one of the most powerful means of unification known up till then—tonality. Even for the lay listener the return to the main key is a clearly perceptible principle of unification. Berg seeks a similar means of consolidating the larger harmonic phases of his work. He finds this means in closing each act with a sort of cadence which always leads to the same chord; but this chord is disposed in a different way each time. The general structure of the work recalls the A–B–A scheme, because of a certain parallelism between Acts I and III which, in a sort of symmetry of duration, enclose the much longer Act II. Furthermore, Act II displays a very close-knit symphonic structure, while Acts I and III are much more loosely formed.

The five scenes of the first act may be considered as *genre* pieces which characterize the principal personages of the drama in order of their appearance—always in relation to the central character, the soldier Wozzeck. These scenes take the musical forms of a *Suite*, a *Rhapsody*, a *Military March* and *Lullaby*, a *Passacaglia*, and an *Andante Affetuoso* (*quasi rondo*).

The second act is a symphony in five movements—*Sonata-form, Fantasy and Fugue, Largo, Scherzo,* and *Rondo con introduzione*—each of which corresponds to one of the five scenes.

Finally, the five scenes of the last act give rise to a series of six inventions: Scene 1, *Invention on a theme*; Scene 2, *Invention on a tone*; Scene 3, *Invention on a rhythm*; Scene 4, *Invention on a chord,* followed by an orchestral interlude in the form of an *Invention on a key*; Scene 5, *Invention on a steady movement in eighth-notes.*

This subdivision of the opera [6] obviously recalls the "Neapoli-

---

[6] It is important to note that the use here of certain "old forms" has nothing to do with a spirit of archaism, or with the "Back to . . ." movement of several years later. In fact, alongside of certain traditional formal schemes, Berg used very different, often very daring devices based on entirely new and original principles.

tan tendency" to set pieces; but, at the same time, a more profound analysis of the whole work indicates that the Wagnerian
concept of the "music-drama" is also applicable to *Wozzeck*. Such
a hypothesis is permitted by the interpretation of the events on
the stage in terms of a self-sufficient musical structure, as well as
by the use of the leitmotivic technique as the foundation of
thematic development.

First, let us consider the musical unity of the work. Aside from
the cadences to the same chord which close the various acts, the
structural unity is created: 1) by *thematic unity* (one of Berg's
characteristic qualities, which we emphasized in the preceding
chapter, and which, in this work, is the result of the abovementioned leitmotivic technique); 2) by the devices of extreme
variation applied to every portion of the work; 3) by the subtle
transitions—often based on the well-known technique of liquidation—which accentuate the interrelationships of the various set
pieces. Furthermore, the numerous changes of scene required by
the dramatic action of the work necessitated a great number of
symphonic interludes. Berg treats these either as *independent
pieces,* complete in themselves (in which case they elaborate the
previously heard themes) or as *codas* to the immediately preceding scenes, or as *introductions* to what is about to take place;
sometimes, indeed, the two latter forms are combined.

Several examples will clarify this. The Suite which constitutes
the first scene begins with a Prelude, dominated by sixteenth-
and thirty-second-notes. This Prelude is followed by a Pavane,
which begins with eighth-note triplets. Example 40 shows the
subtle transition between the two movements. The tag-end of
two notes, D flat and E flat, is preserved and used; the rhythmic
superposition of these two notes is gradually transformed into a
new, *horizontal* rhythmic expression.

Ex. 60

The Pavane is followed by a Gigue, a Gavotte, and a three-part Aria. Then comes a retrograde recapitulation of the Prelude, which imparts a remarkable unity to this first scene. The orchestral interlude which connects this scene with the next is a typical illustration of the way in which Berg makes close-knit contrapuntal elaborations out of such pieces. In fact, this interlude is the development section of the Suite. It begins with a canon on the theme of the Pavane, played by the trumpets, horns and trombones, and accompanied by triplets in the harp. Then, after a canon on the theme of the Gavotte (woodwinds, violas, and 'celli), comes a combination of an element of the Gigue with the beginning of the Gavotte—and so it goes throughout. Quite aside from the musical unity achieved in this way, we see how important the recrudescence of counterpoint is to Berg as an acquisition of contemporary polyphony.

The second scene, a Rhapsody, is not an improvisation like most romantic rhapsodies. Here, too, a very firm structure is erected on the basis of purely musical variation. At one point Wozzeck exclaims, "Something is dancing with us there under the earth." These words are accompanied by a motive taken from the *March* of Berg's *Three Orchestral Pieces*, Op. 6. Aside from the fact that this kind of self-quotation belongs to the very essence of dramatic music (a subject to which we shall return at the close of this chapter), it is significant that this motive plays an important part in the rest of the opera, and thus becomes one of the numerous leitmotivs which secure the thematic unity of the work.

The third scene, a March and Lullaby, is connected to the fourth, a Passacaglia, by a new orchestral interlude, which begins by developing certain elements of the preceding scene, and continues as an introduction to what is to come. This introduction is elaborated by means of devices which adumbrate the fundamental principles of the twelve-tone technique. This is but a further proof of the "contemporaneity" of Berg's compositional consciousness, as well as of the absolute necessity of the new technique, the principles of which appear every time that the coherence of the musical speech calls for strong structural devices.

In effect, the development ends with the chord A–D sharp–B–F. The A remains as a pedal-point; over it, the solo viola plays a melody which unfolds the three other tones horizontally (*unification of melody and harmony*). This melody, which is subsequently taken up by the solo clarinet, presents the exact intervals and rhythm (in diminution) of the theme of the Passacaglia (next scene), *which is a twelve-tone row*.

This Passacaglia, perhaps the most complex scene of the entire opera, is rich in interesting devices. The twenty-one variations which follow the exposition of the theme display the most elaborate contrapuntal workmanship. Let us note as well that the seventh variation presents the theme in two-note clusters (in the solo strings), thus giving us a foretaste of one of the most typical twelve-tone procedures. Finally, numerous earlier motives are developed here; others, heard for the first time here, will play a constructive role in what follows.

I should like to quote another example, which shows how a certain coherence of sound-forms, (due to twelve-tone principles) succeeds in underlining the "unity-in-variety" of the various scenes of the drama. We shall concern ourselves with passages taken from the Scherzo (Scene 4) of Act II. The first section of this Scherzo, which consists of three parts—Scherzo 1, Trio 1, Scherzo 2—is, as in certain symphonies of Schumann, repeated after its first exposition. The method of repetition is extremely subtle.

Example 51 (a and b) shows two important figures in the exposition of the Trio. These two figures are alike, for the chords of b are composed of the same notes which appeared in a. The

recapitulation of the Trio—a musical parody of a sermon—appears
in the form of a chorale (c) which merely spreads out the chords
of b.

Ex. 51

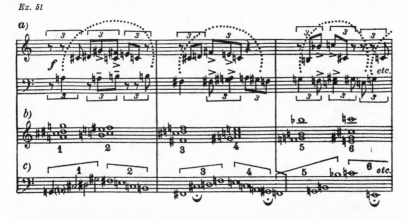

It seems to me that the following examples contain other important elements. The first scene of Act III, *Invention on a theme*,
uses several direct tonal reminiscences. On the one hand, these
are typical of Berg's fundamental spiritual attitude (the sense of
the past) and thus adumbrate the incorporation of tonal functions
into the total resources of chromaticism. On the other hand, the
tonal reminiscences constitute those "foreign" elements which,
like the self-quotation, permit the operatic form to develop its
complete meaning; from this viewpoint, the fifth variation of the
scene in question, written explicitly in F minor, is very revealing.
Dramatically, this variation represents the reading of a fairy-
story; musically, the tonality of this variation is borrowed from
a world of the past, a fairy world. The other tonal element of
this scene is found in the connection between the antecedent and
the consequent of the theme. These two sections are harmonized
with two triads (in the relationship of tonic-Neapolitan sixth)
which are superimposed. This superposition closes the scene; while
the chord dies out, the basses play softly, almost inaudibly, a
low B, which appears as a tone foreign to the chord—and which
is the principal constituent of the following scene, *Invention on a*

tone. In this scene, which brings back many of the preceding motives, the B appears in all possible or imaginable forms—as a pedal-point in the bass, as an upper voice, as a middle voice, in octaves throughout the orchestra, in every position, in every sonority.

Finally, an orchestral interlude brings the B to a unison in the middle register, where it can be played by nearly all the instruments of the orchestra.

Ex. 52

The *crescendo* which rises from the *pianissimo* entrance of the stopped horn to the *fortissimo* of the whole orchestra (without percussion) has proved to be a literally hair-raising "effect" at every performance. Our example shows that the successive entrances do not occur arbitrarily, but according to a precise rhythmic pattern (*rhythmic canon between strings and winds*) [7] which will play an important part in the following scene, *Invention on a rhythm.*

Finally, I should like to mention a previously indicated detail of the orchestral interlude (*Invention on a key*) between Scenes 4 and 5. Musically, like the funeral music in *Götterdämmerung*, this interlude develops all the important themes associated with the principal character.[8] The key of D minor, every resource of which is exploited here, is abandoned in the middle of the piece; this permits a progressive condensation of the total resources of chromaticism which culminates in the following chord, containing all the tones of the chromatic scale:

[7] Note that this canon gives rise to a staggered rhythm which is one of Schoenberg's characteristic devices. We shall see how far Webern carries such procedures.

[8] The beginning of this passage is part of the symphony which Berg undertook in 1913 and which he abandoned for his *Three Orchestral Pieces*, Op. 6. (Cf. Chapter VII, note 8, § 37). The incorporation of this passage into *Wozzeck*—a genuine dramatic gesture—was suggested to Berg by his wife.

Ex. 53

This chord, treated as a dominant, brings back the key of D minor.

All these examples—which could have been infinitely multi-plied—furnish, I think, valid proofs of the hypotheses which we stated at the beginning of this section. The reader has already seen how such musical devices create the very essence of opera. The following discussion will present further support for this view.

42. *Lulu.*—Berg's second opera, the libretto of which combines Wedekind's two tragedies *Erdgeist* and *Die Büchse der Pandora*, is even more sharply characterized by those dramatic and musical qualities already found in *Wozzeck*. However, the two works are really quite different. In the first, the closed forms of the various scenes, clearly defined in content and character, lent themselves to a musical structure which preserved this "fragmentation" and incarnated it in forms borrowed from instrumental music. Here, on the other hand, the drama calls for a strict working-out of the destiny of each character. Hence, the principal element of the musical structure becomes the human voice, which, on the one hand, unfolds in typical vocal forms (arias, recitatives, ensembles) and, on the other hand, undergoes even more varied treatment than in *Wozzeck*. Thus, Berg makes fuller use of the possibilities of dramatic music. In fact, the constant alternation of all possible and imaginable modes of singing is the essential characteristic of *Lulu*. The coloratura style of Lulu's part symbolizes that unreal and dreamlike sphere in which the strange heroine of this drama moves. It is very significant that Berg assigns the roles of the male characters in the third act—those who will be responsible for Lulu's death—to the same singers who, in the first two acts, took the parts of the men for whose death Lulu was responsible. Thus musico-dramatic unity is obtained by means of vocal unity.

The orchestra, too—smaller and simpler than that of *Wozzeck* —clearly serves to maintain a *unity of sonority*. Certain personages of the drama are partially characterized by an instrumental tone-color which persists throughout the work; changes in dynamic and orchestral character completely differentiate passages of similar thematic material; the distinction between the accompanying functions and the dominating functions is more sharply drawn here than in *Wozzeck*; the principal law appears to be the direct and plastic expression of the vocal parts, which Berg underlines with an orchestration of exemplary transparency.

While in *Wozzeck* the musical forms were determined by the dramatic character of the various scenes, in *Lulu* they are used to develop the *total appearance* (as Berg used to say) of the various characters, and hence are built on a larger scale. For example, one character may be designated throughout by the sonata form, another by the rondo form, or by the pentatonic scale.

The thematic unity of the work is brought about by the twelve-tone row which determines all the musical "events" of the opera. The original tone-row gives rise to the themes associated with the principal character. Other figures derived from this row are subordinated to other characters or to specific dramatic moments. Thus Berg succeeds in developing the entire structure of his opera from a single musical form, just as the entire dramatic structure is derived from the central character.

Finally, the structure of *Lulu* emphasizes the synthesis, already found in *Wozzeck*, of the "symphonic" tendency and the "fragmentary" tendency of the music-drama. In fact, while the different acts are clearly subdivided into different scenes, which consist, in their turn, of many separate pieces, the fusion of all these elements into a living whole takes place here with unusual force, thanks to the various abovementioned procedures. Some of these procedures have to do with those fundamental problems of dramatic music raised in the last operas of Monteverdi— problems which had apparently ceased to concern subsequent opera composers. For example, if we compare Monteverdi's attitude towards the functional and dramatic role of orchestral tone-color with that of Berg, we immediately see the relationship (in spite of the three centuries which separate them) between two of the greatest music-dramatists of all time.

As in the case of *Wozzeck,* we must verify such general assertions by means of specific examples. This time, it is less important to point out all the connections between one scene and the next, since, as we just said, the thematic unity of the work is assured by the twelve-tone row and its various derived forms.

In examining this more closely, we shall comprehend not only the "musical penetration" of the dramatic structure, but also certain special aspects of the new technique, which stress once more Berg's effort to link the musical present with the musical past.

Example 54a reproduces the original tone-row. Example 54b shows a typical fragmentation of this row.[9]

This fragmentation makes possible the following form,

from which is derived one of Lulu's most important themes:

One of the most important characteristics of chromaticism is that its simplest organization is the chromatic scale—a "row" based on a single interval, the half-tone. Two other "rows," though based on other intervals, resemble the chromatic scale in that they use the same interval throughout. These are the circle of fifths and the circle of fourths. Their structure is different from that

---

[9] Cf. *Introduction to Twelve-Tone Music.*

of the chromatic scale, but their essence is the same. These two rows may be deduced from the chromatic scale very simply. Let us examine the ascending chromatic scale. If we take the first note, say C, and count up seven half-tones, we find G; again counting up seven (going to B and then starting over again from the beginning) we find D; repeating the process, we find A, and so on. The same process may be used to deduce the circle of fourths, if the number *seven* is replaced by *five*.

Berg applies these two procedures to the original row of *Lulu*. The first procedure gives rise to a row

Ex. 56

which engenders the following "minor-like" theme characteristic of Alwa's elegiac character:

The second procedure gives rise to a row

Ex. 57

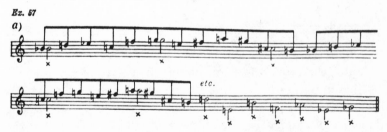

the fifth of which (G–D), superimposed on five-tone groups, creates that pentatonic quality typical of Countess Geschwitz' exotic character.

b)

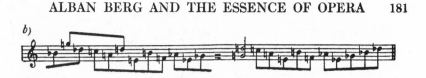

Another simple procedure enables Berg to deduce a row

Ex. 58

a)

which gives rise to the following theme, the "major-like" character of which fits the virile nature of Dr. Schoen, to whom it belongs:

b) Allegro energico (♩ = 80)

The general character of the dramatic action is designated by the motive in fourths (cf. Ex. 40a in the previous chapter), deduced from the original row as follows:

Ex. 59

a)

The work begins with a triple exposition of this motive, which, in its transpositions, sounds every tone of the chromatic scale.

b) ♩ = 80

It is to be noted that the original row is not used thematically until Lulu's aria in the second act—that is, at the culmination of the drama:

Ex. 60

Wenn sich die Men.schen um mei.net.wil.len umgebracht haben

All these examples perfectly illustrate the various characteristics of Berg's style, which are now sufficiently familiar to require no further discussion.

We must again stress that the strictest conception of musical structure governs each scene of the drama. Because of the development of the *whole character* of each personage, the various scenes are less distinctly separated than in *Wozzeck*; likewise, instrumental forms play a lesser role here. Nonetheless, each scene is a perfectly self-sufficient whole, but the interlocking of these scenes bespeaks the Schoenbergian spirit of *Durchkomponieren* and accentuates the synthesis of the two tendencies of opera.

In addition, the functional use of instrumental tone-color to characterize certain personages (Schichgold—chamber-music sonorities, the Athlete—chords on the piano, etc.) represents, as we know, a profound reactivation of certain essential laws of dramatic music.

Given the era in which Berg lived—an era in which opera had degenerated to the point where it deserved nothing better than Schoenberg's ironic description—it is not his least merit to have returned to the very sources of operatic tradition and to have reactivated, with amazing and convincing force, the true meaning of this tradition.

It is to the remarkable efforts of an exceptional musical mind that we owe these two exceptional masterpieces, the operas of Alban Berg.

43. *The essence of Opera.*—If there is any truth in Goethe's affirmation that a thing perfect in its own *genre* always surpasses the limits of that *genre*, it is in the realm of the opera that such a

truth is most striking. No other musical form is so difficult to realize, for its principal rule appears to be the absence of all rules. That is why the operatic form always runs the risk of total failure; the further it progresses towards consummation and perfection, the more urgently it requires its own destruction. Dramatic music does not, as has often been supposed, reproduce scenic action in order to elevate it to a symbolic plane; music penetrates action in order to absorb it completely. Just as the music of Orpheus wakes the dead and frees them from Hell's prison, even so operatic music, soaring above the characters, tears them away from their dramatic destiny and *rebuilds* them in tones. Thus, the dialectic structure of the action in *Der Freischütz* appears only in the musical analysis; Max's destiny is not revealed till the end of the second tableau, at the beginning of the recitative, where the melody adumbrated by the clarinets in the overture accompanies the words, "Ah! darkly yawns the dread ravine!"

So every opera is *Orpheus,* and it is no accident that this very subject furnished the earliest libretti. But, because it is Orpheus, the opera must surpass itself, must transcend itself; in constituting its musical expression, it must know where to place the cesura which creates form and at the same time destroys it. It is not, then, merely a matter of romantic irony that Mozart's *Don Giovanni* stops to recall *Figaro,* or that Hans Sachs reminds Eva of the fate of the characters in *Tristan und Isolde* to the strains of its opening. Such self-quotation belongs to the very essence of dramatic music.[10] Perhaps this is why Bach, Brahms, and Webern never tried their hand at opera. Their immanent sense of form would never have let them write those two measures *too many* without which no opera is complete.

Alban Berg, the conscious architect of dramatic music, also

[10] My friend Henri Kahnweiller has called my attention to a similar case in *Feuersnot,* Richard Strauss's second opera, composed to a libretto of Ernst von Wolzogen. The hero, who has deprived the inhabitants of Munich of light and fire on St. John's Eve, tells them that he is punishing them for having driven away a great magician. To tell us who this magician was, the last verse of this passage is sung to the motive of Siegfried, while the motive of Valhalla appears in the orchestra. The text confirms these reminiscences: "Da triebt ihr den Wagner [daring one] zum Tore hinaus"; and the librettist joins his name to that of the composer: "Der stellt sich immer wieder zum *Strauss* [combat]. *Wohl zogen* manche. . . ."

proved to be more than that. We have already seen how some of his non-dramatic works betray his operatic mission. The *glissando* in the fourth song of Op. 2, the ascending passage in all four instruments in the last measure of Op. 3—these are operatic gestures, transcending song and string quartet. And is not the use of the postcard texts for Op. 4 a dramatic gesture, born of the necessity to destroy form that it may be saved? When the *Chamber Concerto* is developed from the musical letters in names dear to Berg, when the *Lyric Suite*—that accompaniment to an invisible opera—quotes, at its climax, from a work of the composer to whom it is dedicated—these peculiarities show our composer striving ceaselessly to transcend form in the direction of drama.

It is from this viewpoint that we should consider Berg's incorporation of instrumental forms, products of another realm of polyphonic activity, into the realm of opera. This process is doubly significant because

1) It is another example of that destruction of formal equilibrium which we have stressed so often; this destruction takes place here in exactly the opposite way from that which we noted in the instrumental works.

2) Berg proceeds to a kind of synthesis of all past acquisitions of polyphony. The opera, that vocal form *par excellence,* the only one which has succeeded in maintaining the awareness of the necessity for song in all its forms ever since the amazing rise of instrumental music, and which, in our own day, is almost the only possible domain in which the art of song may and must flourish—the opera, then, becomes the ideal meeting-place of all polyphonic acquisitions, whatever their original source.

Certain typical features of *Wozzeck* and *Lulu* may also be considered as genuine dramatic gestures. The self-quotation in *Wozzeck* (the motive from the *Three Orchestral Pieces,* as previously stated) finds its counterpart in *Lulu.* After the dialogue between Lulu and Alwa the latter, soliloquizing, sings, "You could write an interesting opera about that one!"; he is accompanied by the strains of the beginning of *Wozzeck.* Also, when in Act II, Scene 3 of *Wozzeck* (the *Largo,* central point of the entire work)

Berg uses a chamber orchestra identical with that used in Schoenberg's *Kammersymphonie* (a supreme homage to his master!), such a gesture, like all the others, is imbued with that spirit of drama the presence of which we have tried to reveal.

Finally, it is from the same viewpoint that we should consider Berg's use of dance music and movie music in *Lulu*.[11] Too clearheaded to exaggerate to himself the importance of such innovations, he was merely following his sure dramatic instinct. Once the importance of such gestures is admitted, we may say that the spectacle of opera is entirely made up of all kinds of gestures. It is these—from the most varied purely musical gestures of the composer to the sublime or ridiculous gestures of the *primadonna*— that give us dramatic music at its most grandiose and at its most perishable. That is what the author of *Wozzeck* and *Lulu* understood better than any one else. With gestures such as that enigmatic repetition of the crescendo on B after the murder scene in *Wozzeck*, or that citation of the beginning of *Wozzeck* in *Lulu*, Alban Berg tears his creatures away from the Land of the Shades— their own images—and guides them, having re-created them by virtue of musical forms, through that narrow gate which leads *beyond* these forms.

44. *Homage to Berg*.—In these two chapters, we have tried to give as complete a picture as possible of the principal aspects of Berg's work. We have also tried to give this work its proper place in the evolution of polyphony (in general) and in the Schoenbergian universe (in particular). Perhaps we have succeeded in describing one of the most important aspects of the contemporary phase of musical speech. I think that some of the important elements in Berg throw a strong light on certain peculiarities of

[11] The dance music is played by a little orchestra on the stage (as in *Don Giovanni*); Berg used this same device in the tavern scene of *Wozzeck*. This kind of expansion of the stage-spectacle is another aspect of that "destruction of form" proper to dramatic music. The movie episode occurs in the middle of the second act, and serves to connect the two halves of the libretto, Wedekind's two tragedies. Dramatically, the film shows us Lulu's life from her arrest to her escape from prison; it shows her essential transformation, which causes her to lead a completely different life after her escape from prison. Musically, this entire passage is accompanied by an orchestral interlude which may be considered the central development section of the work.

Schoenberg's language which were not, perhaps, so obvious in our analyses of Schoenberg's own works. It is in the same spirit that we shall approach the work of Webern, from which we shall try to extract certain principles that are implicit, but not always explicit, in the music of the founder of our school. Schoenberg seems to have been well aware of this state of affairs. Therefore, far from taking umbrage at the success of his disciples (as is sometimes the case), he never missed an opportunity to speak up for them.

Thus, on the occasion of the first Düsseldorf performance of *Wozzeck*, the program contained the following tribute, written by Schoenberg, in which I wholeheartedly join:

It is with joy that I take advantage of the occasion to confer recognition upon the work and activity of my pupil and friend Alban Berg. It is he and our mutual friend, his colleague Anton Webern, who most powerfully affirm my influence as a teacher; at the time when I suffered from the cruelest artistic oppression, they supported me so firmly, so reliably, so affectionately, that nothing in this world could be finer.

But if anyone would like to believe that it is only gratitude and friendship which induce me to express my admiration, let him not forget that I can read music; that, in notes which seemed like hieroglyphs to all the other musicians at that time, I could see what had been thought and I could form an idea of the talent which was revealed. I am proud because my certainty that this impression was accurate made it possible for me to guide a richly gifted nature in the way that it should go; to help him to the most marvelous unfoldment of his originality and to the greatest independence. But *he* brought the indispensable treasure of character to the first hour he ever spent with me; and he will keep it to the last hour of his life.

I should like to say: Friendship above all.

Yet I must say: Art above all.

But here, too, I need not hesitate; here the demands of friendship and art are united; here the friend can praise the artist and the artist can praise the friend; in fact, both must do so if they want to be fair.

And I want to be fair. So hail to thee, Alban Berg!

PART IV

ANTON WEBERN

The Awareness of the Future in Contemporary Music

No work destined to become
classic may resemble the classic works which preceded it.
JUAN GRIS

CHAPTER IX

Webern's Participation in the Schoenbergian Acquisitions

45. *The instruction of Schoenberg.*— (A) . *Awareness of the "fundamental compositional problem" and of counterpoint.*—Anton Webern was born in Vienna, December 3, 1883. His musical talent displayed itself early. At the time when he began his first serious work as a composer, he also started his musicological studies with Guido Adler at the Vienna Conservatory, and eventually completed his doctorate in musicology. Adler entrusted him with the editing of the Heinrich Isaac volume of the *Denkmäler der Tonkunst in Oesterreich.*

The most important event of his youth (as with Alban Berg at the same time) was his meeting with Schoenberg, which took place in 1904. Webern's period of apprenticeship lasted, like that of Berg, from 1904 to 1910.[1] As we know, it was precisely during these years that there took place those profound changes in music to which Schoenberg contributed more than anyone else. The close contact of Berg and Webern with their master caused them, too, to participate directly in these musical happenings. We have already had occasion to become convinced of this in the case of Berg. What, then, of Webern?

Webern's first published work, the *Passacaglia* for orchestra, Op. 1, already shows us how the composer immediately takes his

---

[1] It goes without saying that it is difficult to fix this period definitely, since both Berg and Webern later published mature and finished works which date from 1907–08. One can only say that everything they wrote until 1910 was entirely supervised by Schoenberg, whereas after 1910 they worked independently. It is true that, even much later, most of their works owe a great deal to the numerous meetings and discussions with Schoenberg (I am thinking especially of the direct part taken by Schoenberg in the composition of Berg's *Wozzeck*) .

place in a tradition to which he will always belong. Furthermore, the *Passacaglia* contains certain typical elements which foreshadow Webern's later works.

Like Berg's *Sonata*, Op. 1, which is a product of the same year (1908), this work seems to be an attempt to solve a special problem of musical composition in the most perfect way possible. The already familiar conditions of this problem (suggested by the strict instructions of Schoenberg) may be stated as follows: to derive an abundance of thematic forms from the least possible musical material in the smallest possible space, while at the same time holding all these forms to a strict unity, so that in spite of the brevity and condensation of the work the variety and wealth of thematic forms will not create confusion.

The same problem confronts us in Berg's *Sonata;* this is natural, for not only are both musicians composing in 1908 under the strict supervision of their master, they are also being profoundly influenced by his *Kammersymphonie* and Second Quartet, works which are very characteristic in their treatment of the important problem stated above. However, in their earliest works we may already feel the profound inherent contrast between the temperament of Berg and that of Webern—especially in the way in which each of them approaches this problem.

Step by step, Berg and Webern follow the evolution of their master; as soon as he penetrates into a new realm the two disciples follow him there immediately. But, while the genius of Berg always strove to establish a connection between the discoveries of Schoenberg and the past—thus profiting by the "retroactive" elements in Schoenberg's work—the genius of Webern is concerned with the *possibilities for the future* inherent in this work, and thus succeeds in *projecting* its particularly novel and radical elements. Although this contrast between the two musicians is not very noticeable in their earliest works, certain of its features may already be seen.

It is interesting to see how each of our two composers attacks the problem stated above. For Berg, the solution lies in the use of the *sonata form* (the classical form *par excellence*) which he submits to a rigorous discipline and to which he applies the special technique of developing *melodic fragments,* which assures the connection between the various constituent parts of the work. In spite of some passages of rather complex contrapuntal writing, the chief emphasis is placed on the harmonic structure of the work. Aside from the fact that Berg makes several more or less exact quotations from Schoenberg's *Kammersymphonie,* it is especially in the domain of harmony that he shows the influence of his master. This is clearly to be seen in the harmonic conception of the *Sonata* (which, as we will recall, is constantly under the control of tonal degrees), especially in the passages dominated by whole-tone chords and fourth-chords. Let us also remember that these combinations were *invented* by Schoenberg, while Berg introduces them logically and prudently by gradually altering other chords of known classifications. This was the first example of Berg's constant desire to connect his master's discoveries with the past.

The case of the *Passacaglia* is visibly different. The choice of this form already shows the desire not to be tied down to a stereotyped formal pattern, since the passacaglia is less a formal scheme than an architectural possibility. Furthermore, it is evident that, in choosing this form, Webern is *primarily preoccupied with counterpoint.* In this connection, we must recall that strict contrapuntal style was restored to dignity by Schoenberg after it had virtually disappeared for nearly a whole century. At this period, it represented one of the most daring and "advanced" elements of Schoenberg's style; it was Webern's mission to take possession of it, and he was to remain preoccupied by this problem throughout his career. Therefore, it is now possible for us to say that one of the major goals of Webern's work is an ideal of pure counterpoint carried to the limits of possibility.

Besides, the *Passacaglia,* although (like Berg's *Sonata*) its general tone resembles that of the *Kammersymphonie,* carefully avoids any too-obvious reminiscences.

The analysis of Example 61, which reproduces the beginning of the work (the theme and first variation) already reveals typically Webernian qualities: predominant dynamic level of ppp, discreet presentation (interrupted by rests) of the theme, subtle orchestration (the combination of flute and muted trumpet is constantly used by Webern). On the other hand, this passage also shows qualities derived from Schoenberg, which Webern transforms according to his own needs.

Ex. 61

a) Moderato ($\text{♩} = 42$)

Let us analyze the theme (measures 1–8). Its extreme precision is due to the following characteristics: 1) none of its notes (except the tonic) is repeated; 2) neither its highest tone nor its lowest tone is repeated, so that these two "extremes" appear with special force; 3) the juxtaposition of the three motives of the theme (1, 2, 3) is extremely economical and perfectly clear. In fact, motive 2 is a strict retrograde inversion of motive 1 (Ex. 61b).

b)

These two motives bear the mutual relation of *antecedent-consequent*; this group is followed by a coda, motive 3, based on V–I, which is prepared by the preceding leap of a fourth (NB).

Though all these qualities are largely due to Schoenberg's strict instruction, it is nonetheless true that Webern's personality is clearly revealed in the choice of thematic intervals. The juxtaposition of minor seconds and minor thirds is one of Schoenberg's typical means of breaking the bonds of tonality. Therefore, it is quite logical that Webern should have cherished, all through his career, a particular predilection for these intervals.[2]

Let us analyze the first variation. In addition to the theme, we find its harmonization and its first countersubject. In spite of the small number of chords, the harmony displays many tonal functions, all organized with typically Schoenbergian efficiency. The functions are as follows: First chord, II_{6}^{5}, typical of the cadence in minor. Second chord, III^6 in its augmented form; the fact that this chord is used in its first inversion, so that its bass is the dominant of the key, gives the progression of the first two chords a cadential feeling which clearly expresses the tonality of D minor. The third chord could be a kind of Neapolitan sixth; it is not used here according to the stereotyped formula of that harmony, however, for it has a minor third and it is not followed by the usual cadence. Its real function is to introduce the subdominant minor region, of which (like the Neapolitan sixth) it is the sixth degree. To this same region belong the fourth and fifth chords, which are, respectively, III (augmented) of F minor and I^6 of B flat minor (subdominant region of F minor, submediant region of D minor). The sixth chord is the celebrated "Tristan chord" transposed to D minor. It is what Schoenberg calls a "roving" harmony; its function here, just as in *Tristan,* is to introduce

---

[2] It is remarkable that the first six notes of the theme of the *Passacaglia* could be the beginning of a twelve-tone row like one of those which Webern chose in his later works (the one in the *Variations for Orchestra,* Op. 30, is built on these very intervals). Let us also note that these same intervals compose one of the principal figures of Berg's Quartet, Op. 4.

the dominant.[3] Finally, the seventh and eighth chords are V and I.[4]

All this is produced, we must reiterate, by the strict discipline of Schoenberg; however, let us note one special quality contained only implicitly in Schoenberg's teachings, a quality the radical nature of which was bound to appeal to Webern, and which gives his harmony strength and originality. It may be stated that no chord is repeated here, so that every note in the melody is harmonized with its very own chord—the height of musical economy!

Let us analyze the countersubject. It is built on a single initial cell, x, the descending minor third; its sequel, x', enlarges this interval into a major third. There follows a variant, y, which introduces a passing tone, thus causing a rhythmic change as well; here, the first and last tones build a minor third. Then comes x' (again the major third), then y (minor third) and a new rhythmic variant of y, y', in which the first and last tones build a major third. Next there is an exact sequence of y'; the occurrence of such a sequence for the first time constitutes a new element. Finally, the countersubject ends on y transposed, thus reintroducing the minor third at the close.

It seems unnecessary to continue here with the analysis of Webern's Op. 1, since the whole work is based exclusively on principles analogous to those which have just been revealed. But I must repeat that the brief passage which we have just analyzed contains, in embryonic form, Webern's essential qualities, which he will continue to affirm throughout his evolution, and which will be increasingly purified. Coming from the pure tradition of composition incarnated in his master, Webern takes up its most radical, forward-looking elements. It is this ideal of strictness, economy,

---

[3] Schoenberg is not much concerned with the explanation of this chord, since its "roving" character justifies it completely. However, as Schoenberg says, it may be considered as II of A flat minor, which is related to D minor through many simple chords. Thus, VI of A flat minor is identical with II (as an artificial dominant) of D minor; the Neapolitan sixth of D minor is V of A flat minor, and the Neapolitan sixth of A flat minor is V of D minor.

[4] It must also be noted that the harmony uses nothing but strong steps. The root-progressions are as follows: ascending second, descending second, ascending fourth, ascending second (no change of root between the fifth and sixth chords), descending second, and ascending fourth. Cf. Schoenberg, *Theory of Harmony.*

and absolute purity which will eventually produce a novel and original language.

Webern's contrapuntal preoccupations are even more profound in his next work, the *a cappella* chorus *Entflieht auf leichten Kähnen*. This piece is built entirely on canonic principles. It begins with a strict canon in two real voices, each of which is doubled in thirds or sixths. The middle section of the work, dominated by a sextolet motive, is a canon in four real voices. The recapitulation of the first section is at first literal, but soon varied. Except in the last two measures, the two-voice canon is strictly carried out. This recapitulation is also characterized by the use of the lowest note and the highest note in the whole piece; neither of these "extremes" is repeated.[5]

46. *The instruction of Schoenberg.—* (B) . *The tendency to suppress repetition.—*Up until now, in spite of its great purity, Webern's work had clung to the principle of repetition. This may be seen in many details of the *Passacaglia* and in Op. 2, where the beginning of the recapitulation uses *unvaried* elements of the exposition. However, Webern gradually escapes from this ruling principle in the course of his next works. The songs with piano accompaniment, Op. 3 and Op. 4 (in which Webern definitely breaks the bonds of tonality) prove characteristic in this respect.[6]

[5] These notes are the high A of the sopranos (m. 23) and the low F sharp of the basses in the penultimate measure.

[6] Thus we see that Webern, like Berg, participates in the evolution of the Schoenbergian language. In fact, the suspension of the tonal system takes place almost simultaneously in Berg and Webern. There is another curious similarity, too. It is in Op. 2 (songs) that the suspension takes place in Berg; it is followed by a string quartet. It is in Op. 3 and 4 (songs) that the same process occurs in Webern; his next work, Op. 5, is for string quartet.

The *Five Movements* for string quartet, Op. 5, are even more characteristic. Repetition appears only in the form of certain juxtapositions of two similar motives (as in Ex. 62a NB); otherwise, everything becomes variation.

Let us observe the contrapuntal elaboration which is immediately lavished on the first theme. First exposed by the first violin, it is taken up and finished by the second violin, which transforms it rhythmically by shifting the accents, while the first violin plays a counterpoint derived from the theme. This typically Schoenbergian shifting of accents is later carried to extremes by Webern.

The three appearances of the second theme in this piece clearly show us how Webern has virtually made variation into an exact science. This second theme is first exposed by the 'cello in its low register. The accompaniment is furnished by a *tremolo* in the viola. (Ex. 62b):

In the course of the development, the theme is given to the viola, in the middle register of the quartet. The major thirds previously used in the accompaniment are now transformed into broken minor sixths ('cello *pizzicato*). A little later, the second violin, also *pizzicato,* is added to this accompaniment pattern. A new element is the pedal-point on E in the first violin. (Ex. 62c.)

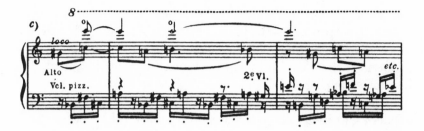

The last appearance of this idea is in the high register of the first violin. Thus all four instruments participate in the elaboration of the whole. (Ex. 62d.)

The four other movements of Op. 5 clearly indicate the same intention to avoid every literal repetition. Furthermore, the second and fourth movements display that tendency to extreme brevity which will soon be one of the essential characteristics of the art of Webern.

47. *Webern's first independent works. Culmination of the minia-ture form and the "Klangfarbenmelodie."*—The next two works, six pieces for large orchestra, Op. 6 (dedicated to Schoenberg) and four pieces for violin and piano, Op. 7, are even more de-pendent upon the devices which we have just been observing. The dimensions become smaller and smaller. This peculiarity demands further attention. It goes without saying that its source is Schoen-berg's *Sechs kleine Klavierstücke,* Op. 19, the first musical work to dispense with all repetitions and sequences. Furthermore, it is evident that such purity could be attained only in pieces of re-duced dimensions, since, at least in the period which concerns us, large forms cannot do without repetition as a means of articula-

tion.[7] Besides, the most radical element in Schoenberg's method of composition is this very desire for continually renewed invention, which, implicit in all the great masters of the past, becomes explicit in Schoenberg's technique of perpetual variation. Again, it is not surprising that this aspect of his master's instruction, more than any other, should have captured the imagination of Webern. Webern's need to express himself in short fragments thus becomes comprehensible.

In this connection, let us again recall the differences between Webern and Berg. The latter was also influenced by Schoenberg's Op. 19, as witness his four pieces for clarinet and piano, Op. 5. In this work Berg is preoccupied with avoiding repetitions and sequences; nevertheless, these clarinet pieces are, in essence, *reductions* of the large classical forms. Surely one of the reasons for Schoenberg's use of short forms during this period is his reaction against the style of "heavenly length" abused by post-romantic composers. Berg is especially drawn to this aspect of the problem, and so finds still another way of bridging the gap between the language of the past and that of his master. When we hear Berg's pieces, we are struck by the fact that each of them lasts but a moment (though this moment is longer than in the corresponding pieces of Schoenberg or Webern). On the other hand, according to the previously-quoted words of Schoenberg, Webern expresses "a whole novel in a single sigh"; [8] in other words, his shortest pieces, instead of reducing large forms, contain them *in petto*.

"*Non multa sed multum*—how I hope that is true of what I offer you here." It is in these terms that Webern dedicates his *Six Bagatelles*, Op. 9, for string quartet, to his friend and colleague Alban Berg. These pieces, as well as the *Five Orchestral Pieces*, Op. 10, and the three small pieces for 'cello and piano, Op. 11 (1913–1914) certainly deserve the above Latin quotation. They doubtless represent the most radical effort ever made in the direction which we have just discussed. The brevity of these pieces seems to defy the very idea of time; the longest rarely last more than a minute, the shortest only a few seconds. One can no longer

---

[7] Cf. Chapter I, *Introduction to Twelve-Tone Music.*
[8] Cf. Preface to Webern's *Bagatelles,* Op. 9.

speak of *themes* in this music; the very motives become shorter
and shorter, until a single tone takes over the duties of a motive.
What purity of invention, what economy, what skill of variation
is revealed in these amazing scores! In addition, they show a new
preoccupation, still another side of Webern's genius.

In the final pages of his *Theory of Harmony*, Schoenberg,
after having recalled that a tone is generally conceded to have
three properties, pitch, color (or timbre) and intensity, remarks
how little attention has been given, up till now, to the second of
these properties. Some very judicious observations lead him to believe that some day melodies will be composed which are not
measured by varying pitch-levels alone, but also (even principally) by varying timbres; they will be "tone-color melodies," or,
to use Schoenberg's German term, *Klangfarbenmelodien.*

Such a projection into the future could not fail to stimulate
Webern's imagination; in fact, the idea of the *Klangfarbenmelodie*
obsessed him throughout his career. It appears with the works
which now concern us. That is why I choose, as an example, the
first piece of Op. 10 (reproduced in its entirety in Example 63);
for, although it is perhaps not the most characteristic of the group
with respect to the abovementioned motivic brevity, it certainly
reveals intense concern with the *Klangfarbenmelodie.*

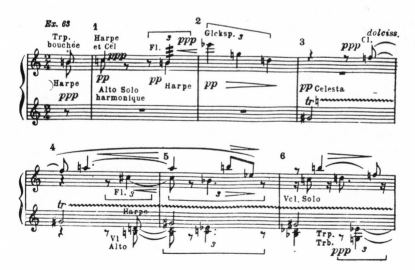

On a first hearing, this piece (like others of the same period in Webern's creation) is utterly bewildering; it does not seem to possess the slightest coherence. However, our analysis will try to show that quite the contrary is true.

The first measure and its upbeat constitute the introduction. The mood, as one might expect, is vague and uncertain. The two notes B and C produce a melody which owes less to the variations in pitch than to the variations in timbre; the changes of instrumentation are subtle and exact. The C is slightly more intense than the B; while the B was played by two instruments, the C is played by three instruments, and the ppp is intensified by the pp of the viola. On the other hand, the tone-color is slightly less intense, since the warm timbre of the muted trumpet is replaced by the cold timbre of the celesta and the viola harmonic. The repetition of the B is less intense than its first appearance both as to instrumental dynamics (the flute replaces the trumpet,[9] which is recalled by the pp of the harp and the crescendo of the flute) and as to tone-color.

The definite motive of the second measure constitutes a transition to the principal section of the piece. In this section, every-

[9] Let us remember Webern's predilection for the combination of flute and muted trumpet.

thing must be clear and plastic; therefore, the *Klangfarbenmelodie* will be excluded on account of its vague atmosphere.

This principal section, measures 6–8, is built on the trill in the celesta, which is derived from the intervals of the introduction. It is subdivided into two distinct phrases. The first of these, measures 3–6, presents an expressive melody of the clarinet, which begins with a major third, varies it by inverting it (minor sixth) and ends (measure 6) with a sort of echo of this last motive, which augments the rhythmic pattern and diminishes the interval. To this is added a counterpoint, composed of two motives of two notes each; the first, a minor third, is played by the flute, the second, a major second, by the 'cello. We also hear thirds in the violin and viola, "punctuated" by the harp.

The second phrase, mm. 7–8, is an answer to the first phrase, or a development of it; its structure is analogous to that of the first, but extremely varied.

The unity between the two phrases is assured by the continuing trill in the celesta, and also by the 'cello, which, after having played the second motive of the counterpoint of the first phrase, continues with the counterpoint of the second phrase. Furthermore, this second counterpoint, in spite of its deviations from the first, is really its *exact retrograde*.

On the other hand, the contrast between the two phrases is obtained by means of the principal melody which passes from the clarinet to the violin.[10] The violin, taking it up, enlarges the minor sixth of the clarinet, and, continuing to vary it, introduces the interval of a major seventh; then the major third (already heard in the clarinet) reappears, and finally we have the major seventh in contrary motion.

Unity and contrast are once more embodied in the low register. Before the first phrase is ended, the thirds in the strings and harp pass to the brasses, which first change to a sixth (thus creating a cesura) and continue in tenths. The trill in the celesta dies out, but before that the flute takes one of its notes, goes a major third

[10] This is the culminating point of the piece, achieved in the orchestration (more sonorous here than elsewhere) and especially in the registration, which, in the widest range of the piece, includes its highest note (B flat in the violin) and its lowest note (F in the trombone).

down (in contrary motion to the violin), reduces that to a second, and finally ends with the ascending major seventh (in contrary motion to the violin). The high G of the violin in measure 9 echoes the second part of the phrase (a pendant to the echo in measure 6) and acts as a transition to the coda.

This transition occurs primarily through a reminiscence (retrograde) of the trill and of the introduction—the tones A and G sharp of measures 9 and 10.

Once again the *Klangfarbenmelodie* plays an important part here. The orchestration of the A corresponds to that of the first B in the introduction; the rhythm is varied. The orchestration of the G sharp corresponds to that of the C of the introduction, minus the harp—the intense harmonic of the 'cello replaces the weaker one of the viola; the note is lengthened, too.

The dying out of the high G in the violin marks the final phase of the transition. The motive heard in the harp is an amplified counterpart of that played by the glockenspiel in measure 2. Note that these two corresponding motives begin and end with the same notes, but in reverse order.

The coda—an abridged counterpart of the introduction just as the second echo was an abridged counterpart of the first—presents a *Klangfarbenmelodie* on the F, which grows in intensity as it passes from the flute to the trumpet (it is interesting to note the juxtaposition of these two instruments, which were separated in the introduction but already imparted a special meaning to the two B's), and which finally dies out in the ppp of the celesta.

We must repeat that the first hearing of this music will plunge the unwary listener into complete confusion, from which only long familiarity can rescue him. The precise details of our analysis may not do away with the difficulties of a first hearing, but they ought to convince the reader that this musical speech is entirely coherent.

48. *The influence of Pierrot Lunaire. Instrumental and contrapuntal problems. First need for the tone-row; adoption of the twelve-tone technique.*—Other major preoccupations appeared in

Webern's creative activity at this time. They are expressed in his numerous vocal works, with accompaniments for various instruments, written between 1912 and 1925. Aside from the four songs with piano accompaniment, Op. 12 (1915–17), written with an economy of means analogous to that of the miniatures of 1913–14, all the other cycles are accompanied by very diverse instrumental combinations.

The two songs of Op. 8 (1913) are accompanied by clarinet (alternating with bass clarinet), horn, trumpet, celesta, harp, violin, viola, and 'cello. The four songs of Op. 13 (1918) call for a thirteen-piece orchestra.

Here is seen the influence of Schoenberg's *Pierrot Lunaire* and *Vier Orchesterlieder*, Op. 22—works in which radical combinations of the human voice with specific instrumental groups tremendously enlarged the field of vocal possibilities. In the two sets of songs which we have just mentioned, Webern seizes on these possibilities and uses them to embody his ideal of the *Klangfarbenmelodie*. However, in the following groups of songs, contrapuntal radicalism in the vocal-instrumental combination, as practised in *Pierrot Lunaire*, becomes Webern's principal problem.

These collections of songs are as follows: *Six Songs*, Op. 14, for voice, clarinet, bass clarinet, violin, and 'cello (1919); *Five Sacred Songs*, Op. 15, for voice, flute, clarinet (alternating with bass clarinet), trumpet, harp, and violin (alternating with viola) (1922–23); *Five Canons*, Op. 16, for voice, clarinet, and bass clarinet (1924); *Three Sacred Folk-Songs*, Op. 17, for voice, clarinet, bass clarinet, and violin (Webern's first twelve-tone pieces), and *Three Songs*, Op. 18, for voice, piccolo, clarinet, and guitar (1925).

Let us glance at the first of these works.[11] First and foremost we note the desire for an extremely close-knit polyphonic texture, which inspires Webern to develop long phrases on a rather large scale. Repetition is still excluded from this polyphony, and the

[11] Like *Pierrot Lunaire*, Webern's Op. 14 changes instrumentation from one piece to the next. The first uses clarinet, violin, and 'cello; the second is written for bass clarinet, violin, and 'cello; the third repeats the combination of the first; the fourth uses the two clarinets and the 'cello; the fifth keeps the two clarinets, but substitutes the violin; finally, the sixth uses all four instruments.

form becomes very free. It is interesting to note the strong individualization of each voice of the ensemble. The musical speech
is rendered even more intense by a vocal and instrumental style
which recoils before no difficulty. The continual changes of register
and the constant use of the extreme registers make these songs
very complex, but also very remarkable in their force of expression.

The last song of this collection presents a somewhat different
aspect. Counterpoint is still the chief concern, but this counterpoint is more traditional and at the same time more radical. Let
us examine the beginning of this piece. The voice presents the first
motive, C–C sharp (quarter-note, eighth-note), which is then
varied by contrary motion and rhythmic diminution (D–C sharp).
Next comes a transposition of the original motive (D sharp–E)
and, finally, a variant of the original motive, C–F–C sharp. The
voice continues in this way throughout the song. Furthermore, the
same principles are at work in the instrumental accompaniment.
It is easy to recognize them in the sporadic appearance of little
two-note motives, all based on the interval of the minor second.

It is obvious that, from some points of view, the application
of such devices marks a return to more traditional forms of counterpoint, since we no longer find that absolute freedom of the
musical figures which we may note in Webern's earlier works,
especially in the other songs of this collection. However, the
passage which we have just analyzed draws our attention to two
elements which will play an important part in Webern's later
works.

First of all, we are again confronted (at least in the instrumental voices) with a very loosely woven style, in which rests
play a preponderant role. When we know how important this style
becomes in Webern's last works, we realize that he had to discipline his thematic workmanship—otherwise this style could never
have been organized into a coherent musical speech.

The other important fact is that this thematic discipline leads
straight to the tone-row system, which soon culminates in the
twelve-tone technique used in all Webern's works after Op. 17.
Therefore, it is not surprising if his next works, the *Five Sacred*

Songs, Op. 15, and especially the *Five Canons,* Op. 16, return even more markedly to the principles of traditional counterpoint.[12]

It is the twelve-tone technique which produces all Webern's works after Op. 17. From then on, we are confronted with motivic work liberated from all traditional constraints. Webern now succeeds in safeguarding the unity of composition, thanks to the strict application of the new musical discipline—so strict as to permit the complete abandonment of traditional thematic principles without any loss of coherence in the musical speech. The application of the twelve-tone technique is still quite rudimentary in Op. 17,[13] and the texture is rather loosely woven. However, greater tensions are set up in the next work, *Three Songs,* Op. 18, which is interesting also from the point of view of twelve-tone technique because of a sort of progression which takes place throughout the whole series of songs.

In fact, the first song uses one single form of the row in all three voices. The second song also unfolds one single form of the row in all three voices at once, but, in addition, uses other variants of the row (inverted and retrograde forms), which are juxtaposed according to the necessities of the articulation of the piece. Finally, the third song superimposes different forms of the row in the different voices.

The polyphonic texture here is unbelievably close-knit. The complexity of the style (of the ensemble and of each individual voice), the most radical use of the most extreme means, the perpetual variation of every sound-form—all this creates sonorities the intensity and opulence of which have rarely been equalled elsewhere. However, the analysis of these pieces according to the twelve-tone technique shows how the unity of the musical speech is secured despite this bewildering diversity.

49. *The return to the large form.*—The following work, *Two Songs,* Op. 19, for mixed chorus accompanied by celesta, guitar, violin, clarinet, and bass clarinet (1926) brings us nothing new after

[12] For a further discussion of pre-twelve-tone music which applies the tone-row system, see Chapter II of *Introduction to Twelve-Tone Music,* which also contains an analysis of Webern's *Canons,* Op. 16.

[13] *Introduction to Twelve-Tone Music,* Chapter III.

Op. 18. There is the same close-knit polyphony, the same use of extreme means, and the same intensity of the musical speech. However, let us note that the choral parts are, in order to simplify the problems of intonation, constantly doubled by certain instrumental parts; this occasionally leads back to the idea of *Klangfarbenmelodie*.

The String Trio, Op. 20 (1927), marks an important turning-point. Here we have the return to large form, made possible by the use of the twelve-tone system. Not only will Webern never abandon this means of expression hereafter, he will constantly seek to augment its resources. This return is principally facilitated by a recrudescence of the classic forms. However, it must be noted that these forms are very freely used in the Trio, and that, in the course of the following works, they will be gradually transformed into an entirely new technique of form.

The Trio consists of two movements. The first is related to the rondo form; the second is a sonata form. A single glance at the score is sufficient to reveal that, in spite of this return to classic forms, Webern does not abandon any of the numerous acquisitions of his preceding works. The musical speech is as intense, varied, and rich as ever. Furthermore, the Trio is astonishingly successful in its combination of two styles—the close-knit texture manifested in Op. 14 and Op. 18, and the transparent, loose-knit texture which, after the next work, becomes Webern's primary concern.

Example 64 reproduces the beginning of the four appearances of the "refrain" of the Rondo. The first presents nine short motives, separated by rests, and yet inextricably interlocked.

Ex. 64

As always, the instrumental style calls on the utmost resources of
the instruments. Despite the complexity of this writing and of the
resultant polyphonic texture, the different musical figures are
clearly articulated and sharply differentiated.

Let us compare this first exposition to the first recapitulation
of the refrain. (Ex. 64b.)

Though the purely acoustical aspect has changed a good deal,
the actual variation is still slight; roughly speaking, it is only a
matter of the inversion of the mutual relationships of the voices.
For example, the top voice, the violin, had first unfolded motives 2,
5, and 9. These same motives, slightly varied in register and
rhythm, are unfolded by the 'cello in the course of the first recapitulation. The middle voice, the viola, which first unfolded motives 1, 6, and 8, passes to the high voice, the violin, in the course
of the recapitulation. Finally, motives 3, 4, and 7, first unfolded
in the 'cello, are now taken up by the viola. Let us note that all

these motives, in spite of their variations, remain perfectly recognizable.

The second recapitulation of the refrain subjects the polyphonic ensemble to further variation. (Ex. 64c.)

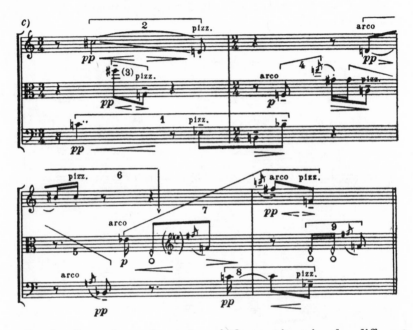

In the first place, the order of the motives in the different voices is no longer maintained; in the second pieces, certain motives are broken up into several voices. The same goes for the last recapitulation, in which this "disjunct" style is carried even farther:

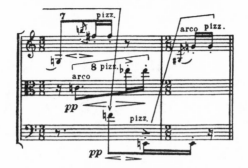

It goes without saying that the sonata form of the second movement depends on similar principles of variation.

From the preceding discussion, a certain number of conclusions must be drawn. The work of Webern, from its very beginnings, is directed towards the conquest of a language dominated by the idea of perpetual variation. During the period of the "little pieces," this ideal is realized in the complete abandonment of the idea of repetition, which necessitates the simultaneous abandonment of large form. However, large form could not be banished forever, and, as it could hardly do without the element of repetition, it was necessary to find a way of reintroducing this element in a legitimate way while depriving it of its static character. That is why, after Op. 14, Webern proceeded to forge an efficient contrapuntal tool, and, in so doing, came to the twelve-tone-row technique. This technique finally produces the *String Trio*, which proves that Webern can restore the large form to its previous dignity. However, his work does not stop here—the Trio is only a preparatory step to new problems. The twelve-tone technique, which is used somewhat chaotically [14] in the *Trio*, is placed *in the service* of classical forms, whereas in the following works the technique, used with unprecedented strictness and discipline, will create its own forms. On the other hand, the problem of counterpoint will again be approached according to principles which, based on the experiments of earlier works, will engender the greatest purity—a quality essentially due to that strictness and that discipline.

[14] Cf. *Introduction to Twelve-Tone Music*, Chapter IX.

CHAPTER X

The Projection of the Schoenbergian
Acquisitions into the Future

50. *General characteristics of the new phase.*—In defining Webern's genius as the incarnation of the most radical side of Schoenberg, we have understood one of its most important aspects. It is true that, up till now, Webern's effort to achieve purity has led him into paths which, though they may branch out from Schoenbergian instruction, have a character all their own. But it is not until the Symphony, Op. 21, that Webern's originality appears in full force. Up until now he had hardly written a page which— exaggerating a little—might not have been written by his master. Now, Webern's style becomes so original that it can be recognized in every measure. Certainly, the influence of Schoenberg can still be felt; but, on the one hand, it exists only *a fortiori*—insofar as it governed all Webern's past evolution of which, naturally, this new phase is a logical consequence—and, on the other hand, this influence is now manifest only in Webern's fidelity to the twelve-tone technique, of which—typically—he seeks out the most radical implications.

It is 1928. Webern is forty-five years old. He has just finished his Symphony, Op. 21, for clarinet, bass clarinet, two horns, harp, and strings (without the double-bass). It is his fifth twelve-tone work, his second since the return to large form. Thus, it might seem that this work is only a prolongation of what has gone before. That is true—and yet it is so different that, even today, some listeners who can appreciate Webern's work up to Op. 20 admit that they are thrown completely off the track when they hear most of the following works. The very appearance of these scores is disconcerting. Their bare bones frighten us. A few notes seem to have been scattered at random without any apparent reason. Hearing this music produces a similar impression. The musical speech is chopped up by continual rests. There seems to be no melody, no harmony; as for the rhythm, it appears incomprehensible. The instrumental style, too, proves problematic, reduced as it is to the emission of isolated tones, without the slightest concern for sonority as such. The whole produces the effect of a world of chaos ruled in the most arbitrary manner.

And yet, it will be easy for me to show that these scores are neither chaotic nor arbitrary—more yet, that there exist few scores so strictly constructed, few in which the architectural conception is of greater purity. But I know in advance that I can convince only a very few people of the *necessity* of such purity, of the necessity of carrying an experience so far. But this experience exists; it is, for some of us, one of the most valuable experiences ever undergone, and we may console ourselves for its present incomprehensibility by thinking about the future, when it will be recognized just as every genuine experience of the past has been recognized. But this certainty, as well as the certainty of the inevitable failure of our effort to convince most readers of the necessity of Webern's last works, should not keep us from making the effort.

Let us not indulge in apologetics or esthetics. Let us limit ourselves, as we have thus far done, to the analysis of the scores. In showing the coherence of their structure, we shall make them easier of access to some, at least.

51. *The Symphony, Op. 21.*—The first movement of the Symphony is based on canonic principles throughout. It displays the application of the purest possible counterpoint, stripped to its barest essentials. But this return to traditional forms of contrapuntal style is accompanied, on the other hand, by numerous radical innovations, the results of Webern's past activity. Thus, only patient analysis reveals that the Symphony begins with a double four-part canon in contrary motion.[1] (Ex. 65.)

---

[1] Cf. *Introduction to Twelve-Tone Music,* Chapter IX, where this beginning is reproduced and analyzed from the twelve-tone viewpoint.

Especially striking here is the way in which the instrumentation participates in the individualization of the various parts; here
is Webern's experimentation with the *Klangfarbenmelodie* carried
to its utmost limits. For example, one of the themes of the double
canon is exposed as follows: the first part of the statement is

divided into three motives; the first (I) is exposed by the second
horn and is imitated (in contrary motion) in the answer by the
first horn (I'); the second motive (II) is stated by the clarinet
and imitated by the bass clarinet (II'); the third motive (III)
is stated by the 'celli and imitated by the violas (III').

Thus we see that Webern was concerned with producing a
certain homogeneity in the imitations of the different motives,
along with variety in the presentation of the whole theme.

The same principle governs the parallel evolution of the other
canon, but the instrumentation of the different voices is more complex. Given a subdivision of the first part of its theme into three
motives, we see that the first (1) is stated by the harp, continued
in the 'celli, and imitated (in contrary motion) by the harp and
violas (1'); the second motive (2) is stated by the second violin
and harp, and imitated by the first violins and harp (2'); the
third (3) is stated by the second horn and harp, and imitated by
the first horn and harp (3').

Let us also observe the extremely loose-knit texture, and the
perpetual variation of the diverse elements. Certain groups of two
notes pass from one voice to another, but their functions differ
according to the motives in which they participate. Though the
rhythmic patterns appear to be very simple, the alternation of
accents imparts great complexity and refinement—qualities which
will be even more evident in the following works—to the rhythm
of the Symphony. It must be especially noted that the counterpoint used here, which is purely classical in its essence, depends
on a systematically and constantly applied law which is at the
opposite pole from the traditional laws of counterpoint. This law
consists in the perpetual crossing of voices, which was avoided at
all costs in traditional counterpoint, but which was progressively
introduced in Webern's previous experiments.

The whole first movement of the Symphony unfolds according
to the principles we have just described.

The second movement is a theme with variations. Certainly,
this is a classical form but, in its present treatment, Webern's
language proves to be completely novel and original even from
the structural point of view.

The theme itself is conceived in a very special way; its melody uses only the original form of the basic twelve-tone row of the work, and the accompaniment is derived from the retrograde form.

Ex. 66

But the economy of this presentation is accentuated by the fact that the second half of the theme is the retrograde form of the first half, so that the whole theme is identical with its retrograde form. The rhythm is symmetrical in both halves of the theme, but it is this very symmetry which subtly changes the accentuation in these two sections. In this first statement, the most significant variation is that of the dotted quarter-note, which falls the first time on a weak beat (B flat) and the second time on a strong beat (E natural).

The first variation displays great contrapuntal virtuosity. It is a four-part double canon in contrary motion, given to the strings. This canon has, in addition, the following characteristics: 1) from the middle onwards, all the voices play backwards; 2) the canon is reversible—it may be read from beginning to end, in which case it appears in its inverted form, or it may be read in its original form if the music is turned upside down and the appropriate clefs are added. Example 67 reproduces the top voice of this canon.

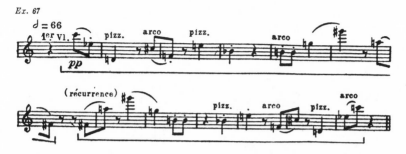

Ex. 67

This example proves that Webern has achieved complete mastery of the most complex contrapuntal problems. However, it must be said that this is no mere game, no futile exercise. On the contrary, the entire meaning of this variation comes from the very structure of the theme. Thus, the theme of the canon simply unfolds successively, on the horizontal plane, those two elements (melody and accompaniment) which, in the first presentation, appeared simultaneously in the vertical plane. Here, the rhythmic symmetry, another structural characteristic of the theme, completely changes the various elements in the two halves (original and retrograde) of each voice, for all the accents are displaced.

The other variations are also concerned with the development of certain basic aspects of the theme. One of the most significant in this respect is surely Variation V, which, constantly turning around a central point, arrives at a state of quasi-immobility. It is the harmonic structure of the tone-row of the theme which is developed here. The special feature of this structure is that the first four notes and the last four notes of the row (and consequently of the theme) are grouped into two chords the characteristic intervals of which are exactly alike; Webern gives these two chords to the high strings and the low strings, respectively. The four "central" tones of the theme produce quite different intervals, which are played by the harp. (Ex. 68.)

Furthermore, the inversion of the original tone-row of the theme, transposed to A flat, gives the identical chords. If this version is used and the horizontal unfoldment of the four "central" tones is maintained, these latter will be slightly varied; instead of E–E flat–A–B flat, we shall have E flat–E–B flat–A. Webern uses this

characteristic, along with a certain shifting of the accents, to
introduce an element of variety into the five successive presentations of the harmonic aspect of the theme.

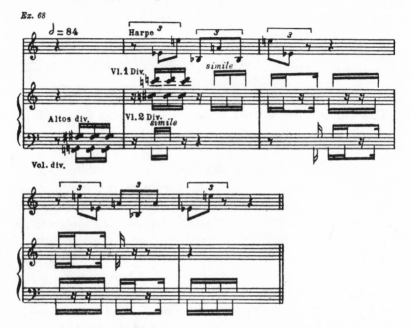

Finally, we must analyze the Coda, which amalgamates the
two elements of the theme into a remarkable unity.

The original line of the theme (which was presented as the melody
in the first exposition) may be followed from the harp (F) to the

'cello (G sharp–G) to the first violin (F sharp, B flat, A) to the harp (D sharp, E) to the violin (C) and finally back again to the harp (C sharp, D, B). All the other tones, going back to the beginning—harp (B, D, C sharp), violin (C), harp (E, D sharp), violin (A, B flat, F sharp), 'cello (G, G sharp) and harp (F)— make up the retrograde version, which was given to the accompaniment at the beginning of the movement.

Needless to say, the variation of a single initial figure here reaches its utmost limits; we see that Webern has not abandoned the state of mind which guided him thus far in his evolution, but that, on the contrary, he is constantly discovering new ways of expressing this state of mind. Again, I draw attention to the "retrograde symmetry" of this passage (in which its real correspondence to the theme consists), which once more displaces the accents in all the motives, except in the seventh E–D sharp played by the harp.

This Symphony, which, I repeat, marks an important step forward not only in Webern's own work but also in the evolution of music in general, calls for still further comments. If we compare it to Webern's preceding works, even to the Trio, Op. 20, we are struck by the extraordinary economy of means which governs its conception. But, in addition to this, there is a manifest desire to draw on the very sources of the art of music. Thus, it goes without saying that the forms used—canons and variations—are the oldest and most "fundamental" manifestations of the polyphonic art. The concern for the utmost economy, combined with the longing to discover the essential meaning—the *original* meaning, one might almost say—of a musical figure, bring about the existence of a strange dialectic in the work of our composer. It is manifested as follows: on the one hand, Webern's musical thought is constantly enriched by the inclusion of new possibilities; on the other hand, it becomes ever more concentrated with each new acquisition. The result is that the language thus constituted attains, at one and the same time, the greatest complexity and the greatest simplicity. For example, let us take the rhythmic aspect of a score like the Symphony. This aspect is so simple that it is ultimately expressed in an almost perfect symmetry; yet this

symmetry is so refined that it becomes synonymous with absolute asymmetry. It may also be said that Webern's mastery of
this realm will soon become such as to enable him to compose with
rhythms which use almost nothing but equal values and yet are
just as asymmetrical as ever. Furthermore, his amazing knowledge of variation brings him to the point of almost complete immobility; his mastery of harmony and counterpoint, and the abundance of his melodic inspiration, bring him to the culmination of
all these elements in their simplest expression—the isolated tone.[2]

With the Symphony, Op. 21, there begins a new phase of an
art which, nourished by all possible sonorities, now makes silence
one of its essential elements.

52. *Consolidation and amplification of Webern's new acquisitions.*
—The next work, the Quartet, Op. 22, for violin, clarinet, tenor
saxophone, and piano (1930), is even more dependent on the principles observed in the Symphony. Like the first movement of
Op. 21, the first movement of the Quartet makes abundant use
of the art of the canon. Again, the strict canon in contrary motion

Ex. 70

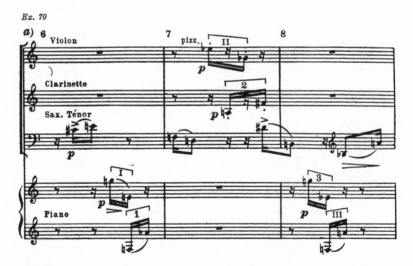

[2] One might well say, as did one of my friends, a great admirer of Webern's art,
"When you have learned to appreciate a melody of Webern, all others, beautiful though
they may be, are just so much marshmallow-whip in comparison."

is most frequently used; the different motives of each part are again distributed among various instruments. Elsewhere [3] I have quoted the beginning (so strikingly bare) of this work. In order to give a more complete idea of it here, I reproduce the following passage, which corresponds to the exposition of the principal theme of the movement. (Ex. 70a.)

This theme is exposed like a *cantus firmus* in the saxophone. Around this *cantus firmus* there is elaborated a two-part canon in

[3] In my *Introduction to Twelve-Tone Music*, Chapter IX.

contrary motion. The statement is heard alternately in the piano and in the violin, the answer in the piano and the clarinet (*vice versa* from the middle of the canon onwards). There is to be observed in this canon a further refinement not known to the analogous passages of Op. 21; the various motives in the two parts (I–X) are rhythmically shifted.

The principle of variation is highly developed in this movement,[4] as witness the recapitulation of the principal theme, in which it is stated in the following form:

The theme is varied, not only in its registration, but also in its instrumentation. Instead of being played by a single instrument (as was the case in Ex. 70a), it is played by three alternating instruments, and so is constantly changing in color. Furthermore, the piano plays the complete inversion of the canon of the beginning. Thus the entire character of the ensemble is altered. The theme, which had but a single color (saxophone) in the exposition, now has a variable color; the canon, which had a variable color in the exposition, now has a single color (piano).

I shall not discuss the important second movement (one of the longest ever written by Webern) other than to say that its freedom of form, knowledge of variation, and limpidity of style are even greater than in the second movement of the Symphony. However, it is necessary to draw attention to the following fact: in the two works which we have just been analyzing, it seems that Webern is trying to achieve a certain uniformity of instrumental style

---

[4] The general form of the movement is very clearly set forth: introduction, principal theme, middle section (an expanded variant of the introduction), recapitulation of the principal theme, and coda (a new variant of the introduction). (ABABA.)

which suppresses, as far as possible, the individual characteristics of each instrument. *All the instruments are treated alike.* The question of sonority as an embellishment of musical speech does not arise at all; the only thing that matters is the relief into which a given voice in the polyphonic texture may be thrown by the specific sonority of this or that instrument. It is as if Webern wanted to deprive music of all outer adornment, leaving only its inner musical meaning. We shall see that this new preoccupation soon leads him to compose his first work for piano alone, and to take up anew the form of the string quartet, abandoned since 1913; in other words, he uses those instrumental combinations well calculated to eliminate the slightest trace of "ornamental" tone-color.

It would doubtless be beyond the powers of any human being to maintain the tension which produced the Symphony and the Quartet. That is why the following work, the *Three Songs*, Op. 23, for soprano and piano (1934), returns to a more traditional style. This work, perhaps one of Webern's most successful vocal compositions, is a wonderful moment of relaxation after the colossal and exhausting effort of the two previous works. Example 71, which reproduces the beginning of the soprano in the first song, shows how rich and intense Webern's melodic invention (in a traditional sense) has remained. A breath of Schubert is felt in these measures, where a ravishing melody is supported by a tender accompaniment, of exemplary purity, in the piano.

Ex. 71

It goes without saying that none of this excludes that solidity of structure, that sense of balance, and that polyphony at once complex and transparent to which Webern has accustomed us. The last

song, in particular, seems to me a striking example of all these
qualities, for it is amazing to see here the manifestation of
Webern's contrapuntal mastery in forms which are not strict
a priori, and in which all discipline comes from a great freedom
of expression constantly under the control of a profound sense of
the economy of means.

I think this is the only valid example of a new acquisition in
the realm of the song with piano accompaniment since Schoenberg's Op. 15.[5] In fact, we have seen that after this work Schoenberg completely abandoned the genre. Berg did not return to it
after his Op. 2, in which he underwent the influence of Schoenberg's songs, Op. 6, and *Erwartung.* Webern, having undergone
the influence of these works and of Schoenberg's Op. 15 in his
songs Op. 3 and 4, returns to the same realm in his Op. 12. This
return is justified by his attempt to adapt the genre of the song
to the demands of the miniature form, an attempt which had never
been made before. But, as the miniature form was only a transitory
phase in the evolution of polyphony, there was to be no sequel to
the effort of Webern's Op. 12. Now, since the twelve-tone technique made possible renewed activity in all fields of instrumental
and vocal music, it was bound to reactivate the song with piano
accompaniment—as witness Webern's Op. 23. And yet, the mere
application of the new technique is not sufficient to assure that the
activity which interests us will be resumed. It was still necessary
to dispense with the traditional forms of the *Lied* and to derive
an entirely new structure from the special handling of the twelve-
tone style. It is this radical compositional attitude which characterizes Webern's last period, and which undoubtedly explains

⎯⎯⎯⎯⎯

[5] Cf. Part I, Chapter IV, § 19.

why he was the only one to attempt a task which, since Schoenberg's Op. 15, seemed foredoomed to failure.

I cannot discuss the *Concerto for Nine Instruments,* Op. 24,
and the *Three Songs,* Op. 25, for they are still unpublished and I
have been unable to become acquainted with them.[6]

Op. 26, *Das Augenlicht,* a sort of cantata for chorus and orchestra (played at the ISCM festival in London, 1938), throws a
new light on all the problems which we have discussed in connection with the preceding works. Here is the intense lyricism, the
melodic warmth of the *Three Songs,* Op. 23, combined with the
nudity of Op. 21 and 22. The juxtaposition of chorus and orchestra
gives Webern the opportunity to attack new problems of equilibrium of sonority. The chorus is treated alternately in harmonic
and contrapuntal fashion. The very special orchestra[7] operates
on the same principles of instrumental style which were active in
Op. 21 and 22. The form, which owes nothing to any preconceived
scheme, is very strictly worked out. The alternations of the contrapuntal and harmonic passages of the chorus, as well as the
fluctuations of instrumentation (orchestra alone, *a cappella* chorus,
chorus and orchestra together) confer an ideal plasticity to the
structure.

The contrapuntal parts display, in addition to Webern's usual
mastery, certain new preoccupations. While Op. 21 and 22 used
mostly canons in contrary motion, here the crab canon plays a
great part. As an illustration of this, we choose the first entrance
of the chorus, in measure 8. (Ex. 72.)

The sopranos and tenors sing such a canon in retrograde motion.
(Note that the rhythm is the same in both voices.) To this the

---

[6] Since I wrote these lines I have become familiar with these two works. The
first furnished the subject for my abovementioned lecture, *What Is Twelve-Tone Music?,*
during which Webern's Op. 24 was performed and analyzed. This concerto is not only
Webern's purest work but also, in a sense, his most radical. My study of it never obliged
me to change my ideas about the evolution of our composer, as I have already
expounded them. On the contrary!

As for the *Three Songs,* Op. 25, they represent a prolongation of Op. 23, although
in some ways they are more traditional. In other respects, they might be considered
preparatory studies for the two cantatas, Op. 29 and 31.

[7] Flute, oboe, clarinet, alto saxophone, horn, trumpet, trombone, tympani,
glockenspiel, xylophone, cymbals, harp, celesta, mandolin, eight violins, four violas, and
four 'celli.

Ex. 72

orchestra adds another canon, also in retrograde motion. Here, from the rhythmic point of view, we are confronted with the typically Webernian procedure of displacement of accents, with equal metric values in both voices. In the same way, the four motives of the theme of the canon (I, II, III, IV and I', II', III', and IV') reveal, in their instrumental style, that "symmetry of timbres" familiar to us since Op. 21—the last phase of the problem of the *Klangfarbenmelodie,* as it now presents itself to Webern's mind.

Let us also note that this passage is of the greatest interest from the point of view of the tone-row technique. In fact, the double canon of this example uses a different form of the twelve-tone row in each voice. Thus, the four possibilities of the row are superimposed, used simultaneously. If we consider the soprano part as the original form of the row, the tenors present the retrograde form, in which case the statement of the orchestral canon (motives I, II, III, IV) uses RI, while the answer of the canon (motives I', II', III', IV') uses I.

It is evident that this complex passage confronts us with new and subtle possibilities of variation in musical speech.

CHAPTER XI

The Last Works of Webern; the Culmination
of Contemporary Polyphony

But, when we have discovered in language an exceptional power of absence
and of denial, we are tempted to consider the very absence of language as
part of its essence, and silence as the ultimate possibility of speech. . . .
But this silence is in no respect the opposite of language, its repudiation
or its condemnation; on the contrary, it is taken for granted by words—it
is their preconceived basis, their secret intention; more yet, it is the only
condition on which speech is possible, if speech is the replacement of a
presence by an absence and the pursuit, through presences ever more
fragile, of an absence ever more all-sufficing.

MAURICE BLANCHOT
Mallarmé et le Langage.

A. *The Piano Variations,* Op. 27.

53. *Fundamental problems of Op. 27.*—Purification, utmost economy of means, precision and laconicism of musical speech—all
these qualities thus far revealed in the evolution of Webern—find
their most perfect embodiment, in a way which can, perhaps,
never be surpassed, in his piano variations, Op. 27.

As previously mentioned, this is Webern's first work for piano
alone. This extremely significant fact is, I believe, explicable
on the basis which I shall now indicate. In the first place, we must
remember Webern's marked desire, so obvious in the last works,
to deprive musical speech of all outer adornment, even the least
distracting. As we have seen, this desire led Webern to elaborate
an instrumental style all his own, which displayed a tendency to
deprive the different instruments of their specific tone-colors, and
to reduce them all to unity or to virtual anonymity. Evidently the
piano, with its special timbre, was bound to mark the culmination
of any evolution in the direction of such musical "nudity." But
this is not the whole problem. In addition, we know that Webern's

polyphony was not always like that of his last works; it knew periods of incredible abundance, wild profusion of rich and complex melodic lines. Now it is obvious that the piano, an essentially rhythmic and harmonic instrument, is not very suitable for such complicated counterpoint, since its unity of timbre tends to obscure the individual melodic lines rather than to bring them out. However, as we have elucidated above, the new phase of Webern's polyphony is so pure and refined that it embodies a curious paradox: the greatest complexity and the purest simplicity are allied in music which seems to be made of only a few notes.

It must, then, be stated that, on the one hand, Webern had to arrive at this extreme condensation of musical material in order to be able to use the piano as an ideal instrument, and that, on the other hand, the piano gave him the opportunity to compose a score which, more than any of his earlier works, embodies that ideal of musical nudity and purity for which he strove throughout his development.

One other thing is important; the music which concerns us is in the form of piano *variations*. This, too, is revealing, for throughout our study we have observed that the principal problem of Webern's evolution is the very one in which Schoenberg's radicalism expresses itself by means of a grandiose synthesis of the genuine tradition of Western music. This is the problem of perpetual variation, starting with a minimum of material, as an essential element of musical speech. This synthesis culminates in the twelve-tone technique, which perfectly embodies such a state of mind as the basis for musical work, since the very technique— or tool—used by the twelve-tone composer already consists of the perpetual variation of the minimum of material. Thus, in the last analysis, it is possible to describe every twelve-tone composition as a set of variations on a twelve-tone row.

The actual form of theme and variations has been rarely used by Webern, but always at significant moments. His work begins with this form—what could be more revealing?—and the only other example I know is the second movement of the Symphony, Op. 21, a score which marks the most decisive turning-point of his career.

To each phase of musical language there correspond forms which are proper to it and which embody the very *essence* of this language. The modal language elaborated the *motet* form, in which each strophe ended with a typical cadence on some degree of the mode. The tonal language, in its beginnings, perfected the *fugal* form, which gave adequate and intense expression to the tonic-dominant relationship. Later, the evolution of the tonal language created a form which permitted and encouraged this very evolution—the *sonata* form, which introduces more complex relationships in addition to the essential tonic-dominant relationship. According to the above definition of the twelve-tone technique, it is clear that the most suitable form for the new language is the *variation* form. This was understood by all the great twelve-tone composers. Schoenberg uses the variation form in his Op. 29, 30 and 31—that is, in the works where he first feels the necessity of building specific forms with the technique which he has created. Berg and Webern follow his example (Berg in *Lulu* and in the last movement of his last work, the Violin Concerto).[1] However, in all these scores, the variation form is still relatively traditional. It remained for Webern to draw the utmost consequences from the problem which confronted him; and that is what he does in his piano variations, Op. 27.

54. *The structure of the theme of the first movement.*—The principal traditional element preserved, up till now, in the variations of Schoenberg, Berg, and Webern was the *theme* upon which all such variations were built. Even the daring second movement of Webern's symphony presents, at the beginning, a clearly defined theme with a melody and an accompaniment. It is true that the variations which follow are not so much variations of the theme proper as elaborations of its various structural elements. This process is carried even further in Op. 27.[2]

At first glance, this score does not remind us in the slightest

---

[1] Again we see that Berg feels the need of associating this form with some positive element in the past. Let us recall that the variations in *Lulu* and in the Violin Concerto are based on chorales.

[2] The following analysis may be supplemented by the notes on the same work in Chapter IX of my *Introduction to Twelve-Tone Music*.

degree of any traditional theme and variations. Instead of the customary indications—Theme, Variation 1, Variation 2, etc.—still used in the second movement of the symphony, we have here three separate movements, which, taken all together, suggest the form of a sonatina. Each movement of this "sonatina" develops one special structural element which gives rise to its own particular devices of variation.

The architectonic element of the first movement is set forth in eighteen measures. (Ex. 73a.)

Ex. 73

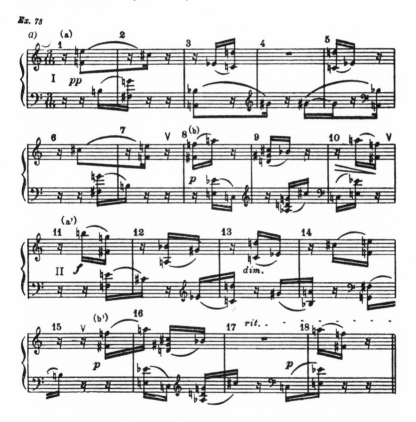

It produces two variations, but its own construction is already dependent on the principle of variation. Roughly speaking, this passage may be subdivided into two sections: the first (I), measures 1–10; the second (II), in which the same musical material is handled differently, measures 11–18. There is no precisely defined melodic theme in any of this, but the idea of a statement which is to serve as a basis for variations is carried out with respectful fidelity to the example of the great masters of the past. A more thorough analysis will prove this.

The first section itself is subdivided into two distinct segments (a and b). The first segment (a), measures 1–7, includes that *Spiegelbild* (mirror-image) characteristic of Webern's last works.[3] Again we note the ruling principle of rhythmic "asymmetrical symmetry." Webern even adds a new and piquant detail; from the middle of measure 4 (where the "mirror" is situated) the long note-values (eighths) become short (sixteenths), and vice versa. This first segment is, then, the antecedent. The second segment (b), in which the musical speech becomes more concentrated, and in which there appears for the first time (measure 9) a chord of three notes struck together and another of four notes, is the consequent. Here, too, we find a slightly modified *Spiegelbild*.

The second section (II) of this passage (measures 11–18) may be considered as an answer to the first section, and also as a coda. We have already noted that it makes strict use of the material of measures 1–11. It is easy to see how this material is varied in the two segments (a' and b') which correspond to a and b of the first section (a', 11–15; b', 15–18). The texture becomes more and more close-knit, and finally produces, in the last segment, a sort of *stretto* (measures 15–16) which begins with an aggregation of two notes, continues with one of three notes and one of four notes, and ends on a single note. The two closing motives also ended the first section, but here they are rhythmically shifted. Furthermore, the two segments of this second section once more depend (with a few changes) on the principle of the *Spiegelbild*.

Surprising and unusual though this passage may appear, there

---

[3] From the viewpoint of the twelve-tone technique, the *Spiegelbild* is obtained by the superposition of the original and retrograde forms of the row, which change hands in the middle. One may also analyze the passage, according to Serge Nigg (doubtless the first French musician to make a complete analysis of a twelve-tone work), as follows: measures 1–4, right hand, first six tones of the row in their original order, left hand, last six tones in reverse order; measures 4–7, right hand, first six tones in reverse order, left hand, last six tones in original order. Both ways of analyzing the treatment of the row reveal the same technique, which is continued throughout the movement.

is no doubt that its structure is perfectly coherent. Even more, this structure is obviously and logically modelled on that of the great masters of the past. Before we verify this assertion, need we say that this is no artificial archaism like that of the "neo-classicists"? The novelty of the language alone would suffice to prove this. On the contrary, such respect for "old" structural principles simply proves that there are, in musical evolution, certain constant elements which remain immutable in spite of the fluctuations and metamorphoses of the musical language from one period to the next. These constant elements are none other than certain architectonic principles which impart coherence to musical speech.

Thus, the passage which we have analyzed conforms to the division of the theme into two principal parts, each of which is, in turn, subdivided into two segments. Examples of this structure abound in classical music. For instance, from Beethoven's sonatas I can cite, without looking too far, the theme of the variations in the second movement of the *Appassionata,* the theme of the second movement of Op. 109, and the *Arietta* of Op. 111. In fact, the structural analogies of the last-named theme with the beginning of Webern's Op. 27 are striking. Its two sections both end on the tonic (if the second strong beat of the first ending is counted as part of the first section); this is the equivalent of the abovementioned identity of the closing motives of the first and second sections of Webern's theme. In Beethoven's theme, too, each section is subdivided into two segments; the second segment is not (as nearly always in Beethoven's earlier works and those of his predecessors) a mere *sequence* of the first, but, as in Webern's example, it is a genuine *variation.* Furthermore, in both themes, the first segment of the second section is a variation of the first segment of the first section. In Beethoven, the variation is produced by the shift from major to minor—an essentially harmonic procedure. In Webern, the variation is essentially contrapuntal and rhythmic; a and a′ are, then, more closely related, since the variation is produced by inversion of parts and rhythmic transformations. The same may be said of the second segments of both parts. Both in Beethoven and in Webern, their function is to "weigh down" the music with heavier harmonic aggregations. In both works, it is only in these segments that there occur passages directly conceived in chords pure and simple. Again, the lapse of time between the composition of the two works is responsible for the fact that Webern's coda develops the preceding material in a more economical manner, since it is a variation of the material included in the second segment of the first section (b).

If these comparisons demonstrate that the functions and inner meaning of the various corresponding segments display real analogies, if not entire identity of conception, it goes without saying that the structural means vary from Beethoven to Webern, and correspond exactly to the differences in language and technique.

In Beethoven's example, the structure is primarily governed by tonal functions. The boundaries of the scheme are the harmonic polar areas: first segment, I–V; second segment, V–I; third segment, VI (relative minor)—III; fourth segment, V–I (equivalent to the second segment).

With Webern, the structure results from the handling of the twelve-tone row. The scheme is as follows: first segment, O and R superimposed; second segment, I and RI superimposed; [4] third and fourth segments, repetition of the same conditions.

In Beethoven, there are other structural means—the melodic unity (theme) of each segment, and a certain symmetry of the various segments. In Webern, both unity and symmetry of the various segments are produced by the *Spiegelbild* principle. It is evident that Webern's structure is, all in all, more asymmetrical than that of Beethoven; but this is only the natural result of the "progress" of the idea of variation during the generations which separate these two musicians.

Attention must also be drawn to the amazing piano style of this passage of Webern. From this point of view, too, the passage surprises most listeners and performers, who find it too "skeletal." In reality, it is quite otherwise; but, to realize this, one must have grasped the wealth of polyphonic complexity in these few measures. Only then one understands that no other piano style could

---

[4] This, then, is a "complete" twelve-tone presentation. Cf. my *Introduction*, Chapter V, section "The theme of variations."

give a purer and more accurate representation of this polyphony. The superposition of the various figures, the way in which both hands extend or limit the register—all this shows a profound knowledge of the possibilities of the piano, possibilities which Webern has mastered completely. Thus, a genuine pianistic technique is created—even though the interpreter must undertake a work of meticulous and patient preparation in order to give a convincing realization of the composer's intent.

55. The two variations of the first movement.—The first eighteen measures of the first movement are followed by another eighteen-measure passage which may be considered the first variation. The texture is more irregular, the musical speech more rapid, the piano style more virtuosic. Furthermore, whereas the first passage was preponderantly *piano, forte* predominates here.

The general structure of the "theme" is preserved; the first variation, too, consists of two sections, and the various segments are again handled according to the *Spiegelbild* principle (and, from the point of view of twelve-tone technique, treated exactly like the corresponding segments of the "theme"). The proportions and functions of the two sections of the variation correspond approximately to those of the two sections of the "theme." The proportions are as follows:

First section, "theme"—10 measures
First section, variation—11 measures
Second section, "theme"—8 measures
Second section, variation—7 measures

As for the functions, the second part of the variation displays a higher degree of musical concentration than the first part, as already in the "theme."

However, there are important structural changes in the variation. In the first place, in spite of similar proportions, the two sections of the variation are amplified in comparison with the corresponding sections of the "theme." Each of the new sections is composed of three distinct segments instead of two. Furthermore, there is no more recapitulation in the course of the variation, for each segment uses a different transposition of the row. However, the presentation of the different forms of the row still retains the *superposition* of original and retrograde order, as well as the *alternation* of original and inverted forms.[5]

Finally, the last eighteen measures of the first movement of our "sonatina" bring back a form analogous to that of the first exposition.[6] Four new segments display the same rhythmic structure, the same piano style, and the same nuances. However, the relationships between the voices are inverted. Here is the first segment of this second variation.

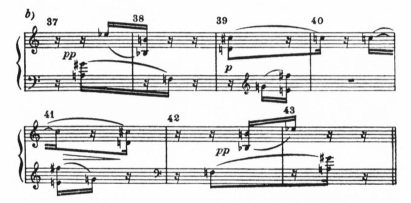

There are two other innovations: 1) in spite of the continued alternation of original and inverted forms, the second variation, like the first, uses different transpositions of the row in every

---

[5] It might even be possible to analyze the first eighteen measures of the movement as a theme (first segment) followed by three analogous variations (other three segments). This principle could then be extended to the next eighteen measures, which might be analyzed as six new variations of two distinct types (first type—first three segments, second type—last three segments). One could proceed throughout the entire movement in the same way. Such an interpretation is not entirely unfounded, since all the segments display the same structure (superposition of an original form and its retrograde =*Spiegelbild*). However, one detail shows that our first interpretation conforms more closely to the inner meaning of the total structure; the different segments do not all necessarily contain the same number of notes. The first segment has to contain twenty-four tones; but since the last tone, B, of the row-form which is used fulfills the same function in the next row-form, and is not repeated at all in the next segment (which leads to a sort of recapitulation of the first segment)—since, too, the notes B flat and B are played only once each, because of certain factors in the tone-row—the entire second segment has only twenty tones. Twelve-tone analysis shows such inequalities throughout the work. In this sense, it is impossible to confer an autonomous value upon the various segments.

[6] This movement thus acquires a clear ABA form.

segment; 2) the chords of the last measure of the second variation [7] (which did not exist in the last measure of the theme) clearly mark this measure as an *ending:*

56. *The second movement.*—The second movement, which we reproduce here in its entirety, presents a different type of variation. Furthermore, it marks the point of highest tension in the work; as it is the *central* movement, this proves how structurally logical the entire plan is. In fact, the function of this movement is analogous to that of a development (elaboration) section. This developmental character is manifest in the tense and precipitate character of the musical speech, which is caused by the rapid pace, the constant alternation of *piano* and *forte,* the continual changes in register (including the juxtaposition of extremely disparate registers), the rhythmic irregularity, the changes in accentuation, and the strictly contrapuntal treatment (which we shall study later).

The "theme" is exposed in the first eleven measures; the last eleven are the variation (Ex. 74a). The theme may again be classified as binary; its first segment extends from the beginning through measure 4, its second from measure 5 to the first double bar. The relationship between these two segments is not that of "model–sequence," but rather that of *"statement–varied answer."* It is easy to see how the different motives of the second segment vary those of the first. The same observation is applicable to the second half of the movement, which takes up practically all the motives of the first half, but gives them a different setting.[8]

The principal interest of this piece lies in its contrapuntal

---

[7] The last chord is the longest of its kind in the whole piece.

[8] Ex. 74a gives a clear idea of the relationship between the "theme" and the variation. It is as if the motives of the "theme" had been put in a hat, shaken up, and drawn out at random to make the variation. Needless to say, despite this chaotic appearance, the variation is strictly derived from the theme.

structure, and in the way in which this structure is derived from the tone-row. It may immediately be said that this contrapuntal structure determines the form of the piece. Thus, the form owes nothing to any preconceived scheme, but is elaborated on the basis of certain twelve-tone laws.

Ex. 74

First of all, let us note that the whole piece is a strict canon in contrary motion. This is the great difference between it and the preceding movement, which simply superimposed original and retrograde forms of the row. The subject of the canon is first announced in the left hand, and imitated at the distance of an eighth-note by the right hand. This order is changed in measure 5, and reestablished in measure 8—only to be changed again in measure 17. Here, the imitation becomes the subject, and vice versa; the order of the hands also changes, but is restored a measure later.[9] We shall say no more about the utter novelty and authenticity of this polyphonic style. Again, anyone who has grasped the deeper meaning of the polyphony of this passage will be convinced that this style is its ideal expression.

From the twelve-tone viewpoint, the four fragments of the canon use the following transpositions:

1. Superposition of I 7 and O 5.

2. O 12 and I 12.

3. O 7 and I 5.

4. I 2 and O 10.

[9] Cf. Ex. 74a. The slurs mark the various segments of the "theme" and of the variation; the dotted lines mark the passage of subject or imitation from one hand to the other.

When we compare the aggregations which result from these different superpositions, we discover that the same aggregations constantly return, and that they use only those intervals proper to the whole-tone scale—the unison, the major second (or minor seventh or major ninth), the major third (or minor sixth) and the augmented fourth (or diminished fifth). This law of the twelve-tone system, which applies to every twelve-tone row, may be formulated as follows: the superposition of any form of a row and the inversion of that form will always produce the same intervals (those of the whole-tone scale) if the initial notes of both forms build any one of the intervals of the whole-tone scale. If the initial notes build some other interval—minor second, minor third, fourth, fifth, major sixth, or major seventh—the superposition of the two forms will always produce this set of intervals.

It is not Webern's least merit to have discovered and applied such a law, which is responsible for the genuine contrapuntal *necessity* and the utter harmonic rightness of this canon.

57. The third movement.—Conclusion.—The third and last movement (by far the most significant in its dimensions), also has its "theme" followed by five variations, the last of which functions as a coda. In its dimensions and in its number of variations, in the varied levels of its musical speech, this last movement is the logical and remarkable culmination of the whole—further proof of Webern's masterly sense of balance.

The "theme" is of a gentle and *cantabile* character. (Ex. 75a.) In places, it is even monodic. The form is ternary, approximately ABA.[10] A glance at our quotation shows that here, too, each segment is already the variation of the preceding one. Thus, the second segment literally quotes the first, inverting the relationship of the voices; since the first segment comes from an original form of the row while the second comes from an inverted form, the second segment is the strict inversion of the first. Finally, the third segment is another repetition of the first section, in retrograde

---

[10] Themes for variations constructed in this way are also not lacking in classical music. Remaining within the limits of Beethoven's sonatas, we may cite the theme of the first movement of Op. 26.

motion this time. Thus, by returning to its point of departure, the
passage becomes a full circle, and so acquires strong unity and
genuine plasticity.[11]

Ex. 75

The five variations which follow use the structure of the
"theme," but expand its proportions. The first variation is of a
more decided character. It is largely based on a quarter-note
rhythm; also, it makes great use of the major seventh, which had
been exposed horizontally in the theme and which is heard verti-
cally here.

The second variation is again gentler. The sevenths are used
melodically. In addition, there is a new motive, consisting of
a twice-repeated tone; and there are three-note chords.

The third variation accentuates the agitated character of the
first. The three-note chords of the second variation persist, but a
new eighth-note motive makes its appearance. The *Spiegelbild*
principle is utilized.

[11] The two dotted lines indicate the separations between segments.

The fourth variation brings excitement to its highest pitch. A new element, syncopation in quarter-notes, plays a predominant part. Finally these quarter-notes turn into eighth-notes and produce a little stretto:

The high A, struck three times at the end of the variation, is the highest note in the whole work, and is heard here for the first and only time.

Finally, the fifth variation moves in a dynamic range of p–pp, and closes ppp. It juxtaposes single tones and three-note chords, all of which fall on weak beats of the measure. The *Spiegelbild* principles are used once more. The last measure presents, for the first time, the low B– the lowest tone of the entire composition.

I have already sufficiently stressed that these variations mark the culmination of Webern's most recent tendencies. However, the above analysis of this work demands certain conclusions. If it is true that the entire evolution of musical language is synonymous with the evolution of the principle of variation, it is obvious that Op. 27 is not only the culmination of its composer's work, but also the culmination of our musical language.

It is the first piece of music in which a composer has approached the concept of pure variation.

In our commentary on this work, we constantly put the word "theme" in quotation marks—for good reason, since the variations reproduced no *thematic* aspect of the "theme." This means that in this work *everything is variation*, or, to put it another way, *everything is theme.* This is especially striking in the last movement, where the lack of any recapitulation whatsoever does away with any semblance of hierarchy among the various sections of the movement.

Webern's piano variations are, then, a basic contribution to the "athematic" method of composition.[12]

B. *The String Quartet, Op. 28.*

58. *General and twelve-tone aspects.*—The String Quartet, Op. 28, commissioned by Mrs. Elizabeth Sprague Coolidge, was completed in 1938.[13] If the preceding work, using the piano as its means of expression, had achieved the maximum purity of sound reduced to its bare essentials, the work which now concerns us marks the culmination of contrapuntal style. This work, composed for the instrumental group best qualified to present such a style—a group which can reduce music to its essentials—is, so to speak, made of *nothing but counterpoint.* Almost all the first movement, certain parts of the second, and most of the third use strict canonic forms. The other passages do not use such strict devices, but their working-out is equally rigorous.

From every other viewpoint Op. 28 is a logical sequel to the previous works. The prodigious assurance of the instrumental style (which, as always, exhausts the utmost possibilities of the

[12] Cf. *Introduction to Twelve-Tone Music,* Chapter X.

[13] This quartet was published during the war by Boosey and Hawkes in London. Since I have not yet been able to secure the printed score, I am depending on the manuscript copy which I have owned since 1938. I know that Webern had certain doubts as to the original order of movements. Among other things, he was asking himself if opening with a slow movement and following it by two fast movements would not disturb the equilibrium, or at least be misleading. He had thought of reversing the order of the first two movements; Rudolf Kolisch, who, with his quartet, had performed the work in question several times, thought the original order should be kept, and I agreed with him. But it is possible that Webern decided on the opposite solution, in which case the publisher had to abide by his decision.

[The order of the movements is reversed in the printed score.—Tr.]

instruments) is realized in amazingly economical fashion. How different from the brilliant virtuosity (already carried out with equal self-assurance) of the *Five Movements* for string quartet, Op. 5, or with the style (so expansive in its concision) of the *Bagatelles,* Op. 9! Nothing could give a more vivid picture of Webern's immense progress than the comparison of the purely "physical" aspect of his various scores for string quartet, the composition of which spans nearly thirty years of intensive and clear-headed work.

In its dimensions, Op. 28 is one of Webern's most important works. The forms of the various movements are extremely free; the architecture is more solid than ever. Here, too, *everything is theme*; the variation of the different elements attains, especially in the last movement, incredible intensity.

The most striking feature, however, is the economy of the musical figures. This economy is made possible and even stressed by the structure of the twelve-tone row, which uses only the intervals of minor second, minor third, and major third.

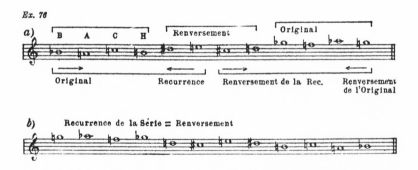

This row, built on the name of BACH, has certain striking characteristics. It is divided into three segments of four notes each; the second is the inversion (or transposed retrograde) of the first, the third a transposed repetition of the first (a). If the row is divided into two equal halves, the second half is the retrograde inversion of the first half; or, if the second half is read backwards, it is the inversion of the original form of the first half (b). The final result is that the retrograde form of the entire row is the same as its inversion. Such a row [14] allows only half as many possibilities as one without such characteristics—hence a more drastic fundamental economy.

Thus we see Webern so greatly concerned with economy that he even deprives himself of the possibilities offered by certain "richer" twelve-tone rows.

Furthermore, we note that this row is made up of six two-note motives, each a half-step. By stressing this interval particularly (especially in the second movement), Webern succeeds in reducing given "thematic" material to a minimum, so that all the wealth of musical discourse must result from the knowledge of variation, the mastery of counterpoint, the extraordinary feeling for architecture, equilibrium and formal logic, and the magnificent imagination which creates inconceivable diversity from the given minimum.

59. *The first movement.*—The first movement is the simplest, and is thus admirably suited to the "introductory" role which it plays in the original manuscript.[15] Its general structure is clearly three-part, ABA. The first part is a long "endless canon" (see the double bars). Here is its beginning:

Ex. 77

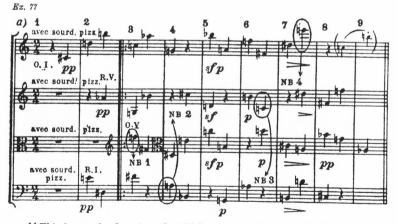

[14] This is not the first time that Webern uses such a row. In that of the Symphony, Op. 21, the original form was identical with the retrograde, so that it, too, furnished only half as many possibilities as ordinary rows.

[15] Cf. note 13 of this chapter.

The contrapuntal characteristics of this passage are as follows:

1) Canon between first violin and viola; both voices unfold the original form of the row, divided into two motives of six notes each. However, the imitation is not literal, for it makes use of two devices of variation—the familiar rhythmic shift, and certain changes in register.

2) Canon between 'cello and second violin; both voices unfold the retrograde forms of the row, depriving each form of two notes according to a subtle procedure of twelve-tone style (NB1, NB2, NB3, and NB4).

Four motives (two of three notes, two of two notes) build each voice. The same devices of variation used in the first canon are applied here to the imitation between the two voices.

Even more interesting is the harmonic structure of this passage. First and foremost, we are struck by a certain harmonic symmetry, which emphasizes the structure. In fact, from the second beat of measure 2, we hear chords of three and four notes arranged as follows: a three-note chord, a four-note chord, then (up till the first beat of measure 5) four three-note chords. From the second beat of measure 5 onwards, the same pattern appears in reverse order: four three-note chords, a four-note chord, and (on the first beat of measure 8) a three-note chord.

Examining the structure of these chords, we discover the same symmetry.

The chord on the second beat of measure 2 corresponds to that on the first beat of measure 8; it is its inversion according to the

tone row scheme (A=A'). The same is true of the chord on the
first beat of measure 3 and that on the second beat of measure 7
(B=B'); and so it goes throughout. Of course this symmetry is
varied, since it employs not only inversions according to the tone-
row scheme, but also changes of register and rhythmic shifts. Let
us also notice that, in the progression of these chords, no two alike
ever follow each other.

  All this is essential, for it shows that Webern's counterpoint is
no mere play of melodic lines, but is constantly subjected to the
strictest harmonic control. The mastery of the musician is such
that he has succeeded in allying the strictest and most independent
counterpoint with a harmony no less autonomous (since this harmony is a coherent whole quite aside from any other considerations). Here, then, is the perfect example of the total interpene-
tration of horizontal and vertical elements, in which the structure
of each helps to bring out the structure of the other.

  The middle section of this movement is more animated and
of looser texture; Webern thus creates a necessary and legitimate
moment of relaxation between the austere outer parts of the movement. This relaxation is further emphasized by the fact that the
middle section begins with a canon (that is, it takes over a strict
element of the preceding section) and little by little turns to a
freer style. (Ex. 78.)

  Let us examine this passage for a moment. It is a double canon
in contrary motion (between the upper voices on the one hand,
the lower voices on the other). Rhythmic refinement is carried to

Ex. 78

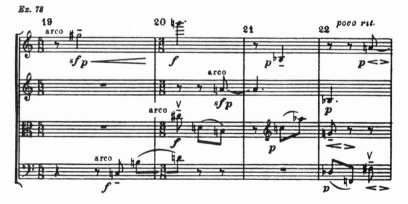

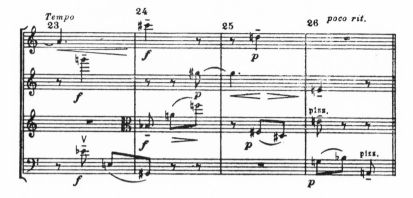

extremes in the canon of the lower voices. Note also the reversal of the statement-answer relationship in measure 23.

The recapitulation presents a picture analogous to that of the exposition. It goes without saying that this recapitulation is highly varied. From the contrapuntal viewpoint, we note a change in the relationship between the voices. Thus, at the beginning, the first violin and viola play the retrograde form of the canon, while the second violin and 'cello play the original form (which is now the one to be deprived of one—not two—notes). All this also brings about harmonic variants. For example, in the passage corresponding to Example 77, we find four four-note chords instead of two.

60. *The second movement.*—The second movement is a sort of "theme with variations." Its dimensions are greater than those of the other two movements, and its form is more complex. Furthermore, as we have already indicated, its economy of means is amazing. The beginning of the movement, which we reproduce here, gives some idea of this. It is a sort of principal "theme" in four sections (I, II, III, IV), the structure of which reminds us of the beginning of the piano variations.[16]

It is important to note that this entire musical discourse uses only a few motives (mostly of two notes only) which are always

---

[16] It is, in fact, A–B; A, statement, B, answer and coda. Each of these phrases may be subdivided into two segments which also bear the mutual relationship of statement and answer. As in the piano variations, B begins with a re-exposition of the first segment of A.

Ex. 79

played by the same instruments. Thus, variation can be produced only by changes in accent and duration.

This passage is even more skeletonized than the beginning of Op. 27, where the variation was produced by the reversal of the relationships between the voices, while here the constant return of the same notes in the same register results in a sort of *immobility*. The four fragments of the phrase use forms of the tone-row chosen in such a way as to permit the almost unvaried repetition of motives which have been stated once and for all.

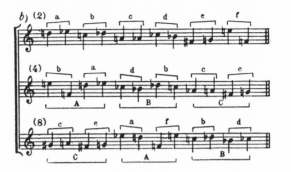

Thus, the whole phrase is an unfoldment of the following chord:

This, then, is the culmination of Webern's dialectics. In composing such a passage as this, the musician has completely transcended the "classical" idea of the theme as such, for nothing could be less like a "classical" theme. Webern transcends this idea because he immediately deprives his "theme" of the static quality which more or less characterizes "classical" themes. The Webern "theme" is already a sort of development *a priori*; it is *entirely made up of variations*, and so is essentially kinetic. And yet, this movement carried to extremes finally becomes synonymous with total immobility, since variations and developments, those essentially *mobile* elements of musical speech, are finally applied only to a single chord, a relatively static element which, in this case, imparts to the various motives their true meaning and their very essence.

61. *The third movement.*—The third movement of Op. 28 is, in my opinion, one of Webern's most shining successes. His contrapuntal knowledge finds here its highest and most perfect expression. The larger structure of the piece is, like that of the first movement, A–B–A. A is a long canonic passage, B is freer, and the recapitulation of A is again an extended canon.

Ex. 80

Example 80 reproduces the first phrase of the beginning of the movement. We see that it is a double canon, simultaneously in contrary motion and retrograde motion; thus, the 'cello part is both the inversion and the retrograde of the first violin part, and the same relationship subsists between second violin and viola. The variation of the different motives, their rhythmic shifting, their "asymmetrical symmetry" produced by retrograde motion—

all this culminates in the acme of subtlety and mastery. I think
that I have familiarized the reader sufficiently with these ideas so
that he can analyze the details of this passage himself. All the
rest of A (and its recapitulation) is elaborated similarly.

B is no less interesting. It uses no fixed contrapuntal form but
is nonetheless strict. The beginning (Ex. 81a) consecutively exposes three motives (x, y, z) which are variants of the motive
BACH.

Each of these motives has its special rhythm; y moves in notes
of equal value, z is syncopated, and x is subdivided into two
similar motives, the second of which is rhythmically shifted. Y is,
then, characterized by a masculine rhythm, and z by a feminine
rhythm, while x combines the two. Example 81b shows us the
superposition of these three variants, x, y, and z. This entire middle

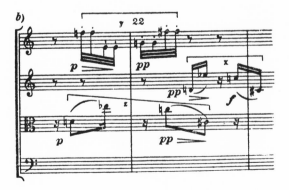

section is a grandiose development of the BACH motive, which undergoes bewildering variations and gives rise to counterpoint of extraordinary richness (and sobriety!).

C. *Conclusion*

62. *The work of Webern and tradition.*—Thus we complete our examination (still too superficial) of the work of a composer who, in my opinion, represents the greatest advancement in the evolution of the art of music. It seems to me that this hypothesis may be taken seriously, since we have tried to show how, from the very beginning, Webern's work has attacked the most fundamental and radical problems of the evolution of music, and how his latest works have furnished novel and pure solutions to these problems. This frees us from the necessity of recapitulating the various phases of Webern's activity as well as the numerous acquisitions revealed in his music.

For greater completeness, our analysis should have included two other works which play an important part in Webern's total output. I am thinking of the orchestrations of Schubert's *German Dances* and of the six-part fugue of Bach's *Musical Offering*. These two scores are so perfectly realized, and present such tremendous problems, that it is impossible to study them here in detail. (It is to be hoped that they will soon be the object of a special study.) However, we must emphasize that, in the special and general preoccupations which they reveal, these two orchestrations prove that Webern's genius—so eccentric at first glance— has remained in contact with the great and genuine musical tradition of Western Europe. To tell the truth, in undertaking such tasks as these, Webern was merely following the example of his master Schoenberg, whose orchestrations of Bach (two chorale preludes and an organ prelude and fugue), far from being mere exercises in hedonism like most such attempts, participate significantly in that spirit of *reactivation* on which we have tried to shed new light. In fact, the special characteristic of Schoenberg's orchestrations (carried even farther in the Bach orchestration by Webern) is that they try neither to "embellish" the original sonority of Bach's music with gratuitous instrumental effects nor to clarify the polyphony of their "originals" by means of an orchestration replete with academic respect for the "style" of Bach's time. Schoenberg's respect for the works of his great predecessors is of a completely different character. This respect is an *a priorism*, in the sense that the work of Bach *must be perfect* (and thus needs no "embellishment" or "clarification" of the polyphony) simply because it is from this work, and that of the other great masters, that we derive all our criterions of artistic perfection, as well as the very structure of the musical language which we understand and speak. What decides a Schoenberg or a Webern to undertake such orchestrations is a purely compositional need, on the same level as the necessity which governs the conception of their other works. They use the scores of their predecessors as *models* (again in the sense in which an artist paints a picture "after" one by a great master of the past) which may help them to realize certain precise problems of musical composition. Thus, their orchestrations become original works, the sonority of which is rather that of Schoenberg or Webern than that of Bach or Schubert. This is especially striking in Webern's orchestration of the fugue of the *Musical Offering*,[17] which confronts both performer and listener with the same problems as would be presented by any of his other works of the same period. This orchestration, finished in 1935, reveals preoccupations analogous to those which we have observed in all his works since the Symphony, Op. 21. The exposition of the subject and that of the first countersubject are quite explicit in this respect. The way in which the different motives of the two themes are distributed among the different instruments is reminiscent of similar devices in Op. 21, 22, and 26, and clearly illustrates Webern's compositional intention.

---

[17] This is rather a special case, since the fugue in question is not written for any specific instrument or instrumental combination. Also, Schubert's *German Dances* have been preserved only in a sketch on two or three staves, without any instrumental indications whatsoever. This would not have prevented any other musician from making orchestrations in the guise of faithful stylistic reconstructions (as witness the many attempts to orchestrate this particular fugue) which can only serve as an *Ersatz* for the orchestrations which Bach or Schubert would have made, and which pay not the slightest attention to compositional problems.

Ex. 82

In whatever realm Webern is active, he always teaches us one of the most valuable of all lessons. The astonishing novelty of his work, especially of the last scores, never belies the tradition which gave it birth. On the contrary, it is this very novelty of conception and invention which assures the continued life of tradition. Have we not seen that it is in Webern's last scores that one of the most traditional of all elements—large form—is realized? We have seen how these scores achieved their goal, but we must now say that the economy of means and nudity of thought is such that, in spite of their considerable dimensions, the duration of all these pieces is still relatively short. It is true that a work like the Quartet, Op. 28, affords a glimpse of truly remarkable possibilities of "expansion," thanks to which Webern's last works attain significant dimensions. These works are the two cantatas for solo voices, chorus, and orchestra, Op. 29 and 31, and the *Variations for Orchestra*,[18] Op. 30, which last nearly twenty minutes.[19] Also, Webern seems to

[18] This work was played at Winterthur, in February, 1943, under the direction of Hermann Scherchen. The first cantata, Op. 29, received its first performance in the twentieth ISCM festival (London, July, 1946) under the baton of Rankl.

[19] I have devoted a study to these three works in the second volume of my work *Meanings of Contemporary Musicians.*

have been working on a chamber concerto in several movements, which was to be even longer; it is not yet known whether or not he was able to finish it.

Those who have followed my reasoning thus far will understand that I am not citing these facts for their anecdotal interest.

63. *Homage to Anton Webern.*—The death of Anton Webern, which took place under tragic circumstances in September, 1945, seems to have gone unmourned both by the music-loving public and by the musical press. This is not surprising, for his very life— calm, modest and retired—passed by unseen. It was marked by no striking events—hence the absence of biographical details in the present study. Thus the silence which surrounds the music of Webern, and which is also part of this music, belongs to the natural order of things. In fact, there is no reason to be surprised at the enormous number of musicians and music-lovers to whom this music "says nothing." Indifference and hostility to Webern's art are the ineluctable consequences of this art, justified insofar as they bear witness to its worth.

That is what Schoenberg understood when, in 1924, he wrote the following preface to the *Six Bagatelles*, Op. 9, of his pupil and friend:

Just as the brevity of these pieces speaks in their favor, even so it is necessary to speak in favor of this brevity.

Think of the concision which expression in such brief form demands! Every glance is a poem, every sigh a novel. But to achieve such concentration—to express a novel in a single gesture, a great joy in a single breath—every trace of sentimentality must be correspondingly banished.

He alone will understand these pieces who is of the faith according to which one expresses in tones what can be said only in tones.

They will stand up against criticism no better than this faith itself, or any other faith.

For, if faith can move mountains, incredulity can make these mountains cease to exist. Against such impotence, faith itself is impotent. In that case, can the performer know how to play these pieces, can the listener know how to accept them? Can performers and listeners who believe fail to communicate this belief to each other?

But what to do with the heathens? Fire and sword may reduce them to peace; but only those can be overcome who have faith.

May this silence resound in their ears!

I, for one, believe that the day will come when Webern's silence will fill concert-halls along with the works of the great masters who are so dear to us—these masters to whose number Webern already belonged in his lifetime, and whom he has now rejoined in silence and death.

PART V

The Structure of Contemporary Musical Speech

Stimulate a future composer to
write in a more dignified manner.

A. SCHOENBERG
Models for Beginners in Composition.

CHAPTER XII

General Foundations of the Musical Language

64. *The essence of musical language.*—If we have succeeded, during the previous sections of this work, in explaining the way in which the evolution of polyphony finds its truest living incarnation in the works of Schoenberg, Berg, and Webern, we must now draw certain conclusions from these explanations. The first necessary conclusion is this: by virtue of the genuineness of their participation in the evolution of polyphony, Arnold Schoenberg and his disciples enter *a fortiori* upon a new phase of the musical language. In order to understand this assertion more clearly, let us examine the idea of musical language more closely.

Just what is this language? Before we give a definite answer to this question, let us note that spontaneous and natural experience proves that musical language *exists*. Take the case of an average music-loving listener or musical amateur. For a number of years he has been attending concerts; he has been hearing compositions most of which were written between the time of Bach and that of Debussy, and which therefore display a comparatively large assortment of different "styles." To such a listener, these works *speak*; they are familiar to him, he comprehends them, he *understands their language*. This understanding has nothing to do with the professional technique of analytical knowledge. Our listener does not analyze; in the first place, he lacks the technical equipment to do so, and, in the second place, when he happens to formulate commentaries on the works which are the objects of his delight or scorn —commentaries which he believes to be "profound" and analytical —for the most part he is simply talking *around* the music. He then abandons himself to purely subjective and personal considerations, which may be suggested by the music up to a point, but which eventually have no further contact with it. And nevertheless, it is evident that he understands this music—otherwise why would he go to hear it?

What, then, is this comprehension? It is nothing else than the awareness—*a priori*, as it were—of the polyphonic structure of the work. Ever since he began hearing music, our listener has been gradually familiarizing himself with certain melodic, harmonic, rhythmic, and orchestral idioms which, taken all together, constitute the elements of the musical language. Perhaps he cannot give precise names to these elements, perhaps he does not even know that they exist as such—in any case, he cannot define their various roles in the articulation and constitution of the discourse which he is hearing—but this does not prevent him from spontaneously comprehending the *oneness* of all these elements—that is, making a synthesis of the components of polyphony and thus realizing, in his own mind, the evolution of musical speech.

Hence there arise two types of reactions, both of which may frequently be observed. On the one hand, the listener, if he is hearing for the first time the work of a composer (or of a period) familiar to him, will not be at all confused by this first hearing. The work will immediately appear to him as a collection of familiar traits, and its complete meaning will quickly be revealed. It may make a more or less powerful impression on him; it may prove to be more or less "beautiful," or "important"; but in no case will it come as a real *surprise*. On the other hand, if he encounters for the first time a work which is not within the boundaries of what he is accustomed to hearing, he will be surprised, even shocked. This can happen in the case of works both older and newer than his usual repertory. There is nothing abnormal about this, for here is what happens. The sound-forms which now confront him do not *speak* to him, because he is incapable of grasping their logic and their meaning. The melodic, harmonic, and rhythmic idioms appear incoherent to him because they use certain devices unheard of in the works with which he is familiar. The melody and harmony use certain "dissonant" intervals; the rhythm is asymmetrical and too complex. If our listener is incapable of grasping the logic of a single one of these elements, how could he come to a conscious realization of the *whole* musical discourse? And yet, we may often observe that the conscientious music-lover need only hear several repetitions of the work which surprised him on first hearing in order to become so familiar with it that, at length, it, too, will *speak* to him—will speak a new and original language, perhaps, but a language just as coherent and articulate as that of the works long familiar to him.

From all this, we may deduce that the musical language *exists*, but not as something established in advance according to eternal and immutable laws. Even more than spoken or written language, musical language is *in a perpetual state of becoming*, inseparable from the sound-forms which embody it and which define it in the very moment of their appearance. The musical language is created as fast as the works of music are created; in other words, its essence resides in its very existence. And, indeed, it is impossible for us to think of any of the laws or elements of this language without simultaneously thinking of the work or works which embodied them.

65. *A priori conception of musical history.*—Thus a new light is thrown on the attitude of Schoenberg's school toward tradition. The first condition of this attitude is respect for the great masters from whom this tradition truly came. We have already touched on this subject (62) but may now go into it more deeply. If we admit that the essence of musical language resides in its existence, this means that our knowledge of the fact that *music is tradition* is in no way identical with our knowledge of the exterior causality which produced the succession of historic events, but that it is the knowledge of the "way of life" of music. To understand any musical element is to be conscious of its historicity, to take it as something which does not simply occur *in* history, but *is* completely historical. Thus we come to a conception of the history of music which has nothing to do with a history of *musical facts*, but which rests upon a strong *structural a priorism* of the evolution of these facts. From this *a priorism* comes a certainty with respect to the constitution of the musical language in the works of the great masters of the past. Evidently, we are free to imagine many facts and to invent many theories about the activity of these masters;

and yet, all these manifestations of our imagination must culminate in essential conclusions which appear in the light of apodictic evidence. For, indeed, the great masters of music have worked in the realm of sound-forms. Their compositional consciousness, depending on such existing forms, has created others, which, in their turn, serve as models for still others in the future. The existence of such forms can no longer be a matter of doubt, any more than the existence of the musical language which is embodied in these very forms. Tradition gives them a stable value, not by making them sufficient for all time, but by rendering possible its own evolution from them. Thus, each sound-form is an element acquired once and for all, an element of musical *syntax*.

Schoenberg, with his amazing lucidity, seems to have understood this better than anyone else. A recent theoretical work, his *Models for Beginners in Composition*,[1] proves it. "The main objectives of this syllabus," says the author in his preface, "are: *ear-training*, development of a *sense of form*, and understanding of the *technique* and *logic* of musical construction." After remarking, among other things, that "often those who have talent think that today one may write everything," after discussing the method which he introduces to arrive at the "coordination of melody and harmony," [2] and after declaring that in this syllabus "great stress is laid upon the concept of variation, because this is the most important tool for producing logic in spite of variety," Schoenberg finally states that the study and analysis of the examples "might stimulate a future composer to write in a more dignified manner."

This last remark, "to write in a more dignified manner," is especially interesting; it is Schoenberg's way of saying that most composers do not achieve that dignity conferred on their craft by a profound, active, and respectful *a priori* knowledge of the great fundamental and traditional problems of composition.

This is the very essence of the question. The examples, with their accompanying analyses and commentaries, contained in the

[1] G. Schirmer, Inc., New York. Second revised edition, 1943.

[2] This is not to be confused with the twelve-tone conception of unity between melody and harmony. (The examples in this syllabus are intended for beginners; they were all written by Schoenberg himself, and are strictly tonal.) What Schoenberg wants is to make the pupil hear the harmony of a passage while he is writing the melody.

little book which concerns us constitute a sort of *phenomenology* of certain sound-forms, based on an *a priori* conception of the great musical tradition. And this phenomenology of sound-forms confronts us, once again, with the following series of assertions: music is a language; in order to be able to compose music in a "dignified manner," one must really know this language, and to that end one must begin by knowing the elements of its syntax.

This syntax is given to us in all the sound-forms invented up till our time. We may, then, deduce it from the past, and if we know how to incorporate this past into our own activity, we shall enrich and advance the language of music. For, just as every sound-form considered by itself has its tradition *behind* it and *in* it, even so all the sound-forms of a given historical moment *imply* all the sound-forms of the past. Or, more accurately, the totality of present sound-forms implies a continuous flow of such forms, each of which implies all the preceding ones. It is this total continuity which embraces tradition *as a whole*—the tradition that has passed to the living present, which in its turn is asserting itself as a tradition, that is to say as a new point of departure for the same tradition.

CHAPTER XIII

The Living Language of Music

66. *The twelve-tone technique as foundation of the living language of music.*—The last assertions of the preceding chapter will now help us to understand some of the problems of the living language of music. First of all, let us note that Schoenberg and his disciples have never tried to deprive accepted musical ideas of their traditional meaning. They have a right to consider themselves *the most traditional of contemporary composers*. Our analyses of the works of these three great masters have attempted to show how the most advanced and radical acquisitions of these works simply prolong the tradition to which they owe their existence. Our general remarks on musical language have now enabled us to comprehend how these acquisitions enrich the language and at the same time respect its very essence.

However, this essence implies the idea of universality, which we have not yet stressed. Indeed, a musical language, if it is to be properly so called, must not be spoken by only a few isolated individuals, but must be accessible to all musicians who want to make use of it. This condition is the inevitable consequence of the previously stated conditions. It is fulfilled when the new acquisitions prove essential to the evolution of polyphony; they can then give rise to the formulation of a technique or a theoretical system, and thus become available to any musician who wants to learn. Schoenberg fulfilled these conditions with the twelve-tone technique, which thus appears as the very foundation of the living musical language. Of course, it would be absurd to claim that one need only master the twelve-tone technique to be sure of participating in the constitution of a contemporary musical speech. The adoption of the new technique is necessary, but it is not enough. Just as in the eighteenth and nineteenth centuries everybody composed in keys but everybody did not play a real part in the evolution of the musical language, so today the use of the twelve-tone technique produces valuable results in some, but by no means all cases. Other, deeper qualities are needed for the achievement of such results. That is why Schoenberg, Berg, and Webern have taught the new technique very sparingly. In their teaching, they have laid most stress on the well-disciplined development of *all* the musical faculties of their pupils. Schoenberg, who likes to tell his pupils that there is still "lots of good music to be written in C major," thinks that if the pupil's musical consciousness is sufficiently "advanced," the profound and detailed knowledge of his craft will inevitably lead him where he must go—probably, that is, to the twelve-tone technique. In other words, the perfect assimilation of the laws of the musical syntax of the past brings the would-be master to this syntax of today—the only one in which his mastery may be expressed.

Therefore, there is no reason to be surprised at the relatively small number of twelve-tone composers; after all, the number of completely lucid musical minds has always been very small at any given time. This means that nearly all those who are now composing in the new technique are on a higher level than other contemporary composers.

However, it is evident that the more the twelve-tone technique is used by an increasing number of composers (and this is taking place today), the less real effort of lucidity will be required to use it, and the more numerous will be the insignificant works composed according to its laws. The same thing happened at the beginning of the tonal system, when adherence to this system was synonymous with logical consideration of certain polyphonic problems, and when the very adoption of such an attitude almost automatically guaranteed, if not a masterpiece, at least a work of value (if only in its consolidation of certain discoveries), a work often useful, in its anonymity, to the geniuses of the present and the future. This explains the high level of nearly all Bach's contemporaries and immediate predecessors; on the other hand, because of the general distribution of the tonal system, many of his successors are completely uninteresting musicians whose works made no contribution to the evolution of polyphony.

In my other book I gave some attention to Schoenberg's other direct or indirect disciples who belong to the school with which we are concerned. What especially characterizes their activity is that, instead of trying to make new discoveries at all costs (as is often the case today), they try to assimilate the discoveries of their masters, and thus to consolidate these discoveries. Here, I think, we see the initial effort and the conscious will to construct a truly contemporary musical speech.

67. *Fluctuations of the living musical language.*—In the last chapters of my *Introduction to Twelve-Tone Music*, I tried to throw some light on the consistent appearance of certain twelve-tone devices in the works of Schoenberg, Berg, Webern, and a few other composers written since Schoenberg's Op. 31. Having asserted that in his *Variations for Orchestra* Schoenberg had reached the stage of complete mastery of all treatments of the twelve-tone technique, I concluded that later twelve-tone compositions simply prolonged Schoenberg's acquisitions. At present, after having become acquainted with many new scores, I am still of the same opinion. I have, therefore, further concluded that this sort of consolidation of Schoenberg's discoveries in the realm of laws governing the twelve-tone row is the first step in the construction of the living musical language. In fact, if all twelve-tone composers handle a common technique in a common way, the technique acquires a collective quality, a universality, which is indispensable to every real language. We can say that all composers of this school use 1) the total resources of chromaticism, 2) a disciplined organization of this material, 3) devices which enable this discipline to engender certain sound-forms, or idioms, that—quite aside from individual differences in talent and temperament—belong to the common syntax of composition.

There should, then, result a certain common denominator for the various melodic, harmonic, and rhythmic idioms. Is there such a common denominator? Yes and no. In a general way, it may be said that the melodic and harmonic idioms, since they always use the same material, and since they are always extracted from this material by a similar process, acquire a certain *resemblance* to one another, in the sense in which such a resemblance existed between the idioms of different composers belonging to the same stage of the evolution of tonality. In the same way, the twelve-tone composers' awareness of the laws of "perpetual variation" leads them to more or less similar procedures in all phases of style—melodic, harmonic, rhythmic, and instrumental.

However, our time has not yet seen the establishment of a new order. Certainly the old order of tonality has been suspended, but that does not tell us exactly what order will succeed it. We have observed in the last works of Schoenberg and Berg a definite effort to re-establish certain tonal structures which can produce functional unity in the total resources of chromaticism. This effort has even been successful. On the other hand, we have discovered in the works of Schoenberg, and especially in those of Webern, numerous elements which strive to transcend any tonal order. Although all these works use the same fundamental devices of twelve-tone technique, the idioms which result from these devices differ according to whether they tend to re-establish or to surpass tonal functions. A simple comparison of two previously cited examples cannot fail to be explicit in this respect.

Let us take our Example 25a, quoted from Schoenberg's Suite, Op. 29, and let us compare it with Example 77a quoted from Webern's Quartet, Op. 28. The twelve-tone devices used here are derived from the same principle, the superposition of different forms of the row. Nevertheless, the idioms engendered by these devices are quite different in every respect. Even without choosing such extreme cases, it would be easy to find a similar state of affairs in many other cases outwardly less characteristic.

All this should make it clear that a certain quality of "disparity" (variety of musical idioms) within "homogeneity" (identity of devices governing the conception of such idioms) is the very essence of contemporary musical speech as it has manifested itself up till now. The evolution of polyphony has reached a stage in which a new order is about to arise, although, perhaps, all the problems of the old order have not been completely solved. This explains the survival, in many works which already outline the elements of a new order, of certain other elements belonging to the old order. Such survivals, which I have explained elsewhere, signify not only that we are living in a period of transition, but also that our living musical language as described here is, in its very fluctuations, the result of living musical activity and of genuine effort, insofar as the musical minds which create it are powerfully drawn towards all the unexplored realms of polyphony. Thus, the various fluctuations of these musical minds are only, as I have said elsewhere, "the pulsations of an intense *life* which imparts to the language of today its vibrant vitality as well as its profound necessity." [1]

68. *Sketch of a new theory of twelve-tone polyphony.*—The role of a prophet would be repugnant to me. I am profoundly convinced that a valid musical theory can do no more than describe a certain number of constant phenomena which are found in a significant number of compositions. In this sense, a theory cannot be formulated until a long time after the composition of the works on which it is based. The fluctuations of our living musical language have, up till now, prevented any more precise theoretical formulation than that of the very generalized laws of twelve-tone technique. We are still too close to the center of things; we do not yet have enough perspective to synthesize the immense total of the acquisitions which characterize the present phase of contemporary polyphony. There is no doubt that such a synthesis, for which this book is a preparation, will be realized sooner or later. That will be a moment of polyphonic evolution at which the present fluctuations have subsided, in one way or another; from then on, it will be possible to teach strictly according to the laws of twelve-tone polyphony. It is probable, also, that the language of music will then be more homogeneous than at present.[2]

---

[1] *Introduction to Twelve-Tone Music,* Chapter XII.

[2] It is true that even today's music will certainly seem more homogeneous to future observers than it does to us. The differences will have been levelled out and the fluctuations will appear smaller; the re-establishment of tonal functions and the transcending of these functions will be less sharply differentiated. This inescapable phenomenon may easily be observed in a glance at the various polyphonic periods of the past. We often confuse two older composers whose works must have sounded and looked entirely different to their contemporaries. Also, the different works of a single composer, in which he was tackling entirely different polyphonic problems, often sound very much alike to us.

Again, I do not want to set myself up as a prophet. I am no historian or esthetician, and I profess theories only insofar as they result from my activity as a composer. This activity, which brings me into constant contact with the problems presented in the works of those who were and are my masters, and who are thus responsible for my development and my experiences, furnishes me with a certain number of elements (drawn both from my contact with the music of others and from the effort which I expend on my own music) which justify me in drawing some conclusions as to the present direction of polyphonic evolution.

This is what I want to formulate as accurately as I can; and this formulation, besides synthesizing the principal observations of our previous study, will, I believe, constitute the basis for a new theory of twelve-tone polyphony.

A. Let us begin by stating that all laws which we have been able to formulate up till now are derived from a single supreme law, the law of perpetual variation. Indeed, it is possible to say that all the melodic, rhythmic, and harmonic laws which we shall try to deduce simply illustrate, in their own realms, one and the same fundamental compositional attitude.

Let us, then, examine the simplest elements first.

a) *Melody.*—The melodic structure of a statement, a phrase, or a theme is elaborated from different motives. Since all these terms might lead to confusion, let us give their Schoenbergian definitions.[3]

The *motive* is the smallest melodic unit. It contains one or more intervals based on a single rhythmic figure.

The *phrase* consists of at least two motives, and thus becomes a small self-contained unified structure. The "school form" usually presents the phrase in two measures. The separation between two phrases is equivalent to a *comma* in written language.

The *sentence* consists of two phrases (or a statement and answer) to which a *codetta,* usually consisting of but a single motive, is sometimes added. The sentence may be a theme in itself (like most of Webern's themes) in which case the separation between

[3] Cf. Schoenberg, *Models for Beginners.*

two sentences is equivalent to a *period* in written language. But often the theme is the result of the juxtaposition of two distinct segments; in this case we have a *period,* and the two segments, *antecedent* and *consequent,* are then separated by a *cesura* (equivalent to a semicolon). The whole sometimes ends with a *coda,* which is an independent statement or phrase.

Schoenberg, in *Models for Beginners,* stresses the devices of variation which should govern the conception of all these elements. In twelve-tone compositions, such procedures become completely conscious, and are under the most rigid control.

In the sentence, variation is applied to the motives; the intervals may be changed while the rhythm remains the same, and *vice versa.* In addition, there are the rhythmic shifts with which we are already familiar.

The answer varies the statement by presenting its motives in a new order and once more changing their rhythm and intervals.

The sentences which follow the first sentence are variants of it—often quite extreme variants, if they come from different forms of the tone-row.

The analysis of one of Schoenberg's extremely significant themes will clarify all this. Example 83 reproduces the beginning of the Fourth Quartet, Op. 37, which is a large period of three sentences.

The first sentence, measures 1–6, is exposed in the first violin. The *statement* consists of motives, I, II, and III. II varies I, using the half-tone motive in the opposite direction and changing the rhythm. III, a rhythmic diminution of I, enlarges the first interval. The *answer* consists of motives IV and V. IV is a variant of II, while V is I with the rhythm shifted; thus the original order of the motives is reversed. Motive VI is a *codetta.* Its rhythm is derived from II and IV, but here has the value of an upbeat; its intervals are derived from I and from the interval which separates II and III (a fifth, which here becomes a fourth).

The second sentence is exposed in the second violin (measures 6–9). The statement, motives VII and VIII, gives the first motive the value of an upbeat derived from the preceding codetta. Motive VIII is a variant of VII; the two intervals of VII are each

made a half-step larger, and the rhythm is changed. The answer, motives IX and X, varies the statement by shifting the upbeat-rhythm to the middle of the measure and leaving it only the interval of a major third, borrowed from VII. Furthermore, this upbeat-rhythm is prolonged into the next motive, which, corresponding to VIII, varies the accentuation and intervals of VIII. The order of the intervals of VIII is reversed; also, the second interval of VIII is made a half-step smaller and the first interval of VIII is inverted. We must also note that the second sentence uses an inverted form of the row, whereas the first sentence was derived from the original form.

The third sentence, the recapitulation of the first, is again exposed in the first violin (measures 9–15). Rhythmically, it is very close to the first sentence, though there are some subtle variants—an added upbeat at the beginning, the omission of the first strong beat in measures 11 and 12, and the extension of the codetta. Melodically, the intervals are entirely different, since this sentence uses the retrograde form of the original row.

I think that these few comments are sufficient to give an idea of how variation is applied to melodic structure in twelve-tone composition.

b) *Harmony.*—The example which we have just analyzed is also useful for the comprehension of harmonic laws, insofar as they can already be formulated from certain works written in the twelve-tone technique.

In my other book I greatly stressed this aspect of twelve-tone composition, and drew attention to the fact that such a passage as this is the perfect illustration of one of the most essential twelve-tone laws, according to which the exposition of a principal idea must be characterized by an extremely strict harmonization of a very well-defined type.[4] In fact, the theme which we are

---

[4] My words on the subject were as follows: (*Introduction to Twelve-Tone Music*, Chapter IX)

"When a piece exposes, for the first time, a theme which is to play an important part, this theme should unfold one or more *complete* forms of the twelve-tone row. If there is a harmonization, it should be systematically and consistently handled in the *same way* throughout the entire exposition of the theme. (One might add a corollary; a second thematic idea, contrasting with the first, should be derived from the forms of the tone-row according to an equally consistent, but different plan. Cf. the two themes

studying has the following harmonic peculiarity: each phrase is harmonized by chords which result from the breaking up of the tone-row form used in the melody into four equal segments. From the twelve-tone viewpoint, there is thus established a harmonic scheme which need not be described further, as it is explicitly shown in our musical example.[5] On the other hand, we must again draw attention to the way in which the spirit of variation is manifested here.

First, let us note the constant changes in the position of all the chords; indeed, none of them is ever repeated in its previous position. Then, we note a progressive increase in the rhythmic variety of the chords, and in their accentuation, throughout the passage. Thus, in the first three measures, a single formula, derived from the molossic rhythm, is used. In the next three measures, this formula is varied; it is shifted so that it crosses the bar-line (NB1), and the same chord (with the metric value of a quarter-note instead of an eighth-note) is repeated three times in succession. Later (NB2) there is even more variety; we now have an iambo-trochaic rhythmic formula.

In the second sentence, variety continues to increase. We note that the principal rhythmic formula (eighth-note—sixteenth-rest —sixteenth-note—eighth-note) continually appears on different beats of the measure. Finally, the third section of the theme uses, pell-mell as it were, all the rhythmic devices thus far heard, and introduces a new one in measure 11. Thus, variety has attained considerable proportions, but there is no incoherence because we have been led to this point gradually.

In closing, let us note the numerous changes of register (like-

---

of Schoenberg's Op. 33a.) Such a rule seems to me neither arbitrary nor gratuitous. Given the highly kinetic nature of twelve-tone composition, the application of this rule, which expresses a relatively static procedure, provides for a certain gradation of musical intensity. Furthermore, the authenticity of the procedure cannot be doubted, since it governs the exposition of the following themes of Schoenberg: theme of the variations, Op. 31, first theme, Op. 33a, first theme, Op. 37. Webern uses the same procedure in the exposition of the theme of the variations in Op. 21." I could add innumerable such examples.

[5] The reader will find many similar types of harmonization analyzed in my *Introduction*. He should also look back at Ex. 66, the theme of the variations in Webern's Symphony, Op. 21, which uses an equally strict harmonization.

wise introduced gradually) which are also produced by the spirit of variation.

These few indications should give some idea of the harmonic laws which we may begin to deduce from twelve-tone composition.

c) *Rhythm.*—Our remarks on melody and harmony have already familiarized us with certain rhythmic problems which are also, of course, governed by the principles of perpetual variation. I should like to add a few more precise details, and especially to emphasize that the genuine polyphonic tradition *does not admit the idea of rhythm for its own sake.* Rhythm is merely an element which is produced spontaneously by horizontal and vertical sound-forms because it articulates the unfoldment of these forms in such a way that musical speech would be impossible without it. In this sense, the "purely rhythmic" experiments of certain contemporary composers [6] seem to me not only mistaken, but quite meaningless, since in them there is no "pure rhythm" (inasmuch as this rhythm operates willy-nilly with melodic and harmonic elements) but simply a tremendous impoverishment of polyphony as such.

It is, then, hardly possible to study rhythm without the melodic, harmonic, and contrapuntal formulae in which it is embodied. In this sense, twelve-tone polyphony is extremely traditional, for it simply develops the possibilities of variety and coherence implicit in the spirit of variation. Another glance at Example 83 will show us how admirably Schoenberg applies this rhythmic variety and coherence to the entire polyphonic structure. The rhythmic relationships between melody and harmony are rather simple in the first phrase. In the second phrase, they become more complex, and tend towards complementary rhythm, which is triumphantly manifested, with amazing wealth and variety of invention, in the third phrase. It goes without saying that the application of such rhythmic complexity and variety to polyphony becomes even more explicit in contrapuntal passages, wherein the varying accentuation of the different voices produces that "polyrhythm" which, from the first contrapuntists to our own time, has

---

[6] I am thinking especially of Stravinsky. (Cf. my previously cited article, *Les Temps Modernes*, No. 7.)

remained the basis of polyphonic rhythm. In this connection, I refer the reader to Example 44b (Berg, *Lyric Suite*) for a simple example, and to Example 80 (Webern, Quartet Op. 28) for a more complex example.

Before closing this discussion of rhythm, I should like to quote another passage of Schoenberg, the extreme precision of which strikes to the root of the matter.

Ex. 84

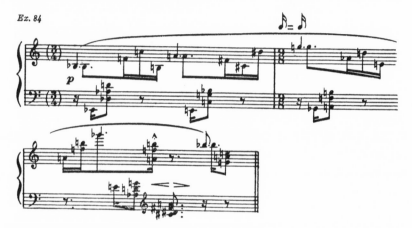

This passage is taken from the piano piece Op. 33a, where it functions as the recapitulation of the first theme. The twelve-tone harmonization is very strict; the rhythm, too, is most instructive. Let us begin with the middle voice. Three times in succession it repeats the same formula—a sort of dactyl plus a third short beat [7]— with rhythmic variants. The first time, it begins on a strong beat, and its second short note falls on another weak beat. The second time, it is composed entirely of weak beats, since the last strong beat of the measure is not struck. The third time, it begins again on a strong beat; but, since the meter is now changed, the rest of the formula is unfolded on weak beats. Because of the new meter, the formula, if repeated again, would no longer undergo rhythmic variation; therefore, the formula is now changed.[8]

The top voice, which merely marks the accents of the middle voice, superimposes a different rhythm of five equal note-values,

[7] Or a trochee with a catalectic ending.

[8] Note, too, the constant variation of the melodic intervals.

which may be considered as a spondee (first measure) followed by a molossus (second measure) .

Finally the lower voices, the actual harmonization, introduce an iambic rhythm which is constantly varied. The first "long" note falls on a weak beat, the second on the strong beat which was not sounded in the middle voice. In the second measure, the same formula is shifted so that it occupies different parts of the two beats where it appears.

Such a carefully balanced superposition of different rhythms creates an extremely rich polyphonic rhythm. In this sense, the term *polyrhythm* seems to me out of place, for one of the conditions *sine qua non* of polyphonic richness and variety is that the rhythm must display the same qualities which are inherent in the other elements of such a musical discourse.[9]

d) *Instrumentation. Registration.*—It is clear that so rich and varied a musical speech must be expressed in terms of an instrumental style which possesses these same qualities. We have already given sufficient attention to the problems of instrumentation which arise in this connection, and we know that the search for the most extreme means of instrumentation is one of the essential characteristics of the spirit of variation and of architectonic purity, in the sense in which we have understood these concepts.

Furthermore, simply reading over all the examples in this book should be enough to show how much care our composers have lavished on the problem of registration. Here as elsewhere it is important to emphasize that this registration is never used as an "effect" for its own sake, but that its infinite variety simply underlines the variety characteristic of the other elements of the musical speech.

More or less, then, all these elements essentially constitute an indissoluble whole. They are mutually inseparable, and it is only because we are trying to analyze, and so must discuss one thing at a time, that we have been setting up artificial distinctions in a realm where everything is the result of a compositional act of syn-

---

[9] In order to indicate more precisely the rhythmic functions of the various polyphonic parts, Schoenberg often uses the traditional symbols of metrical prosody: / = accented, ⌒ = non-accented. Thus he makes it clear that a tone can fall on a strong beat without being accented, and vice versa.

thesis, an act which, with its powerful force of invention under the control of a sovereign mastery, spontaneously and simultaneously encompasses all the constituent elements of musical speech.

B. Having observed how these various constituent elements are produced in twelve-tone music by the spirit of variation, we must now see what are the ultimate consequences of such a compositional technique.

Roughly speaking, we will recall that Webern's work seemed to offer the most complete realization of this technique. The following observations are, then, primarily based on this music.

One of the most important consequences of the state of mind which concerns us seems to me to be the ultimate transcendence of the tonal system.[10] This is obvious, for the preservation of even the most "free" and "vague" tonal functions calls for a certain symmetry which impedes the utmost development of the spirit of variation. In the realm of musical forms, recapitulations, varied though they may be, are necessary for the reaffirmation of certain strong thematic elements without which tonal equilibrium would be menaced. That is why Schoenberg, even in as daring a work (from the formal viewpoint) as his Piano Concerto, Op. 42, has to bring back the first theme in the last movement. On the other hand, we have seen that Webern, in his last works, succeeds in completely eliminating the idea of recapitulation without harming structural unity in any way. As a matter of fact, Webern's last works constitute the first musical experience which entirely transcends the various functions even vaguely reminiscent of the tonal system.

Under what conditions can this transcendence occur? Our observations on Webern's last scores should help us to answer this question. Once again, then, let us analyze the various elements of his polyphony.

a) *Melody.*—Melodically, it is necessary to avoid giving predominance to any one tone in any one voice of the polyphonic

---

[10] For some supplementary remarks on this, see *Introduction to Twelve-Tone Music*, Chapter XI.

structure. That is why Webern uses more and more complete un-
foldments of all forms of the row in all voices. This tendency
reaches its limits in the Quartet, Op. 28. The entire first movement
and most of the third call for the simultaneous unfoldment of
four forms of the row.[11] In places where the row is not so treated,
repetition of one tone in any voice, before the unfoldment of the
eleven other tones, is still avoided, unless it is limited (as in
Ex. 79a) to the constant re-exposition of the same motives for
harmonic reasons. Before we turn to harmony, let us recall that
the perpetual unfoldment of the total resources of chromaticism,
by depriving each individual tone of any special privileges, effec-
tively eliminates all tonal reminiscences.

   b) *Harmony*.—Elsewhere [12] I have emphasized the *false relation of the octave*, which must be avoided in the melody as well
as in the harmony, and which can even take place when only
complete forms of the row are used (for example, between the
end of one form and the beginning of the next). This concept is
fundamental, for, if there is a false relation, the tone involved
automatically acquires special importance. In this sense, the comparison of two examples, one by Schoenberg and the other by
Webern, will be very instructive. Before undertaking this comparison, however, we must state that the twelve-tone technique
has recently led to the discovery of certain principles of the twelve-
tone row which will, I think, play an important part in the future.
It may be observed that the different transpositions of the forms
of the row produce distinct regions, which are determined by the
reappearance of certain aggregations in a number of these transpositions. These regions constitute, then, different harmonic levels,
which can be very helpful in bringing out the structure of a composition [13] or even the coherence of a sentence or period.

   The study of Example 79b, which reproduces the second,
fourth, and eighth transpositions of the row of Webern's Op. 28,
shows that all the two-note fragments which make up these forms

---

[11] The first Cantata, Op. 29, is entirely built in this way; the same device is used
in long passages of Op. 30 and 31.

[12] *Introduction*, Chapter XI.

[13] Passing from one region to another is rather like modulating from one key to
another.

are identical. Furthermore, 4 and 8 display a similar type of fragmentation. Transpositions 6, 10, and 12 also belong to the same region (12 being like 4 and 8, 6 and 10 like 2). The structure of this row includes, then, two different regions, one of which includes the transpositions which we have just named, while the other includes all the rest of the transpositions.[14]

Schoenberg uses similar relationships to emphasize certain tonal functions in his Piano Concerto, Op. 42. Let us look at the beginning of the theme of the last movement.

This theme has a definite tonal character, which is underlined by the pedal-point on F sharp in the middle voice. It uses the row—

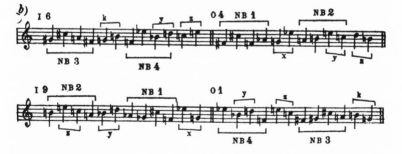

[14] It is true that this row is in some respects extremely simple, and hence has only two regions. Some other rows have three or four. Cf. *Introduction,* Chapter X.

forms I6, O1, O4, and I9; the many interrelationships of which (NB 1, NB 2, NB 3, NB 4, k, x, y, z), show that they belong to the same region.

First, the right hand plays I6 up till the sixth tone. The left hand takes up the same form and carries it through to the end. The right hand then plays the retrograde form of O1, up till the seventh tone. But I6 and O1 are interrelated in that the first six tones of I6 are the same as the last six of O1 (and, vice versa, the first six tones of O1 are the same as the last six of I6). This permits Schoenberg to present the retrograde form of O1 incompletely in the right hand, since the last six tones of this form are being played simultaneously in the left hand. Finally (measure 331 from the third beat onward) the right hand takes up O4 (which is completed in the left hand from the third beat of measure 332 onward), while, at the same time, the left hand takes up I9 (which is completed in the right hand from the third beat of measure 332 onward).

Such handling of the twelve-tone technique gives the harmony complete coherence. Schoenberg's tonal functions result not only from the abovementioned pedal-point on F sharp (which is also underlined by the orchestra) but also from the repetitions, in various registers, of certain tones of the melody (the C sharps in measures 329 and 330, the G sharps in measure 331) and especially from all the harmonic false relations of the octave (some of which we have indicated by means of arrows).

In this sense, Example 79, taken from Webern's Op. 28, is completely different. This example has been sufficiently analyzed in Chapter XI to require no further comment here. Let us simply remark that the limitation of each motive to its own register (symbolized in the chord of Example 79c) is caused by a conscious effort to avoid the slightest false relation.

Furthermore, it is clear that this idea of the false relation of the octave plays exactly the same role in harmony as in counterpoint. Generally speaking, there is no reason to set up separate rules for these two styles, since twelve-tone harmony results either from counterpoint or from the simultaneous sounding of several tones of the row, in which case it is merely a sequence of vertical motives—in other words, again the result of a kind of counter-point.[15]

c) *Rhythm.*—There is not much more to say about the rhythm of twelve-tone music. Here, too, one must carry the spirit of variation as far as possible. The superposition of different rhythms should produce the greatest wealth of rhythmic figures without jeopardizing the coherence of the whole. I have tried to apply this principle radically in my recent *Sonata for Flute and Piano,* Op. 12 (1944) from which I quote the passage on the following page.

This passage, which superimposes on a basic meter of 2/2 numerous subdivisions derived from this meter (12/8, 6/4, 3/2), is simply the ultimate consolidation of a procedure familiar since the beginnings of polyphony. This multiplicity of meters is not meant to be interesting in itself, but to emphasize—or, rather, to express—the varied accentuation between one voice and the next. Furthermore, the accents within each voice are constantly varied.

If we were to formulate a general rule for twelve-tone rhythm, it would be as follows: each measure, in each voice, includes a certain number of feet, which may easily be defined in the terms of Greek rhythmics and metrics previously used in this book.[16] This is the function of the meter, which should not change as long as the number of feet remains the same, and which will not change

[15] Furthermore, it seems to me useless to formulate a law according to which twelve-tone harmony must prohibit the use of major and minor triads, as certain "neophytes" have tried to do. In the first place, every theorist must beware of purely speculative theories. Even the most radical twelve-tone scores of our time exhibit such chords; for example, there are two at the beginning of Webern's Op. 28 (cf. Ex. 77a and b = A–A'). In every way, these chords assume entirely new functions, determined by the tone-row technique. Any tonal reminiscence is *superficial,* not *essential.* It does not necessarily influence the harmonic structure in one direction or another, and the transcendence or non-transcendence of the tonal system is dependent on quite different laws, which we have tried to define above. Twelve-tone music, the attempted synthesis of all the polyphony of the past and of the total resources of chromaticism, should be able to use *every chord* which these resources can produce.

[16] It may be that a given foot does not correspond to a single term, in which case we may amalgamate several of them: iambo-trochee, anapest-dactyl, etc. In any case, the terms themselves are quite unimportant, and are merely used to facilitate analysis and theoretical formulation. The composer does not have to know what the thing is called—he only has to know how to use it.

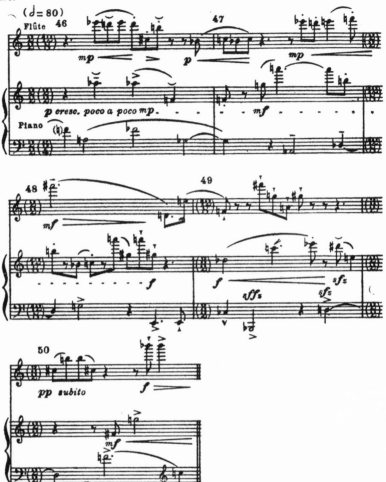

Ex. 86

until that number of feet changes.[17] If the number of feet varies from one voice to the next, a meter which can include them all should be used.

It may be said that, up until now, musical minds have not surpassed certain limits of rhythmic variation, in the sense that,

[17] The bar-line was introduced as soon as polyphony became conscious of these rhythmic concepts. The bar-line has, then, a precise function, and protests against its "tyranny" betray a complete misunderstanding of the real problems of polyphony and rhythm.

in spite of the rich "polyrhythm" of Bach and Mozart, the repetition of one foot over a long period of time has been, so to speak, *de rigueur*. Even today whole phrases are sometimes built on a small number of feet (if not, as often happens in tonal music, on a single foot).[18]

The meter is, then, the sum of the feet contained in the measure. The time-signature (1/2, 2/4, 3/8) simply indicates the monometric, bimetric, trimetric, etc., character (i.e., the number of feet in the measure). The spirit of variation should approach this problem as follows: a) a compound measure (one containing several feet) should vary the rhythm of the feet; as, however, rhythmic *ostinato* should be possible, it can be introduced in several different ways: 1) in a simple form (cf. Ex. 44b, *Lyric Suite*), 2) in a more complex form wherein the *ostinato* passes from one voice to the next while the other voices are governed by the previously stated principle of rhythmic variation;[19] b) one can consider the measure, whatever its metric definition, as a monometer, in which case each successive measure must have a different character.

Generally speaking, the rhythm of the polyphonic texture should be elaborated from the superposition of different feet, even in strict contrapuntal forms like the canon. In this respect, Webern's last works, especially the last movement of the Quartet, Op. 28, furnish us with many valuable examples.

I realize that the above "sketch" is really just that; but, as I have said before, it seems to me impossible at the present time to draw any more definite conclusions from the twelve-tone laws now known to us. However, I think that even this incomplete and schematic effort deserves credit for throwing a little light on a realm which is still enveloped in outer darkness for most musicians and music-lovers, even though some few understand its essential nature. In any case, my ambition in writing this book was not to

---

[18] In this connection let us recall that all tonal music has a tendency to submit to iambic meter. Trochaic meter is second in importance. The dactyl expresses "graceful" motion, while the anapest expresses energetic and "propulsive" motion. Finally, the spondee is used only in grave and solemn motion.

[19] The entire first movement of Schoenberg's Third Quartet, Op. 30, is written in this way.

exhaust the subject, but simply to stimulate, and to provide a valid basis for, future research. Such as it is, this study will some day serve as a foundation for a *treatise on twelve-tone composition*.

Again let me emphasize that all our observations have been based on the certainty that the compositional problems studied here owe their very existence to the evolution of the great fundamental laws of polyphony, which constitute the true tradition of Western music. This tradition, which has never ceased to enrich the language that expresses it, now culminates in a new phase (as legitimate and as important as all the preceding phases) of that language. We have tried to formulate the basic syntax of that language, as it is (or should be) used in contemporary music. The abovementioned treatise of composition, which cannot fail to be written some day, will prove that there has thus been constructed a truly contemporary musical language, in the most generally accepted sense of that term.

Conclusion

The very struggle towards the
heights is sufficient to satisfy a
man's heart.

ALBERT CAMUS
Le Mythe de Sisyphe.

We have come to the conclusion of a work intended to familiarize the reader with what seems to us to be the keenest expression
and the most important manifestation of the art of music in our
time. We have tried to fulfill this task by analyzing, as thoroughly
as possible, the works of the three great masters who determine
the present state of music. We have considered these works from
the double viewpoint of their specific acquisitions and of the tradition which is enriched by these acquisitions. Such an analysis
surely imparts to our effort a certain logic, perhaps even a certain
persuasive force. And yet it is evident that all the analyses and
all the commentaries which fill these pages are insufficient, because
they say nothing about what is really essential. How, indeed, could
they make any claim to revivify the emotion, the extraordinary
creative power, the tense striving to reach the summit of artistic
activity, which produced every composition, every measure discussed in these pages? The admission of the ultimate impotence
of any work of criticism is enough to strike despair to the heart
of anyone who undertakes such a work in honest and clear-headed
fashion. The uselessness, even the sterility of such a book as this—
at least in its major ambition, which is to throw further light on
its subject—becomes even more obvious when one stops to consider that only those who want to be convinced are open to con-
viction—only those, indeed, who will some day come face to face
with certain problems, book or no book—and that the influence
which a theoretical work can exert on those who are not yet ready
to grapple with these problems is, so to speak, nil.

But then what is to be done? Ought we to let the works speak for themselves—these works which all in all can well afford to dispense with commentaries and justification, simply because their most eloquent justification is their existence? But these works are played very infrequently; and, when they are played, their unfamiliarity causes most of the listeners to miss their essential quality, and, far from retaining a strong and valid impression of them, to be confused and even irritated by works which they have not the slightest desire to hear again.

Certainly, we could content ourselves with a passive and resigned attitude; we could say that, since the value of these works is beyond discussion, they can wait—their value will impress itself on the world without our doing anything to force the issue. After all, a masterpiece is in no hurry; it transcends time; it can be misunderstood or ignored—all this is quite unimportant, and the time will come when its beauty will be revealed without any outside assistance.

Certainly! I often feel this way myself—the more so as I know all too well how empty is the noisy and fashionable agitation of a great many musicians. In this sense, the silence which, up till now, has almost completely surrounded Schoenberg and his disciples, a silence which has protected them from fashion, snobbery and the like, not only honors them but perhaps even serves their interests.

But this silence has lasted long enough, and this is why.

We know what Schoenberg's activity means; we know the noble task which he has fulfilled. We have compared the musical situation created by this genius with that in which the genius of Bach unfolded. Like Bach, Schoenberg succeeded in a great renewal; for, just as the death of the modal system brought to life the tonal system, which was definitely constituted in the work of Bach, even so the classic tonal system, dead since Wagner, is transmuted, in Schoenberg's work, into the system which we have been trying to define.

But it is evident that such a renewal cannot take place without a violent reaction. In this respect, too, our time is exactly like the period which immediately followed Bach. His work, together with the theoretical formulations of Rameau, marks the culmination and the codification of the acquisitions of several centuries of musical activity—principles which were to determine the entire musical evolution of the future. But let us remember the extreme impoverishment of music which then took place. Between 1750 (Bach's death) and about 1780 (burgeoning of the true genius of Haydn and Mozart) what has music to offer? On the one hand, a few successors of Bach, among whom only Johann Christian Bach, on account of his concessions to depraved public taste, acquired a certain reputation; on the other hand, some "local" schools like that of Mannheim, where, just as in the work of K. P. E. Bach, there are developed certain forms which perform the useful and necessary (if thankless and obscure) task of bridging the gap between Johann Sebastian Bach and Mozart. But what these thirty years principally have to offer us is that eyesore, the "style galant," which depends on a number of pleasant and sterile formulae, and which therefore commands the entire allegiance of most musicians and music-lovers. Even Mozart and Haydn are contaminated for a long time by this style; they have to make a real effort to rid themselves of it and to establish a connection with an authentic musical tradition. For example, it was not until he rediscovered and applied the complex laws of Bach's polyphony that Mozart succeeded in attaining the level of his own genius.

This excursion into the past would doubtless be superfluous if it did not furnish us with the key to the contemporary musical situation. Just as the seriousness, austerity, and complexity of the art of Bach and Rameau finally exhausted the musicians and the public of 1750, about 1925 most musicians, and the public, turned aside from the difficult path of Schoenberg.

For, though that historic moment, exceptional from the viewpoint of the elaboration of certain polyphonic problems, which marks the beginning of this century seems to have favored the development of many powerful musicians fully aware of these problems,[1] of all those who participated in this historic movement

[1] In addition to Mahler, Schoenberg, and his disciples in Austria, we might name Debussy, Dukas, Ravel, and Satie in France; Reger and Strauss in Germany; Scriabin and Stravinsky in Russia; Bartók and Kodály in Hungary; de Falla in Spain, and even Puccini in Italy. Each of these contributed in his own way to the overthrow of tradition—and to its continuation.

only a few had the courage to follow their experiments to the bitter end. Most of them, frightened by their own temerity, beat a speedy retreat. Now, it happens that the less glorious human actions are, the harder we try to justify them; that is why we have so many theories about the impasse in which certain pre-1914 experiments ended—the "Back-to-Bach" movement, as well as "neo-classicism" and "neo-objectivism," which are neither classical, objective, nor "neo."

There emerges from this pitiful debacle only the austere and clear-headed Arnold Schoenberg, surrounded by his faithful and no less clear-headed disciples, Alban Berg and Anton Webern. These men, whose whole life was love of and respect for genuine musical values, complete altruism, and repudiation of mediocrity, are a shining example only to those who care more for absolute truth than for the satisfaction of their personal cravings and the demands of the public. But the search for truth is attacked as a mere "laboratory experiment"; this well-worn formula completely satisfies most weak and lazy minds, which will ever defend their own petty interests against the menace of the "supra-personal." Thus it becomes easy to have a clear conscience about giving in to one's predilection for facility and compromise, which is so well expressed in the "style galant" of our day—a style which characterizes most of our composers, from Stravinsky and Hindemith down to those of the lowest rank, many of whom are tremendously successful. This success must be protected from anything which might endanger it. There is one sure way to protect it—to join in a conspiracy of silence about the works of composers who express genuine musical values.

This would be sufficient reason to break that silence. As long as silence merely protects the works dear to my heart from the pollutions of fashion and snobbery, I, too, shall gladly be silent; but all my convictions about the "supratemporality" of masterpieces will not keep me from speaking if the chief function of this silence is to protect the peace of mind of those who are menaced by these masterpieces.

But peace of mind may not be bought so cheaply. Life continues in spite of everything, and with it are perpetuated the true values. Arnold Schoenberg, Alban Berg, and Anton Webern are not the last of their kind. Younger, less well-known musicians, mostly functioning away from the "official" musical scene, have understood the meaning of a great lesson. Just as, between Bach and Mozart, lesser geniuses had the courage to do their duty—always modest, always indispensable—even so these musicians, very few of whom are known to the public, follow their elders in consolidating a new, rich, universal musical language. To this must be added the role played, ever since Schoenberg's beginnings, by a certain number of interpreters, who have used every opportunity—and often made their own opportunities—to propagate a language which they had learned to speak often with great difficulties, and which they tried to communicate at all costs to every available audience.[2]

This, then, is the crux of the problem. All these musicians—composers and interpreters—have done their work. They have finally created a situation in which the truth inherent in the works of Schoenberg and his school has a chance of winning out. New generations of musicians—composers and interpreters—have made their appearance. Among these musicians we may observe a passionate concern with the problems raised here; either the music of most of the "official" composers of their countries does not satisfy these newcomers (because they have the necessary perspective to judge the poverty of music which might have passed for new, daring, or original work several years ago), or the hearing of some of the works which we have been studying has made them keenly aware of certain genuine musical values.

[2] Some of them should be mentioned here: the Rosé Quartet which, before World War I, introduced Schoenberg's first two quartets; the Kolisch Quartet; Marya Freund, doubtless the best interpreter of *Pierrot Lunaire* (which she spent more than a year learning); the previously mentioned conductors Erich Kleiber and Hermann Scherchen; the pianists Eduard Steuermann (who transcribed many of Schoenberg's works for the piano, and who gave the first performances of most compositions for or with piano by Schoenberg, Berg, and Webern) and Erich-Itor Kahn (who gave the first performance of Op. 33a, in the first recital devoted to all Schoenberg's piano music); the violinists Rudolf Kolisch (who played a part analogous to that of Steuermann, and founded the Kolisch Quartet) and Louis Krasner (who commissioned Berg's violin concerto and was the first to perform Schoenberg's). Space permits me to cite only a few of these musicians; I have probably omitted some important ones, for I cannot remember them all and there are certainly many whom I do not know about.

Among these musicians (to whom there must also be added an infinitesimal but ever-increasing fraction of the musical public) there are some who, through lack of preparation, familiarity, competence, or maturity, cannot yield unaided to the art of a Schoenberg, a Berg, or a Webern. They might, indeed, be discouraged or misled by their reading of the scores, or by the few isolated performances in the concert world. This book should serve, then, as a necessary guide for these musicians; for the young composer, to inspire him to the serious and profound study of compositional laws; for the young interpreter, to familiarize him with certain principles without which he could not possibly *re-create* the work of his choice; and, finally, for the enlightened music-lover, who, if he does not completely understand the technical problems, will at least have grasped the meaning of that "struggle towards the heights" which we have described, and will thus—if only emotionally—have lessened the distance between himself and an art of which the very origin and essence were previously unfamiliar to him.

It is to all these that I address myself—with no hope of providing them with anything "definitive." Whatever my experience in teaching, whatever my vanity with respect to my own knowledge, I completely lack that overweening ambition which gives some people the illusion that they can successfully acquit themselves of such a superhuman task. The only thing that I can hope to do is to pass on the enthusiasm of my own research, and thus to inspire my readers to *seek* in their turn.

Furthermore, the silence which has, up until now—especially in France—surrounded the school of Schoenberg has certainly been responsible for many of the vagaries of musical activity during the last few years. There is no cause for despair, however. Even error can be fruitful—if it is denounced one day, if it is brought face to face with Truth.

That, and nothing more, is what this book has tried to do. If it succeeds, the effort which it has cost me, and the breach of silence which it constitutes, will be justified.

INDEX

BIBLIOGRAPHY

I. Collections of essays devoted to Schoenberg.
Armitage, Merle (ed.). Schoenberg. New York, 1937.
Arnold Schönberg. Munich, 1912.
Arnold Schönberg zum fünfzigsten Geburtstage, 13. September 1924.
(Sonderheft der Musikblätter des Anbruch.) Vienna, 1924.
Arnold Schönberg zum sechzigsten Geburtstage. Vienna, 1934.

II. Other books (including biographies and works of general reference).
Krenek, Ernst. Music Here and Now. New York, 1941.
—,—. Studies in Counterpoint. New York, 1940.
—,—. Ueber neue Musik. Vienna, 1937.
Leibowitz, René. Introduction à la musique de douze sons. Paris, L'Arche
(in preparation).
—,—. Qu'est-ce que la musique de douze sons? Liège, 1948.
Newlin, Dika. Bruckner, Mahler, Schoenberg. New York, 1947.
Perle, George. The Twelve-Tone Row. Chicago, 1941.
Reich, Willi. Alban Berg. Vienna, 1937.[1]
Wellesz, Egon. Arnold Schönberg. Leipzig, 1921.

III. Articles, prefaces, etc.
Hill, R. S., "Schoenberg's Tone-Rows and the Music of the Future," Musical
Quarterly, XXII, 14-37, January, 1936.
Reich, Willi, "Alban Berg," Die Musik, XXII, 5, 347-53, February, 1930.
—,—, "Anton Webern," Tempo (London), March, 1946.
Searle, Humphrey, "Webern's Last Works," Monthly Musical Record, De-
cember, 1946.
Sessions, Roger, "Arnold Schoenberg," Tempo (London), 1944.
Stein, Erwin, Prefaces to Schoenberg's Third Quartet and Berg's Lyric Suite.
Vienna, 1926.
Wellesz, Egon, "An Alban Berg MS at Oxford," Tempo (London), 1946.
—,—, "Arnold Schönberg," Revue Musicale, April, 1926, 12-25; July, 1926,
11-23.
Webern issue of "23," Vienna, 1933.

---

[1] This work contains analyses of all Berg's works by Berg himself, Krenek,
Reich, and Wiesengrund-Adorno.

DISCOGRAPHY

SCHOENBERG:

Buch der hängenden Gärten (Nos. 5 and 12 only), Erica Storm and Mosco Carner—
C-DB 1303, in *Columbia History of Music,* CM-361
Gurre-Lieder, Philadelphia Orchestra (Stokowski)—VM 127
Pierrot Lunaire, Erika Stiedry-Wagner and ensemble conducted by composer—
CM-461
Postlude, in *Genesis Suite,* Janssen Symphony of Los Angeles—JS-10 (Artist Records)
Six Little Piano Pieces, Jesus Maria Sanroma—V-15862, in VM-646
Verklärte Nacht, Minneapolis Symphony (Ormandy)—VM-207
                          St. Louis Symphony (Golschmann) DM-1005 (Victor)

Transcriptions:

    Bach-Schoenberg: *Komm, Gott, Schöpfer, heiliger Geist* and *Schmücke dich, o*
    liebe Seele, Berlin Philharmonic (Horenstein)—D-CA8056

BERG:

Lyric Suite (Suite Lyrique), Galimir Quartet—Vox 181
Violin Concerto, Louis Krasner and Cleveland Symphony (Rodzinski)—CM-465
Wozzeck (Excerpts)—Charlotte Boerner and Janssen Symphony of Los Angeles—
JS 12 (Artist Records)
—, Gertrude Ribla and Philadelphia Orchestra (Ormandy)—English Columbia LX-
1158-59

WEBERN:

String Trio, Kathleen Washbourne Trio—D-K904 (Decca)

WORKS OF ARNOLD SCHOENBERG[1]

String Quartet in D Major (1897). Lost.

Op. 1. Two Songs for baritone and piano   )

Op. 2. Four Songs with piano accompaniment)   (1896-98)

Op. 3. Six Songs with piano accompaniment   )

Op. 4. *Verklärte Nacht,* string sextet (1899). Version for string orchestra (1917; revised 1943).

     Gurre-Lieder, for solo, chorus and orchestra (1900-01; orchestration finished 1911).

Op. 5. *Pelleas und Melisande,* symphonic poem (1902; orchestration finished 1903).

Op. 6. Eight Songs with piano accompaniment (1905).

Op. 7. First String Quartet, in D minor (1904-05).

Op. 8. Six Orchestral Songs (1903-04).

Op. 9. Chamber Symphony, for fifteen instruments (1906).
     Version with doubled strings, Op. 9b.

Op.10. Second String Quartet, in F sharp minor (1907-08).

Op.11. Three Piano Pieces (1908).

Op.12. Two Ballads with piano accompaniment (1906).

Op.13. *Friede auf Erden, a cappella* chorus (1907).

Op.14. Two Songs with piano accompaniment (1907).

Op.15. *Das Buch der hängenden Gärten,* fifteen songs after Stefan George (1908).

Op.16. Five Orchestral Pieces (1909). (Peters).

Op.17. *Erwartung,* monodrama (August 27-September 12, 1909).

Op.18. *Die glückliche Hand,* drama with music (1909-13).

Op.19. Six Little Piano Pieces (1911).

Op.20. *Herzgewächse,* for soprano, celesta, harmonium and harp (1911).

Op.21. *Pierrot Lunaire,* for reciter and five instruments (1912).

Op.22. Four orchestral Songs (1913-15).

Op.23. Five Piano Pieces (1923). (Wilhelm Hansen, Copenhagen.)

Op.24. *Serenade,* for seven instruments and bass voice (1923). (Wilhelm Hansen, Copenhagen.)

Op.25. Suite for Piano (1924).

Op.26. Wind Quintet (1924).

Op.27. Four Pieces for Mixed Chorus (1925).

Op.28. Three Satires for Mixed Chorus (1925).

Op.29. Suite (Septet) (1927).

---

[1] Unless otherwise indicated, published or taken over by Universal-Edition, Vienna. Works marked with an asterisk published by G. Schirmer, New York.

Op.30. Third String Quartet (1926).

Op.31. Variations for Orchestra (1927-28).

Op.32. *Von Heute auf Morgen*, one-act opera (1929).

Op.33 (a and b). Two Piano Pieces (1932).
(Op.33b, New Music Edition, San Francisco and New York.)

Op.34. *Accompaniment to a Film-Scene*, for orchestra (1930). (Heinrichshofen, Magdeburg.)

Op.35. Six Pieces for Male Chorus, *a cappella* (1930). (Bote und Bock, Berlin.)
Three Songs with piano accompaniment (1933). Unpublished.
Suite for String Orchestra* (1934).

Op.36. Concerto for Violin and Orchestra* (1936).

Op.37. Fourth String Quartet* (1937).

Op.38. Second Chamber Symphony* (1906-1940).
Version for piano four hands, Op.38 B.

Op.39. *Kol Nidre* for reciter, chorus and orchestra* (1938).

Op.40. Variations on a Recitative for Organ (1943). (Gray, New York.)

Op.41. *Ode to Napoleon* for reciter, string quartet, and piano (1942).* Version for reciter, string orchestra, and piano (1943), Op.41 B.

Op.42. Concerto for Piano and Orchestra* (1942).

Op.43A. Theme and Variations for Band* (1943).
Version for symphony orchestra, Op.43 B.

Op.44. Postlude to a Suite from *Genesis*, for orchestra (1945). (Unpublished.)

Op.45. String Trio (1946). (Bomart, New York.)

Op.46. *A Survivor of Warsaw* for reciter, male chorus, and orchestra (1947). (Bomart, New York.)

Op.47. Fantasy for Violin and Piano (1949). (Unpublished.)

Transcriptions

Various realizations and instrumentations of eighteenth-century works for the *Denkmäler der Tonkunst in Oesterreich* (1912).

Orchestral transcriptions of Bach's organ chorale preludes *Komm, Gott, Schöpfer, heiliger Geist* and *Schmücke dich, o liebe Seele* (1921).

Orchestral transcription of Bach's organ prelude and fugue in E flat major (1928).

Orchestral transcription of Brahms' G minor piano quartet, Op.25* (1932).

Concerto for 'Cello and Orchestra, after a concerto for cembalo and orchestra by G. M. Monn* (1932).

Concerto for String Quartet and Orchestra, after Händel's *Concerto Grosso*, Op.6. No.7* (1933).

Three German Folksongs, arranged for four-part *a cappella* chorus: *Es gingen zwei Gespielen gut, Der Mai tritt ein mit Freuden,* and *Mein Herz in steten Treuen* (1948). (E. B. Marks, New York.)

Unfinished Works

Die Jakobsleiter, oratorio (begun in 1913). Text completed and published by
Universal-Edition.
Moses und Aron, three-act opera (begun about 1929).

Theoretical Works

Harmonielehre (1909-11). Published in English as *Theory of Harmony* (Philo-
sophical Library, 1947).
*Models for Beginners in Composition** (1942).
Projected works: *Counterpoint*
                Fundamentals of Musical Composition
                Structural Functions of the Harmony
                Style and Idea (essays and lectures)

WORKS OF ALBAN BERG[1]

Seven Early Songs with Piano Accompaniment (1905-07; orchestrated 1928).

Op. 1. Piano Sonata (1908).

Op. 2. Four Songs with Piano Accompaniment (1908-09).

Op. 3. String Quartet (1909-10).

Op. 4. Five Songs with Orchestral Accompaniment (to post-card texts of Peter Altenberg) (1911-12.) Unpublished except for the fifth song, which appeared with piano accompaniment in the review *Menschen* (1912).[2]

Op. 5. Four Pieces for Clarinet and Piano (1913).

Op. 6. Three Orchestral Pieces (1914).

Op. 7. *Wozzeck*, opera in three acts (1917-21, Concert suite 1922).

Chamber concerto for violin, piano and thirteen wind instruments (1923-25; transcription of second movement for violin, clarinet and piano, 1935).

Lyric Suite, for string quartet (1925-26). Transcription of second, third, and fourth movements for string orchestra.

Der Wein, concert aria for soprano and orchestra (1929).

Lulu, opera in three acts (unfinished) (1928-35; concert suite, 1934).

Concerto for Violin and Orchestra (1935).

Miscellaneous

Double fugue for string quintet with piano accompaniment (1907). (Lost.)

Theme and Variations for Piano (1908). (Unpublished.)

An Leukon, song with piano accompaniment (1908). Published in Willi Reich, *Alban Berg.*

Four-part canon on the twelve-tone row of Schoenberg's *Von Heute auf Morgen* written (1930) in tribute to the Frankfurt Opera where that work was staged. Published in Willi Reich, *Alban Berg.*

Schliesse mir die Augen beide, song with piano accompaniment. Tonal version (1907) and twelve-tone version (1926) both published in *Die Musik* (Berlin, 1930).

Transcriptions

Piano reductions of the following:

Schreker, *Der ferne Klang* (opera) (1911).

Schoenberg, *Litanei*   ) Last two movements of
          Entrückung) Second String Quartet
          Gurre-Lieder

Theoretical Works

Analyses of Schoenberg's *Gurre-Lieder, Pelleas und Melisande*, and *Chamber Symphony*, Op.9.

Articles on Music

Numerous articles and essays are collected in Willi Reich, *Alban Berg.*

Radio lecture: *Was ist atonal?* (1930).

---

[1] Universal-Edition, Vienna.

[2] Reprinted in *Musical Quarterly*, XXXIV, 4 (October, 1948).

WORKS OF ANTON WEBERN[1]

Op. 1. Passacaglia for Orchestra (1908).
Op. 2. *Entflieht auf leichten Kähnen,* mixed chorus *a cappella* (1908).
Op. 3. Five Songs with piano accompaniment (1909).
Op. 4. Five Songs with piano accompaniment (1909).
Op. 5. Five Movements for String Quartet (1909; transcription for string orches-
         tra, 1930).
Op. 6. Six Orchestral Pieces (1910).
Op. 7. Four Pieces for Violin and Piano (1910).
Op. 8. Two Songs with accompaniment of eight instruments (1911-12).
Op. 9. Six Bagatelles for String Quartet (1913).
Op.10. Five Orchestral Pieces (1913).
Op.11. Three Little Pieces for 'Cello (1914).
Op.12. Four Songs with piano accompaniment (1915-17).
Op.13. Four Songs with accompaniment of thirteen instruments (1916).
Op.14. Six Songs with accompaniment of four instruments (1917-21).
Op.15. Five Sacred Songs with accompaniment of five instruments (1922-23).
Op.16. Five Canons for voice and two clarinets (1924).
Op.17. Three Sacred Folk-Songs with accompaniment of three instruments (1924;
         only one published, by the New Music Edition, San Francisco and New
         York).
Op.18. Three Songs with piccolo, clarinet, and guitar (1925).
Op.19. Two Songs for Mixed Chorus accompanied by five instruments (1926).
Op.20. String Trio (1927).
Op.21. Symphony for Chamber Orchestra (1928).
Op.22. Quartet for Violin, Clarinet, tenor saxophone, and piano (1930).
Op.23. Three Songs with piano accompaniment (1934).
Op.24. Concerto for Nine Instruments (1934). (Editions Dynamo, Liège.)
Op.25. Three Songs with piano accompaniment. (Unpublished.)
Op.26. *Das Augenlicht,* for chorus and orchestra (1935).
Op.27. Variations for Piano (1936).
Op.28. String Quartet (1938). (Boosey and Hawkes, London and New York.)
Op.29. Cantata No.1 for Chorus and Orchestra (1939). (Unpublished.)
Op.30. Variations for Orchestra (1940). (Unpublished.)
Op.31. Cantata No.2 for Chorus and Orchestra. (Unpublished.)

---

[1] Unless otherwise indicated, Universal-Edition, Vienna.

Transcriptions and Editions

Edition of works of Heinrich Isaac (*Denkmäler der Tonkunst in Oesterreich*).
Piano reductions of Schoenberg's Six Orchestral Songs, Op.8.
Transcription of Schoenberg's Chamber Symphony, Op.9, for flute, clarinet, violin, 'cello, and piano.
Transcription of Schoenberg's Five Orchestral Pieces, Op.16, for two pianos.
Transcription of Schubert's *Six German Dances* for orchestra.
Transcription of the six-part fugue of Bach's *Musical Offering* for orchestra (1935).

Theory

Two series of lectures:
Der Weg zur Komposition mit zwölf Tönen (Vienna, 1932).
Der Weg zur neuen Musik (Vienna, 1933).

Articles

Webern's various articles and essays have not been collected. The first study of Schoenberg's work, written by Webern, appeared in 1912 in a collection of essays about Schoenberg (see bibliography).